FOREIGN INVESTMENT IN CONTEMPORARY RUSSIA

Also by Andrei Kuznetsov (in Russian)

DEVELOPING COUNTRIES IN THE NETS OF
  FINANCIAL DEPENDENCE (*editor with G. Solus*)

FOREIGN INVESTMENT IN THE USSR
  (*with S. Evstratov and N. Kozlov*)

Foreign Investment in Contemporary Russia

Managing Capital Entry

Andrei Kuznetsov
Senior Lecturer
Faculty of Management and Business
Manchester Metropolitan University

St. Martin's Press

First published in Great Britain 1994 by
THE MACMILLAN PRESS LTD
Houndmills, Basingstoke, Hampshire RG21 2XS
and London
Companies and representatives
throughout the world

A catalogue record for this book is available
from the British Library.

ISBN 0–333–60713–9

Printed in Great Britain by
Ipswich Book Co Ltd
Ipswich, Suffolk

First published in the United States of America 1994 by
Scholarly and Reference Division,
ST. MARTIN'S PRESS, INC.,
175 Fifth Avenue,
New York, N.Y. 10010

ISBN 0–312–12041–9

Library of Congress Cataloging-in-Publication Data
Kuznetsov, A. P. (Andreĭ Petrovich)
Foreign investment in contemporary Russia : managing capital entry
/ Andrei Kuznetsov.
p.   cm.
Includes bibliographical references and index.
ISBN 0–312–12041–9
1. Investments, Foreign—Government policy—Russia (Federation)
2. Russia (Federation)—Foreign economic relations.   3. Russia
(Federation)—Commercial policy.   I. Title.
HG5580.2.A3K89   1994
332.6'73'0947—dc20   93–36679
                                                     CIP

To the memory of my father

Contents

Acknowledgements

This book is a revised version of my Ph.D. thesis submitted and approved in the winter of 1992 at the European University Institute in Florence. I am indebted to many individuals and organisations for assistance they provided in my project. I am grateful to the State Academy of Finance, Moscow, and its rector, Alla Griaznova, for giving me the opportunity to come to the European University Institute and begin work on the thesis. Mario Nuti, Vladimir Kollontai and Peter Hertner have patiently commented on parts of the manuscript at various stages of its development. I have benefited from discussions with Charles Ohman, John Flemming, Vladimir Shemiatenko, Jean Blondel, Nikolai Kozlov, Milica Uvalich, Marvin Jackson and Daniel Linotte. Most thanks, however, go to my two thesis supervisors, Susan Strange and Stuart Holland, who have offered constructive criticism and support, made invaluable suggestions, and without whose help the book could not have been completed. I can blame no one but myself for the remaining errors and omissions.

I would also like to express my appreciation to the European University Institute for financing my research at its final stage and the Catholic University of Leuven for providing me with the opportunity to prepare this book. Leuven Institute for Central and East European Studies has proven to provide a very stimulating intellectual environment from which this book has benefited.

My final acknowledgements go to my mother and my wife who not only encouraged me to proceed with this project during its critical moments but also helped me in many practical ways to accomplish it. Anyone who has wrestled with a project like this will recognise what it occasionally cost them. I cannot find the words to thank them.

ANDREI KUZNETSOV

Introduction

Russia, together with other countries of the Commonwealth of Independent States (CIS), has begun the transition to a market economy. This implies that the national economy must become incomparably more open than before in the sphere of international economic relations. It presents policy-makers with the crucial task of choosing an appropriate opening-up strategy. Judging from the controversy over the tactics chosen by the Yeltsin/Gaidar government for internal economic reforms, this can be expected to be a difficult problem involving, as before, many conflicting interests.

This research deals mainly with one aspect of opening up the Russian economy, namely, with policy toward foreign investment. Russian politicians need no persuading that foreign capital can play a very positive role in the renovation of the national economy. However, there is still a lot of confusion and uncertainty as regards both the practical ways of attracting foreign investment into the country and the capital entry management regulations. An observer may notice two prevalent conflicting attitudes on the part of politicians and their academic consultants. One group expresses apprehensions that, unless very elaborate policy measures are worked out, the massive unregulated inward flow of foreign capital may result, in the prevailing erratic conditions, in loss of control over the most important and competitive national industries. The other group in contrast warns against dilatoriness in taking decisions and insists on a drastic *laissez-faire* approach towards economic reform. Both groups refer to the experience of other countries, international practice and modern economic and political theory. There is little evidence of any narrowing of the gap between the two opposed positions. Meanwhile, the situation in Russia and the CIS in general has been characterized, on the whole, by the absence or inadequacy of conceptual, legislative, institutional and material premises for foreign investment.

This study attempts to contribute to the discussion of conceptual grounds for a basic framework for a national policy toward foreign investment in an ex-Soviet type economy with a special emphasis on Russia. The study focuses on four critical aspects of the problem: how to identify those specificities of Russian economic development that require to be taken into account as the opening up strategy is worked out; what conceptual base is appropriate for Russian strategy toward foreign investment; what is the present investment climate in the country and how it may be improved; and what priorities should govern Russian policy in respect of foreign direct investment.

This study does not aim to produce yet another programme of economic reforms in post-Communist Russia. It is written under the premise that market reform is the only plausible way toward the revival of the country. The whole burden of my argument, however, is that economic policy-making in Russia should be liberated as much as possible from any ideological dictat, no matter what its theoretical base. It should be determined neither by the present oversimplified market orthodoxy, nor the old orthodoxy of economic planning. To tackle this matter, I start, in Chapter 1, by demonstrating that the conflict between 'big bang' and gradualist approaches to economic reforms in Russia was principally of a political nature. The application of monetarist doctrine was not conditioned by the actual state of the national economy but rather by other, non-economic, considerations. Meanwhile, the economic situation demanded a much more balanced approach. This was stipulated by the fact that seventy years of the Soviet regime had turned Russia's economy into a very specific entity sharply diverging from the pattern developed in the non-Communist world. Hence, the question of speed and measure has become central to the success of reforms. By stressing the importance of 'pace and measure' I want to highlight the specificity of the transition in question: this is a transformation not to an adjacent but rather to an opposite state. In order to avoid the most negative consequences of the opening-up, it is necessary to address the Soviet economic mechanism as the starting point of the transition to the mechanism of international markets and then to evaluate the distance between them.

The problem of Russia and other ex-Soviet republics is not only a complete lack of experience with private ownership or market-based prices. No less important is the fact that, in the years of socialist planning, *the economy was subordinated to a completely different logic of development.* It has resulted, *inter alia,* in the creation of a number of built-in checks or barriers (Ol'sevich, 1991; Nove, 1991; Nagels, 1993) insulating the economy as a whole as well as its separate sectors and enterprises from the rest of the world. I investigate three of these barriers, i.e. the technological, structural and efficiency incompatibilities of domestic industries with the international market. This leads me to outline a hypothesis that, in the long run, economic degradation cannot be excluded as a possible outcome of hasty integration of former Soviet-type economies into the international market. Being the product of the Soviet economic system, the aforesaid barriers may fall only as the system's legacy is disposed of. However, some forms of destruction may be productive, others not. There is already evidence to show that the task of preparing the economy to become a part of the modern international economic system cannot be entrusted to the market mechanism alone. The question therefore arises whether in Russia, owing to its planning-days heritage and historical background, there is not a strong case for interventionism. Such interventionism in this book is described, following Richard Wade (1990), as the 'new interventionism'. Its important distinction is that it needs to be open to feedback from the market so that state economic policy is subordinated to economic rationality rather than to political ambitions.

Regarding foreign investment, state policy is always and necessarily an important component of the environment for business which is yet to be synthesized. Searching for the guidelines along which such a synthesis will proceed, I outline, in Chapter 2, a conceptual framework for a national policy toward foreign investment. I start from two premises. One concerns what Peter Drucker (1986) describes as the crisis of the modern 'macroeconomic axiom'. The mainstream of economic theory traditionally considers the national economy, especially that of the large developed countries, to be autonomous and the unit of both economic analysis and economic policy while treating the international economy largely as a restraint and a limitation. This approach accounts only poorly, if at all, for the reciprocity of national economies. On the other hand, the 'new' international political economy (Keohane and Nye, 1987; Strange, 1988a, 1988b) has been successful in demonstrating that the interdependence of nations is playing the role of the most influential single factor behind the changing profile of international relations, both political and economic.

This study shows that, for the purpose of economic policy-making, the conceptual notion of interdependence may be successfully interpreted in terms of *national competitiveness* theory. It is introduced in the research as an attempt to supply policy-makers in ex-Soviet republics with a conceptual method to evaluate short-term and medium-term economic policy against the background of the major tendencies of international economic development. The competitiveness in question is a much wider notion than just industrial competitiveness measured by the share of national firms in international trade. For the purpose of this research the term 'national competitiveness' is defined as *the ability to protect or pursue national social and economic interests in the situation of profound international interdependence*. Clearly, the challenge presented by this task exceeds the scope of separate firms and industries. Recent developments in Russia which caused mass impoverishment of the population, made me, in particular, raise the question of the human component of national competitiveness. I also explore whether the traditional measures of competitiveness like export quotas should be abandoned in favour of such indicators as per capita national income, the level of employment and quality-of-life indices.

This study puts into question the causal chain, more economic openness – more competition – higher efficiency – increased competitiveness. This chain does not allow for the fact that the opening up of the Commonwealth of Independent States, taking into consideration its consequences for the modern international economic regime, creates a serious problem for the stability of the latter. Hence, it would be reasonable to expect that the main pillars and beneficiaries of this regime, the US, the EEC and Japan, would take measures to ensure that the integration of the ex-Soviet economy will proceed on terms worked out by the triad and favourable to it. To countervail this pressure an alternative scenario is proposed aimed at increasing national bargaining power by concentrating effort on identifying, preserving and reinforcing existing competitive advantages, and creating new ones already in the early stages of reforms.

Chapter 3 deals with Russia's previous experience as a capital importing country. It is quite common that the pattern of newly industrialized countries is evaluated in the academic literature as particularly relevant to post-Communist economic transition. However, Russia's own economic history can prove to be no less instructive. At the turn of the century in terms of economic development Imperial Russia did something very similar to what South Korea or Taiwan did in the 1970s and 1980s. To an extent this was a result of very skilful foreign capital entry regulations practiced by the Tsarist government. It succeeded first in awakening the interest of foreign investors and later in extracting benefits from a massive inflow of foreign investment. Consequently, within only twenty years, Imperial Russia made great strides towards becoming a major industrialized country. It is particularly suggestive to look for an answer to one of the paradoxes of the first Russian industrialization, namely the willingness of foreign capitalists to invest despite an unfavourable investment climate.

Chapter 4 examines the characteristics of the investment climate in Russia. Since 'investment climate' is a very diversified notion, the research will be focused on two of its most important aspects, political risk and policy risk. As regards the former, the intention is to investigate in more · detail government risk and the consequences, for the prospects of foreign investment, of post-Communist nationalism and regionalism in the former USSR. An attempt will be made, based on the theory of rational government, to disclose the origins of what are claimed to be purely technocratic governments, a distinguishing feature of the majority of post-Communist regimes in Eastern and Central Europe. Nationalism and regionalism will be analyzed along the lines of 'national frustration' theory (Knudsen, 1974) in order to establish whether the post-Communist nationality issues present investors with an opportunity or a threat.

Policy risk in turn stems from uncertainties related to the dynamics of capital entry regulations. Hence the importance of revealing a tendency underlying the genesis of Russia's capital entry management system (CEMS). This part of the book contains an analysis of relevant legislation and relates the attitude of the higher levels of policy to that of the lower levels which were very important under the Soviet system and still retain much of their power.

Chapter 5 continues the examination of the capital entry management system started in Chapter 4, but the emphasis is switched to a more widely defined CEMS. This is necessary to demonstrate that the environment and incentives for investment, forming an integral part of the host-country economy, are to be created in a different way from those aimed at attracting enclave-type investment. The former incentives are largely identical with those that encourage domestic economic growth and rapid expansion of the private sector. Seen this way, any CEMS must include some elements of industrial and regional policy. As it is quite obvious that Russia will never get all the money it needs to renovate its economy through foreign investment, it is legitimate to raise the question of how to concentrate foreign resources into priority spheres.

The problems facing the Russian economy are characterized in this study as largely structural. Therefore an attempt will be made to identify some of the most urgent structural problems to be solved in the coming years and to analyse the role of foreign capital in resolving them. For this reason, I focus on the development of natural resources, environmental challenges and the conversion of the defence industries.

Lastly, in Chapter 6, because this has been a subject of a major debate in Russia, I undertake a more detailed study of one of the prospective forms of foreign investment regulations, the creation of free economic zones in the territory of the ex-USSR. The chapter contains criticism of the official policy (more precisely, of its absence) in respect to the zones. It also addresses itself to the phenomenon of free export-promoting zones with a view to assessing the relevance of this type of economic zone, quite widespread in developing countries, to the needs of Russian economic restructuring.

1 The Challenges of Post-Communist Transition

1.1 THE BASIC APPROACHES CONFLICT

The ex-Soviet economy at the beginning of the 1990s entered into the deepest crisis in its post-war history. Some interpreted its disastrous performance as an inevitable price of change. Others, however, claimed that there was no evidence of structural change; that the economy simply risked degeneration, and that it had lost its way on the path of transition.

After six years of frustrated attempts at increasing economic efficiency without sacrificing the basic principles of a command–administrative system, reforms have taken a drastic turn towards radicalism. The destination of the transition has been defined more clearly. From the famous '500 days' programme to Yavlinski's draft of a treaty on common economic space, to the economic programme of the Cabinet of President Yeltsin, the projects of economic reform more and more explicitly advocated the change from an economy owned and managed by the state to a market driven economy imitating the most daring models of neo-classical economics. In general terms, it was going to be a system in which private property had priority over all other forms of ownership, market forces were given an upper hand in defining the shape of the economy, and the national economy was wide open towards international market.

In academic and political circles, indeed in all the strata of the society, there has been major debate and uncertainty with respect to the scheme and many of its details, especially as regards the economic role of the state and its welfare policy. But that could not deter the process of reforms any more.

With the points of departure and arrival identified as non-market and market systems, the problem of transition lies in the task of determining their reciprocal positions and finding the optimal passage. For this end it is necessary to know how much of a difference there is between the two economic systems; how easily can this difference be overcome, and over what timescale.

This set of questions is the crux of a great controversy. Basically, there are two approaches. One claims that the case of the Soviet Union is unique and demands specific tailor-made measures. The other stresses the validity of the experience accumulated by the variation of countries which have undergone economic restructuring; the general validity of modern neo-classical economic theory, and also of the standard package of 'structural adjustment' recommendations developed by international financial organisations.

Initially the dividing line between the two approaches practically co-incided with the border-line of the country. A clear example was the fundamental multivolume report *A Study on Soviet Economy* (1991) prepared by the IMF, the World Bank, the OECD and the EBRD, and the reaction it provoked in academic circles in Moscow. Giving praise to the objectiveness and the thoroughness of the authors of the report, experts from two leading economic institutes of the Academy of Sciences of the USSR were unanimous in noting its 'cognitive, analytical rather than practical value'.[1] All objections summarised, the practical value of the report was dismissed on the grounds that it did not account for the principal differences between the content of monetary, budgetary, credit and other relations in the Soviet economy and a capitalist economy. Hence, the recommendations of the report, quite predictably biased towards exactly monetary, budgetary and credit instruments, were found inadequate for a situation in which the market was both underdeveloped and overmonopolised, the production of consumer goods was marginal in comparison to the output of heavy industries, the weight of a military–industrial complex was enormous, agriculture was in a deep structural crisis and the population was poor. The 'programme of the four' was criticised as too radical and painful, as putting too much emphasis on purely market measures whilst the specifics of the Soviet system and the necessity to preserve the integrity of the economy required gradualness and the preservation of the elements of the centrally planned system at least in the initial stages of transition.

Within only one year the situation had changed dramatically. First, numerous independent economic centres (former Soviet republics which became sovereign states) have emerged with their own nationally coloured approaches to reforms. Second, in the biggest and most powerful of republics, Russia, some of the most questionable proposals of a radical agenda have materialised into the governmental policy of free-market 'shock' therapy.

This latter development, important as it is, does not signify that one concept has surpassed the other by the strength of its argument. The events in Russia have confirmed what was noticeable initially in the ex-socialist countries of Central Europe: in practical terms the choice between the two approaches is determined in the long run by the balance of political forces. The new political leadership which attained power in the course of struggle against established political structures opted for drastic economic changes in the view that they must even further undermine the positions of old state-party apparatus in the society.

Nor should one disregard the importance of the fact that financial aid from the OECD countries to ex-Soviet economies is made conditional on the choice of the strategy of transition. The interaction of these circumstances made Russia, in terms of a regime theory, a policy-taker strongly influenced by external forces.

As Yeltsin's administration chose to apply a 'shock' therapy[2] to the economy of the country, in the Russian literature the two approaches to reform described above started to be more and more often characterised as evolutionary and radical. The shift of emphasis, however, seemed to be determined by political considerations more than anything else. In analytic terms it is misleading because it contributes to illusions which might have truly damaging consequences for the strategy of national economic development.

(i) The term *marketisation* often used in connection with economic reforms in the ex-socialist countries obscures the essence of the process. The passage to be effectuated by post-Communist economies is not a leap from a non-market to a market condition but rather a shift from an inefficient, distorted and suppressed market to an efficient one. In other words, the problem is to 'get prices right', not just to liberate them from state dictat which was the hard core of all 'shock' therapies. As the experience of several centuries of capitalism shows, there are so many other factors besides government intervention that distort prices, that getting prices right has inevitably become an endless process deeply interrelated with other circumstances. The impression that this type of qualitative transition could be made in one great bound is an illusion, hence even the most radical approach cannot avoid a good portion of evolutionism.

(ii) The propaganda of 'shock' therapy implies the presence of a free market 'in general' and a market economy 'in general'. In practice these are unreal conditions. There may be a 'wild' market of the period of the initial accumulation of capital. This was surpassed in western industrialised countries long ago but is still possible for Russia. There may be a 'civilised' market. The market economy may be an attribute of a depended and exploited country, and it may be a basis for an economy with a high competitive potential. Hence the goal should be to create an efficient modern market economy, not just any market economy. 'Shock' therapy may or may not be instrumental in constructing the basics of modern market structures. It certainly does not exhaust the spectrum of economic strategies which represent the social function of the modern state.

(iii) The opposition of radical to evolutionary change builds an illusion that old structures may simply be disposed of by dismantling them. This amends to nihilism with respect to everything that bears the stamp of a pre-free-market period. In turn this impoverishes and narrows the choice of strategies, allows short-term gains to overshadow longer-term priorities.

The discussion on the two approaches to economic transition initially focused on confronting 'tailor-made' to 'standard' reform packages. This came to be reformulated in terms of radicalism-versus-evolutionism (or even conservatism). The issues concerning the speed of reforms and the hardships of change have overshadowed the principal question of the *origins* of the 'standard' package, and why international financial organisations are so much obsessed with promoting it.

The answer hinges on what Robert Cox (1991, p. 335) has specified as a powerful globalising economic trend towards the achievement of a market utopia on the world scale. This trend is based on the internationalisation of production by transnational corporations. The internationalising process results when capital considers the productive resources of the world as a whole and locates elements of complex-globalised production systems at points of greatest cost advantage. Hence, transnational production, on which the prosperity of western capitalism is based, requires an environment in which (a) capital, technology, and inputs in the production process, as well as finished goods, could cross borders relatively freely; (b) business conditions (the price system, property rights, taxes, market organisation, employment norms, etc) are standardised worldwide in order to relieve the management of transnational complexes and to facilitate the collection of information on costs and revenues necessary to combine these complexes in an optimal manner. The formula of the free market is a very convenient ideology for pushing forward such a standardisation. Agencies such as the IMF and the OECD act as transmission belts for the world economy. In relations with the countries of the 'second world' and 'third world', their priority is to contribute to the creation of this unified environment; national welfare and social policies are consigned to the background. As for the World Bank, it focused its efforts towards the regions of 'absolute poverty' in order to, turning to Cox once again, prevent poverty somewhere from becoming disruptive of growth elsewhere.

There is yet another important feature to distinguish the two approaches. 'Shock' therapy derives from the philosophy that puts trust in the separation of state and economy, while the rival agenda reasserts the recognition of the indispensable guiding role of the state in the development of the nation's productive forces. 'Shock' therapy is an export adaptation of the much publicised hyper-liberal model of Anglo-American capitalism of late.[3] In its social aspect, it generally relies on confrontational tactics. The post-War economic reconstruction of Europe and Japan – the much quoted example of a successful large scale transition – was achieved, however, along the lines of the Keynesian model through conscious industrial policy and consensus-based tactics.

This book is devoted to the problem of opening the economies of Russia and other members of the Commonwealth of Independent States (CIS) to foreign capital. In this realm the competition of the two approaches is espe-, cially fierce. Given the disastrous economic situation, inadequate capital base and slow privatisation, for many providing freedom for foreign direct investment seems a ready-made answer to the economic difficulties of the country. Professor Hans Hirsch from the Institut für Wirtschaftswissen- schaften TH Aachen, for instance, claims that Russian industry cannot be reorganised successfully unless it is managed and owned by foreign capi- tal.[4] One should not be prejudiced against foreign control of enterprises, Hirsch continues, as long as they function efficiently.

In our cosmopolitan age this point of view is no more extravagant than any other. Harvard economist Robert Reich practically shares this approach to the question of control. In several articles and a recent book, *The Work of Nations*, he drives home the argument that the prosperity of America depends less on the strength of American companies than on the strength of the economic activities located within US borders. But the question of control over the economy cannot be dismissed merely by assumption. Even ignoring national defence, there are still many good reasons to believe that control matters. National markets, despite the process of globalisation, remain highly regulated. As Professor Laura D'Andrea Tyson (1991) notes in her critique of Reich, it is premature to rely on market forces to bring high-wage jobs to American shores. This is no less true of any other country.

Nowadays, concerns related to the issue of foreign control concentrate in particular on two points. First, it is usually stressed that the efficiency of a foreign owned firm in market (money) terms is not the same as its efficiency in the terms of public welfare. The economic success of such firms is mea- sured according to the global interests of power centres controlling them which may or may not coincide with the economic interests of the host country. The second point has to do with the task of shaping the structure of the national economy. The most important question is, if foreign companies are in charge, will their investment policy assist national industries to gain a place among major players dominating the technological race, or, on the contrary, will these industries be reduced to the role of simple recipients of technology developed elsewhere? Apprehensions on this account are not all groundless. According to John Dunning, a scholar who has done extensive research on multinationals, outside their domestic environments, global companies mainly produce goods and services, not innovation.

1.2   DEFINING THE CAPITAL ENTRY MANAGEMENT SYSTEM

It is probably impossible to find a publication on foreign investment which would question the significance of the business environment, or the investment climate, as a premise for foreign investment. The literature is far less unanimous as to the role of the state. It is quite often ignored that the investment climate always assumes the economic presence, in one form or another, of the state and, hence, the existence of what may be called a capital entry management system. Major progress in employing foreign capital in the interests of economic reforms in Russia may be achieved if sporadic regulatory efforts of the government evolves into a comprehensive programme of action which does not confine itself to emergency measures to eliminate current bottlenecks. Instead, it should concentrate on a framework for foreign participation on a long-term basis by means of improving the country's investment climate, and establishing an efficient capital entry management system.

In general terms the category *investment climate* is well described in the literature (see discussion in Chapter 4). None the less, it is scarcely elaborated with respect to the ex-Soviet Union despite the fact that the importance of this issue goes far beyond the boundaries of purely theoretical interest. It has practical significance for working out regulations and policies concerning foreign capital inasmuch as it helps to determine priorities within which international investors act and, on this basis, to optimise national strategy towards them.

The 'investment climate' is a multiple category encompassing everything that foreign investors take into consideration when evaluating to what extent conditions in a particular country favour capital investment, including the economy and culture, ideology and politics. In the course of this analysis they seek to use this heterogeneous input for calculating a generalised index of investment risk. When the investment climate is bad, capital exporters estimate their risk as high and the cost of attracting investment for the capital importing economy increases. Hence, for the recipient country, the investment climate is not an abstraction, it is something that has value, and the country may gain or lose wealth according to how the state of the investment climate determines the efficacy of foreign investment.

Modelling the investment climate should become an important stage in developing a well-founded strategy of international economic relations. First of all, it provides a systematic knowledge of the factors influencing foreign investors' decision-making. Second, it gives a new reference point to evaluate the economic situation in the country. Finally, it helps clarify the motives which drive foreign partners. At any given moment, the investment climate is an objective parameter as long as it is related to an actual socio-economic situation in the country. Yet, at the same time, it is subjective because it is always an interpretation of this situation by foreign investors in terms of the efficiency of their investment. In any case, state regulations are important for shaping this notion, whether they are consciously aimed at forming a particular business environment or are contemplated without taking into account possible outcomes for foreign ventures. Even the inertia of the authorities is a factor forming the investment climate. From this point of view one may claim that any country open for foreign capital possesses a certain capital entry management system (CEMS) referring to legislation and institutions, implementing state policy with respect to investment from abroad, or their absence. The entry management system may be defined as a system consisting of public and semi-public agencies, laws, regulations, and programmes established by host country authorities to both regulate and facilitate the entry and subsequent operations of investment and business ventures of foreign firms (Ting, 1988, p. 67).

The CEMS and the investment climate interact. The CEMS makes a component of the investment climate and simultaneously, to a certain extent, it is an external factor able to rearrange this climate. As logical categories, the CEMS and the investment climate cannot coincide absolutely not only because the latter is broader than the former but also owing to the fact that the CEMS represents the recipient side concept of how to channel foreign capital in accordance with national priorities, while the 'investment climate' evaluates the economic situation in terms of maximising premises for the increase of the profitability of investment.

In fact, the entry management system may be justly regarded as an important form of communication. It passes signals to and receive signals from the world investment market and, on this basis, is a tool of adjusting investment conditions both to national interests and to certain established international standards. This communication aspect of the CEMS may be particularly trying for ex-socialist economies which lack this sort of experience. The theory of interpersonal communication opens a gateway for success: it is in seeing the expressed idea and attitude from the other person's point of view, achieving his or her frame of references about the subject being discussed.

The lesson to be drawn from this recommendation in terms of international investment relations is evident: modelling of the investment climate is indispensable when working out the outlines for the entry management system. The second postulate of the communicational theory is no less relevant: the communicational message must be expressed in a clear form or, in other words, regulations should be transparent and self-explanatory.

The CEMS may form itself without a previous plan being a result of non-coordinated actions which have affected in some way or other the international economic relations of the country in question. This is how it has been built in those countries in which the process of integration in the international markets was stretched across time and how it is being built in some others which are in the initial stages of integration into the world markets and are still uncertain about it, with Russia being one of them.

Countries which staked their fortune on export-led growth followed a different scenario according to which, from the start, the CEMS is contemplated as a complex of interrelated measures including the formation of a necessary institutional structure up to a specialised state body responsible for foreign investment. Of the OECD countries, only Greece reported incentive measures specifically intended for foreign enterprises. But, as the experts of the OECD conclude, the international promotional activities of most member countries indicate that foreign investors are targets of certain programmes which aim at substituting foreign ventures for domestic firms when they are in no position to carry out the desired investment themselves (OECD, 1983, p. 17).

In the economic literature the elements of the CEMS used to be classified as positive and negative. The first group usually includes tax incentives, tariff concessions, locational incentives, export processing zones, non-expropriational guarantees, favoured repatriation, one-stop approval, etc. Ownership restrictions, repatriation restrictions, local content requirements, price controls, export ratio requirements, bureaucratic red-tape, lack of patent and trademark protection together with some other restrictions form the second group. This grouping, however, appears to be somewhat biased: it explicitly relies on the increase in the revenue of foreign investors as a criterion for evaluating the entry management system. If this logic is to be followed, the optimal CEMS should be the one that vigorously plays into the hand of foreign investors. In reality, no government wishing to retain public support can agree to identify national interests with the interests of international investors no matter how strongly it is committed to the principles of economic openness.

'Negative' or restrictive elements are an organic component of a CEMS rather than a sign of its imperfection. It is not by chance that many writers investigating the implications of the business environment on foreign investment hold the same opinion as the authors of *Developing with Foreign Investment* (Cable and Persand (eds), 1987, p. 10) who claim:

> [T]he policies that have had the greatest impact both in attracting FDI and ensuring high social returns to the host country are not special incentives, but countries' principal economic policies. Financial, fiscal and trade policies are by far the most important.

The evidence of less developed countries shows that, where governments seek to boost import of capital, entry management systems tend to have typical teething troubles. The balance of interests in relations between investors and the host country is quite often distorted as authorities overshoot the mark in rendering incentives and privileges for foreign owned ventures in hope to send a strong signal to the international business world that foreign capital and technology are welcome. In some cases this eagerness to attract foreign ventures breaks with economic rationality and proves to bring more disadvantages than otherwise.

Even if we put aside the fact that, by doing this, the host country deprives itself of legitimate income, it is not difficult to see that this approach is shortsighted also in the terms of establishing a favourable investment climate. If the purpose of the entry management system is to promote long-term and expanding relations between exporters and importers of capital, as it should be, then *stability and mutual respect* gain especial importance as features of the investment climate. Obvious disparity puts them at peril. This fact becomes ever more apparent (Vernon, 1985).

This does not mean, of course, that incentives or privileges to foreign capital should be avoided. This is neither possible, nor desirable. Even if international corporations, in some cases, do not gain much by these measures, the very fact that the host country is willing to offer them is considered by potential investors as an important declaration of intentions promising a generally benevolent treatment of foreign capital. Nevertheless, a certain conflict of interests between the host country and transnational business is hardly avoidable. At the same time, feverish competition among borrowing countries in the world capital market plays a harmonisation role: it remains a seller's market thus putting limits on the freedom of recipient countries to shape business relations with foreign investors. There is an evident tendency towards unification and standardisation of regulating investment regimes.

Getting back to the two approaches to economic reforms, in the ex-Soviet republics reform-making radicalism and evolutionism are not

necessarily antipodes. Of course, if radicalism is understood as disposition
to hasty actions and evolutionism as a synonym for inertia, then the two
cannot but be in contradiction. However, if radicalism instead is seen as the
declaration of the *resolution* to achieve the result, i.e. the desired effect, not
just any change in the state of affairs in comparison to the pre-reform
period, in the shortest time possible though not at any cost, while evolutionism is regarded as something that stresses the values of continuity and
discretion as factors reinforcing reforms, then the two approaches could
successfully complement one another. This latter concept of the mutual
complementariness of radicalism and evolutionism in contemplating economic reforms when applied to the realm of foreign investment in Russian
economy, suggests, in my opinion, that designing the CEMS for Russia
should have as its starting points the analysis of:

– the particularities of the economic situation in the country;
– the modern theory of foreign investment;
– Russia's own experience with respect to foreign capital.

1.3   THE CHALLENGES OF SPEEDY INTEGRATION

1.3.1   Systems Incompatibility

The emerging regime for foreign capital in Russia and other ex-Soviet republics cannot be investigated properly unless it is duly placed in the context of
the general transition to an open economy which the CIS member-states are
willing to undertake. It is indisputable indeed that, in order to succeed in
restructuring, the economy of the Commonwealth must be much more open.
The experts of the IMF, the World Bank, the EBRD, and the OECD for
example, in their already mentioned report on the Soviet economy, practically put this point in the centre of their concept of reform maintaining that:

> [i]t is ... essential to move as rapidly as possible to a transparent and
> decentralised trade and exchange rate system, in order to hasten the inte-
> gration of the USSR into the world economy. (*The Economy of the
> USSR*, 1990, p. 17)

Otherwise, the report claims, the monopolism of producers, one of the most
characteristic features of the Soviet economy, cannot be eliminated and,
until prices are free to move in response to shifts in supply and demand,
both domestic and external, markets cannot begin to develop.

The general logic of this reasoning raises no objections. None the less one should not fail to note that the questions of speed and regulation are central to this problem. In fact, there is no guarantee that the consequences of a hasty integration of an economy producing over twenty five million different products will limit themselves only to a destructive impact on monopolies. In order to estimate other possible outcomes as well, it is necessary once again to confront the Soviet economic mechanism as a starting-point of the transition to the mechanism of international markets and evaluate the distance between them.

The discrepancy between the two mechanisms was stipulated from the outset by a distinction in the forms of ownership. However, in the course of the development of the socialist economic mechanism this discrepancy was consciously drawn to extremes owing to two factors which had more to do with politics and ideology than with the organic qualities of the economic system itself. The first was that hypercentralism in the political system – the foundation of Stalin's regime – could not be firm enough unless coupled with an equally rigid centralism in economy. The slogan 'economic policy is the main policy of the Party' was used as an ideological gimmick for designing and creating an economic mechanism non-responsive to any input other than the directives of the central authorities. The primitive and erroneous perception of socialism as a society which has to be in every respect diametrically opposite to capitalism was the second factor. Instead of being a successor to capitalism, as envisaged by Marx, Soviet socialism tried to become its alternative.

The logic of constructing socialism in 'one separate country' demanded a degree of political and economic isolation and shaped Soviet strategy towards international markets. The system of foreign economic contacts evolved in the USSR had a two-fold orientation: to protect the national economic system from whatever external signals interfered with the voluntarism of the command economy on the one hand and to compensate for the deficiencies of domestic production through imports on the other. The system evolved proved to be reliable and the Soviet Union, in the course of time, had got the economy into strong autarkic momentum. Creation of the CMEA did not change much as this integrational organisation followed, yet on a larger scale, a traditional 'two systems–two worlds' approach to international economy.

Today, it is proposed that this highly specific economy should be promptly integrated into the world economy. The aim cannot be in question. Yet policy-makers must be fully aware of the obstacles awaiting the country on this path, as well as of the additional costs the opening-up is likely to impose on the economy and decide on the pace of a reform and measures necessary to minimise its burden.

1.3.2   An 'Open Economy' Concept

Since reform is often described in the terms of a transition from a 'closed' to an 'open' economy, it is important to be clear on the meaning of these concepts. Although the two words – open economy – are very common in modern economic discourse, there is still no unanimity as to what they really mean.

General convention is that they should be applied to an economy with considerable foreign exposure. Most often an international trade criterion is used as a cornerstone. In this case an export volume/GNP ratio, a so-called export quota, is utilised to measure the rate of openness of the national economy. It seems, however, that this indicator, used rigorously, could be valid only for qualified purposes. With the export quota of less than 10 per cent, in 1989, the USA would have a very modest performance as an 'open economy', especially in comparison with countries such as Belgium and Switzerland, or, for example, Ireland in which this ratio, in 1989, was 70 per cent.[5] But with the United States expelled from the ranks of open economies, one would unjustifiably narrow the range of plausible explanations for vigorous trade wars in which the US has been almost constantly engaged during the last two decades, as well as for the fact that the USA has been the driving force behind the GATT ever since its foundation. A study *Is the US a spendthrift nation?* by Lipsey and Kravis, two National Bureau of Economic Research experts, suggests that while the fraction of world markets held by US corporations exporting from the territory of the United States has steadily dropped during the last quarter of a century, such losses have been offset by the gains of American corporations exporting from other nations. The existence of 'second economies' is just one argument favouring the claim that big industrialised countries are more open than country-by-country foreign trade figures might suggest.

It is reasonable, therefore, to apply the term 'openness' to describe the situation when there are clear signs, *together with or despite the export share*, that the economic stability and well-being of a country substantially depends on its international performance, and the economy itself is extensively exposed to international competition.

In 1985, when the turnover of the Soviet foreign trade was the highest, it had never exceeded 4 per cent of world trade though the volume of its GNP was about 10 per cent of the world total. Since 1986, the figures of international trade of ex-Soviet economies had been progressively deteriorating to fall, by 1992, to the 1979 level. None the less, the opening-up of post-Soviet economies, at least for the time being, is not so much about their export quotas as about disclosing their markets and their enterprises to the hazards of an alien economic environment.

The problem of Russia and other republics of the CIS is not only in their particularly distorted relative prices, a complete lack of experience of private ownership, little exposure to market system and unresolved constitutional questions. No less, if not more, important is that, in the years of socialist planning, *the economy was subordinated to a completely different logic of development* (see for instance Nove, 1991; Nagels, 1993) which had led to the creation of a number of in-built checks or barriers (Ol'sevich, 1991) insulating the economy as a whole as well as its separate sectors and enterprises from the rest of the world in a more profound manner than conventional tariff barriers and exchange regulation can provide. Some of the most important barriers are as follows.

1.4 BARRIERS TO INTEGRATION

1.4.1 Technological Incompatibility

Domestic machinery and technologies are commonly generations behind their state-of-the-art counterparts in the West. Usually, industrial and technological equipment produced in the country is heavier and less precise, consumes more energy than the models of foreign firms and – this is most crucial – employs far fewer electronic devices, which raises the main obstacle to increasing its efficacy. In particular, minicomputerisation has created a sizable and growing technological gap favourable to the West. It also brought about the shift from the economies of scale of the Fordist-type production to the economies of flexibility of post-Fordism. Since, by design, the majority of the equipment produced in the CIS belongs to a pre-electronic era, it cannot be lifted to modern standards simply through refinement: a new state of technological quality must be reached first. Hence, the engineering industry can only find export markets in some developing countries, but, quite obviously, this is equally true of other national industries as they depend on the input from the engineering industry. Even before having slid into its present depressive condition triggered by the general economic slump, mechanical engineering never contributed, sales to CMEA countries included, more than 15–16 per cent (in monetary terms) to national exports. This was half the share of this industry in the total industrial output of the country three times less than the machine-building component in the exports of the Federal Republic of Germany and the US and half as average world index.[6]

Therefore, the future of this important industrial sector depends on how strong its positions in the internal market will be. On the one hand numerous prognoses predicting that domestic producers will be ousted by foreign competitors as soon as the access to the market of the CIS becomes unconditional seem to fail to recognise in full the degree of the qualitative integrity of the productive forces of the country. Engineering industry is not the only sector of the economy which is below world standards. Its performance corresponds to the average quality of labour, supplies, services and infrastructure in the country. Backwardness as a common feature makes national industries more compatible with one another than with firms abroad thus leaving domestic producers at least a theoretical chance to retain a niche in the domestic market.

On the other hand, over the longer term, this chance is limited. It is based on a disadvantage, rather than on an advantage. It might help enterprises sharing it stay afloat as long as they constituted mutually related entities. In reality, this integrity is breaking together with the collapse of the Union state. In fact, the economy of the USSR – this is often overlooked – had become factually 'open' as soon as it had disintegrated into the economies of sovereign republics. Each is now extensively exposed to influences by the other. In 1991, inter-republic trade involved about 20 per cent of their combined GNP; in the European Community the figure was 14 per cent. The share of purchase of goods from other republics and abroad, in consumption, ranged from 16 per cent in Russia to 31 in Armenia. The share of sale of goods to other republics and abroad, in production, varied from 11 per cent in Russia and Kazakhstan to 27 per cent in Azerbaijan.[7] The ending of many traditional ties has put the industrial complex of the CIS at the brink of paralysis. In the Russian economic literature this development is generally condemned as regressive and counterproductive, leading to catastrophic consequences.[8] At the same time, one can hardly come across an attempt to estimate what has happened from the point of view of modelling the situation of hasty integration in the world market. For enterprises, owing to the barrier of technological incompatibility, disintegrating effects will be even stronger. How many of them will have to be closed down in the absence of relevant regulations necessary to smooth the transition? No such calculations have ever been done, furthermore, they are hardly feasible.[9] Nevertheless, some conclusions may be deduced from the experience of restructuring in Central Europe.

The costs of the integration of East German industry, modern and efficient by CMEA standards, into the economy of the Federal Republic of Germany have proved unexpectedly high. In the territory of the former GDR, industrial production has fallen by one half of the 1985 level and the number of unemployed and short-time workers has reached 2.5 million (a third of the East Germany's labour force). The IMF estimates that to reach the West German levels of productivity by 2001 would require no less than one trillion dollars of investment in eastern Germany within ten years.[10] In 1992 alone, net transfers from Bonn to the east are expected to total about 112.5 billion US dollar.[11] These data put in question the reliability of the often quoted estimate of 20 to 25 billion dollars in foreign aid sufficient, according to Russian economists staying on the platform of the government,[12] to give an impulse to restructuring of the ex-Soviet economy.

1.4.2 Structural Incompatibility

The Soviet Union's economy was a rare example of an industrial economy without revealed comparative advantages. The profile of its sectoral structure and the relative weight of different industries in the GNP was defined by the aspiration for self-sufficiency and the maintenances of military–strategic parity. Participation in the international division of labour played a supportive role and, in fact, was never based on anything like comparative advantages, as a dramatic gap between internal and world price systems made impossible any meaningful comparison. Foreign trade was a state monopoly completely controlled by the central authority. Export policy was subordinated to the needs of industries using imports, hence, selling in world markets was mainly[13] a means to pay the bill for imports.

The notorious dependence of Soviet exports on the sales of oil, timber and some other non-manufactured goods (60 per cent of all exports) is more evidence of the specifics of the Soviet economic mechanism than of particular competitive strength in extracting, mining or other similar industries. In reality, Soviet policy-makers traditionally favoured the export of machinery and equipment in comparison to other goods, also out of consideration of the international prestige associated with the high level of machinery exports.

However, the pursuit of this policy was continually frustrated: domestic manufacturers, being effectively isolated from competitive pressure as much as from the fruits of commercial success, refused to make the additional effort necessary to help their products penetrate foreign markets. Furthermore, they came to view foreign orders as undesirable. As early as 1959, by introducing special supplements to prices, the government launched what later became a long succession of export-stimulating measures. They never really worked.[14] In this context, a stress on the export of mineral resources was the easiest way out the government had at hand. Oil and gas were exported despite the fact that domestic demand for these products was not satisfied and the real cost of production was unreasonably high.

The economy of the CIS has inherited the structural defects of the Soviet economy. In the last twenty years, in the West the composition of industries has undergone profound changes. Labour, material and energy-intensive industries have given way to technology and capital intensive production; the role of services has dramatically increased and their range expanded; front-line technology, modern infrastructure and managerial skill became major competitive advantages; knowledge has acquired the status of a leading export commodity.

By contrast, in the CIS prime processing dominates industry; the relative weight of heavy industries is overwhelming and the per capita consumption of steel kept rising contrary to a world tendency; enterprises are orientated to the mass output of simple articles; services, both for firms and individuals, are scarce and of poor quality, many modern banking, insurance or financial products are simply unknown; infrastructure is obsolete; the degree of commercial utilisation of the results of scientific research has been extremely low.

The logic of autarkic development has brought the industrial complex of the CIS to the point where it can rely on no established niches in the world market and, in the terms of a structure, is lagging far behind other industrialised countries. This latter fact is especially alarming in view of a clear trend in the international economy towards building up an exclusive technological community of a few industrialised countries monopolising research, development and innovation. The competitive gap between these and other countries is increasing. A new system of international division of labour, which will shape the distribution of wealth between countries in the foreseeable future, is under way. The CIS member-states may find themselves being backwashed by this process to the periphery of international economy. The disquieting signs are everywhere. For example, boasting a quarter of the world's graduates, the Soviet Union, in the 1980s, managed to export patents and licenses averaging only 150–200 million dollars a year against 700 million dollars in Japan and eight billion dollars in the United States (*Pravda*, August 10, 1989). Furthermore, no leading industry of the country has a competitive advantage from pioneering technology to ease a start out into the world market.[15]

In this situation the speedy integration of the CIS into international markets will inevitably entail drastic restructuring of the economy. If firms are left to fend for themselves, it will mean the death of entire industries. At the same time, the accelerated pace of restructuring alone can provide no guarantee that the economy which will emerge will be something more than an off-shore assembly platform for transnational corporations, or an indigenous exporter of mineral resources, basic machinery and educated labour.

The 'new' international economics, whilst not denying the importance of underlying differences among countries in shaping the positions of a national economy with respect to other economies, adds that much of international trade also reflects national advantages that are created by historical circumstances, and that they then persist and grow because of other advantages to a large scale either in development or production. Paul Krugman (1990, p. 110) cites journalist James Fallows: 'Countries that try to promote higher-value, higher-tech industries will eventually have more of them than countries that don't', and then concludes:

> Because comparative advantage is often created, not given, a temporary subsidy can lead to a permanent industry. (Krugman, 1990, p. 110)

This plea is addressed to the American government but there are no reasons to believe that this line of reasoning is not valid for the CIS with its huge problem of structural imbalance. Could a market alone be held responsible for settling down such an imbalance, in particular if the market in question is immature and ill-functioning? This question remains open for discussion. What may be suggested at this point is that any answer to it should account for two important realities: first, in one way or another, state interventionism has been an indispensable attribute of all existing economic systems including the most liberal; second, with a few exceptions, everywhere in ex-socialist countries the demolition of an old economic mechanism has been showing much faster progress than the installation of its market-based successor. This may lead to the situation of an economic nonsystem (Nuti, 1992) which is likely rather impede to than help transition.

1.4.3   Efficiency Incompatibility

Efficiency depends on a combination of factors many of which stay beyond what may be described in terms of production organisation proper. By responding to market failures through internalising certain market functions, modern corporations – especially those doing business in international markets – have evolved sophisticated organisations whose ultimate success is secured by developing and implementing a range of product, technological, marketing, employment, advertisement and other strategies. A popular theory on transnational corporations specifically stresses the importance of so-called *intangible* assets as a stimulus for internationalisation (Dunning, 1985). They include not only in-house bred technology and patent rights, but likewise managerial skills, the organisational experience, the knowledge of the market, local contacts, the reputation of the brand, good record with the banks, etc.

In this respect the CIS enterprises are very seriously handicapped by their socialist past. There are factories and plants using modern technology able to produce competitive goods. But this might not be sufficient for them to remain viable in an open market environment. For decades the efficiency of enterprises was evaluated according to how successful they were in fulfilling plan figures: they never had a free hand to pursue their own industrial, technological or commercial policy. The system did not harbour effective incentives promoting innovations, technical progress or quality. Many enterprises have been 'value subtractors' – that is, at world prices the value of the resources they consume is worth more than they produce. There are no figures concerning the ex-Soviet Union; however, a recent study covering manufacturing industries in Poland, Czechoslovakia and Hungary maintains that 20 to 25 per cent of enterprises could be value-subtractors.[16] Excessive centralisation in decision-making and priority for administrative over economic criteria stipulated a particular type of business environment which made for a wasteful economy[17] and left its basic units – enterprises – only poorly equipped for autonomous survival in the face of more competent competitors. The observation of N. Klimov and D. Kuzin,[18] two experts from the Institute of Economics of the Russian Academy of Sciences, is much to the point:

> [I]f in capitalist countries industrial, technological and foreign economic policies are closely interrelated, if any big firm there evaluates its performance and builds its strategy accounting for the global factors of competition, in our country there is neither such coordination of policies, nor even a basic notion of a long-term firm strategy or of those dozens of factors which determine competitiveness.

If the situation remains unchanged, direct clashes between the firms of the CIS and foreign companies in the world market, as well as in the market of the CIS, are likely to resemble a skirmish between militia units and the regular army. To turn once again to the fate of big industry in the ex-socialist countries of Europe: firms with modern plant and boasting a certain standing in export markets, such as Tungsram (lighting equipment) in Hungary and Skoda (automobiles) in Czechoslovakia, have already become the property of transnational corporations. The others face at best a dim and uncertain future, and at worst oblivion.

1.5   ON THE WAY TO 'NEW' INTERVENTIONISM

The above review of only a few of the difficulties awaiting Russia's economy in the course of integration into the world economic system, though necessarily brief, sufficiently serves our goal of drawing attention once again to what is at stake in current reforms. Unlike textbook abstractions, in actual life no variable may be disposed of because it does not fit the model. A long-term economic degradation of the country cannot be just assumed away. 'Shock' therapy hard-liners never lose a chance to stress that the country has found itself in an economic stalemate not because reforms are harsh and hasty but because they came late, adding that 'hidden' degradation was characteristic of the Soviet economy long before the reforms started.

However, references to the past could be as misleading as they are consoling. In real terms the difference between 'hidden' and 'revealed' degradation may be enormous. The main point is the problem of the decline in living standards, and the inevitable unemployment and social tensions provoked by them. Under the administrative–command system, overemployment was the cause of inefficiency in production, and by far the most important sign of economic degradation. But, at the same time, it was also a tool of social policy similar to public works under President Roosevelt's 'New Deal'. It was used by the regime to cushion the social consequences of economic stagnation. Marketisation is eliminating this cushion and the opening of the economy will be the ferment which may speed up the process to the state of explosion.

Being the product of the Soviet economic system, the described barriers cannot be overcome until the system's legacy is disposed of. Internal reforms, in particular the privatisation of property and the establishment of a new type of relations between the business and the state, play a leading role here. Despite all the present uncertainty concerning the pace and the efficiency of these reforms, they should define the speed and the scale of the opening up of the ex-Soviet economy (unless its integration in the world market is seen as an end in itself, which would be a mistake).

The problem of reforming the ex-Soviet economy is very much a chicken-and-egg dilemma. So many factors interact and so many interests interlace that no beginning seems to have indisputable advantages over any other. The reforms by definition are destructive. However, some forms of destruction may be productive, others not. What matters is the scale, pace and sequence of reform. This is wholly valid with respect to the sphere of international economic relations. The warnings that a shift to an open economy should be gradual, well prepared and based on a sophisticated strategy may be heard not only inside Russia. Addressing reformers in post socialist countries, Professor Alice Amsden writes (*International Herald Tribune*, April 10, 1990):

> Without institutional guidelines and vision, freer markets will only squelch the ability [of industries] to compete, and at greater social cost … Many developing countries that lack the machinery to screen foreign investments find the benefits less than costs.

In her conclusions, Professor Amsden refers to the record of those countries which commonly serve as a textbook example of a successful transition from internal to external oriented development: the newly industrialised countries.

Contrary to early publications and the position of the major development agencies tending to present their case as a vindication of a free-market approach to economic development, recent investigations are careful to stress that their success was designed and secured through extensive state intervention. Two of them, by Wade (1990) and Smith (1991), stand out thanks to the scope and the depth of the analysis. Their major finding is that successful export-led growth has generally been based on activist trade and industrial policy. However, this recent flow of literature draws a distinction between what Wade calls 'traditional' and 'new' interventionism: the former tried to eliminate the market, the latter seeks to collaborate with it – to guide, not replace, the market. The important characteristic of the 'new' interventionism is that it needs to be open to the feedback from the market so that state economic policy is to be subordinated to economic rationality rather than to political ambitions.

1.6 SEARCHING FOR A NEW PARADIGM

Clearly the problem with the 'new' interventionism, as with any authoritative action, is that regulators may abuse discretion or use their powers incompetently. In the case of Russia and other CIS member-states, the abundance of goodwill cannot make up for the absence or inadequacy of theoretical and material, legislative and institutional premises for foreign investment. Such an environment has yet to be synthesised. This naturally only brings in the question of what will be the guiding lines along which the synthesis will proceed. There might be different scenarios varying mainly by the relative balance between governmental action and the interplay of market forces.

The synthesis may only work if there is a strategic concept constituting a basic framework for a national policy towards foreign investment. There is no real need that such a concept should necessarily take the form of an official declaration or a programme, although this variant cannot be entirely excluded. It may well be a kind of prevailing general attitude for foreign capital participation expressed through state legislation and practice, entrepreneurial behaviour and public opinion. As any product of the interaction of social forces this attitude is likely to bear the signs of compromise and will be subject to permanent correction. Though there is little doubt that it will be based mainly on the everyday experience and material interests of the main participant groups, it is none the less of great importance what set of ideas will serve as a methodological key for interpreting the facts of life.

The change of attitude towards economic openness in general and towards foreign direct investment in particular is a remarkable sign of the new political and economic thinking in Russia. Foreign investors are now seen, for the most part, as partners in developing the economy of the country. However, this general perception has not yet taken the form of a coherent comprehensive longer term strategy at the state level. Up to now the efforts of the state to regulate foreign investment and adjoining activities bore many signs of haste and emergency. They were mainly concentrated on two objectives. One was to grope for organisational forms facilitating the inclusion of foreign direct investment in the framework of the Soviet economy with its many specific features (in practice so far only the joint venture has been widespread). The other was to adopt some essential legislation intended either to bring juridical norms, affecting foreign investors, in line with prevailing international standards. For example, since being introduced in 1987, norms regulating joint ventures have undergone three subsequent rounds of profound revisions and amendments, explicitly progressing towards further liberalisation. Otherwise, provisional measures have been introduced to close gaps in existing legislation.

Both approaches are of importance, granted the total lack of previous administrative experience in the area, as well as the absence, until late, of any regulations or institutions dealing with this range of issues. But this type of work, as well as forthcoming regulations, may eventually miss their point if there is a lack of a pivotal idea (or criterion) behind them, generalising foreign investment-related aspirations on the national scale and, in this capacity, functioning as a sort of a yardstick for measuring the effects of state policy and the performance of foreign capital itself. This implies the following question: 'What potential advantages may this country expect to get from foreign investment and how can it manage to extract them in reality?'

It seems only logical at this point to advise policy-makers to refer to existing concepts of foreign investment – intellectual products offered by international economics and international political economy, and allegedly combining theoretical insight with the generalisation of actual experience. In reality, of course, this advice cannot easily be followed owing to competition between different theories and, in too many cases, the spectacular inadequacy of theoretical analysis in relation to the practical needs of policy makers. Despite the sincere effort of many scholars to be independent and objective in their research, political and economic theories are known to reflect ideological beliefs and cultural and historical background of their authors. In the case of international relations studies, belonging of the scholar to one of the two existing 'worlds' – developed and developing – usually also shows.

None the less, all the social and economic conceptions that have stayed the test of time cannot but carry a grain of rationality in them. Ernesto Balducci, authoritative modern Italian philosopher, once remarked (*Testimonianze*, No. 2, February 1992):

> In order to create a really planetary civilisation, without any hegemony, we have to resolve conflicts not by force but through revealing the partial truth which every particular case conceals.

This observation holds its force also when applied to the realm of theories. What make possible the coexistence (though not necessarily peaceful) of contradictory explanations of the world around us is in part the complexity of the world itself. Physicists discovered long ago that the observer's perception of reality depended on his position in respect to the investigating item, i.e. on the chosen system of co-ordinates. For this reason both classical and quantum mechanics are right within their own term of reference. Rival economic theories follow the same pattern by applying, quite often, different systems of co-ordinates, presumption and assumptions in relation to the facts they allegedly explore. In this context the choice between a right and wrong theory should be considered in the terms of choosing a proper system of co-ordinates, i.e. the relevance of its premises and the degree to which it relates to reality itself.

For Russian scholars this choice will not be easy. There are clear signs of a general search for a new paradigm to be characterised, among other things, by a rearranged balance between traditional Marxism and modern western theories. It is a natural and important process. However, it is not unfounded to believe that, at least on the initial stage, it will be strongly affected by other than purely scientific considerations. Facing the fate of a dismissed official teaching, Marxism is clearly on the defensive in the country. Western theories, on the contrary, have all the appeal of forbidden fruit, the charm of novelty and can very often count on the support of important academic schools and international organisations. If in the West, for decades, Marxism has been synonymous with radical thinking, in modern Russia, instead, scientific radicalism in economics and social sciences expresses itself in advocating the extremes of free market theorising. Radical 'fashion' may deprive the newly emerging paradigm of many approaches which might prove to be especially relevant for the Russian case.

Below I shall try to put forward arguments in favour of the claim that defining proper terms of reference for opening-up strategy in the transitional economy means directly addressing issues of national competitiveness.

The issue, like the attention paid to it by scholars and politicians, has grown dramatically in recent decades owing to the globalisation of production and markets, and to the new lines of interaction of nations this latter brought into existence. None the less, whatever extensive globalising proceeded up to now, one sixth of the dry land of our planet, harbouring one fifth of the production capacity of the world, has been and still is mainly isolated from this process. The integration of the ex-Soviet republics in the international market system will inevitably affect the interests of traditional and new world economic power centres and add to international rivalry.

One hundred and fifty years ago, Friedrich List wrote that, in the real system of international competition, the nation may rely only on itself; it may not even expect other states not to interfere, as the increasing might of one power threatens the interests, and insults the feelings, of all nations aspiring at independence, wealth and high political significance. A lot has changed in the world since the time this observation was put on paper but it appears to be premature to regard it as dated. In the economic sphere nations continue to vie for wealth. The state of national competitiveness is important since jobs with high value-adding and wealth-generating capacities are rare and by no means can be distributed evenly across nations. The structure of production is such that these 'premium' jobs make only a fraction of all jobs needed to provide for the modern society. Rich countries are anxious to transfer the low tiers of a job pyramid to a foreign production basis. Foreign direct investment is as much a tool of this policy, just as it is an important channel of dispersing modern technology worldwide; most of all it is an indispensable component of the international economic system.

The premises, functions and consequences of the export of capital are numerous, which is probably the reason for the absence of anything like a general theory of foreign investment; instead there are many explanations on foreign investment from different positions and points of view. The following chapter will search for a methodological key to the many investment theories valid for countries in the state of transition.

Notes

1.   For a discussion on the condensed version of the study, *The Economy of the USSR: Summary and Recommendations*, see *Voprosy ekonomiki*, 1991, 4, pp. 37–47; No. 5, pp. 3–27.

2.   In the economic literature the terms 'shock' therapy or 'big bang' are usually applied to any programmes having as their conspicuous feature a drastic and massive change in key economic parameters (see *ECE, Economic Survey of Europe in 1991–1992*, New York: UN, 1992, p. 41).

3.   It is not without irony that in the United States where the Bush administration, with its free-market orientation, for years publicly opposed a collaboration between the government and the private sector, the developements in the Commonwealth of Independent States urged a noticeable change in policy. Seeking to give the United States a leading role in shaping the Commonwealth transition to capitalism, the Bush administration patently supported Federal guarantees for private-sector investments. Moreover, by doing this it fuelled a debate over the need for a more comprehensive national industrial policy, one that would explore other areas that could benefit from the government help and presumably rank them by importance.

4.   *Izvestia*, April 13, 1992, p. 7.

5.   *European Economy*, November 1989, p. 252.

6.   *Voprosy ekonomiki*, 1991, No. 2, p. 105.

7.   *Ekonomika i zhizn'*, February 11, 1992, No. 6, p. 13.

8.   Complex industries with extensive vertical and horizontal integration have suffered most. The steel industry is an appropriate example. One of the most important distinguishing characteristics of Soviet ferrous metal production was its self-sufficiency in raw materials and a considerable usage of scrap as a replacement of pig-iron. This latter fact makes collecting and rechanelling scrap to metallurgical plants vitally important for the industry. Separatism of ex-Soviet republics undermined the traditional links of metal turnover and caused, in 1991, a decline in production equal to 22 per cent of the achieved level (*Izvestia*, April 22, 1992).

9.   According to official statistics, in 1990, forty per cent of state enterprises were either loss-making or achieving minimal profit (*Planovoe khoziaistvo*, No. 3, 1991, p. 31). It would be wrong to deduce, however, that all these enterprises are prime candidates for a close-down if markets are liberalized as many of them were consciously made profitless by plan assignments and others were victims of a distorted price system.

10. *The Economist*, April 6 1991, p. 63.

11. *International Herald Tribune*, April 8, 1992.

12. See, for example, *La Repubblica*, March 26, 1992.

13. Though not solely of course: trade, especially in weapons and military hardware, as an instrument of political influence was also important.

14. See *The Impact of International Economic Disturbances on the Soviet Union and Eastern Europe* (New York: Pergamon Press, 1980).
15. Military industries have considerable technological potential. In certain areas (metallurgy, composites, aeronautics) they hold leading positions in the world and surpass American and Japanese producers. However, the technologies they use are so much specialized on military products that they cannot be utilized for other purposes without enormous new investment, 150 billion US dollars according to official figures (*Izvestia*, March 31, 1992).
16. *The Economist*, September 21, 1991, Survey, p. 13.
17. The following data is helpful in conveying the idea of the scale of this waste: the cost of the equipment bought and paid for by state firms which had not been installed and remained in deposit by the end of 1989 amounted to an astronomic sum of 18 billion rubles. One third of this equipment was ordered from abroad (*Pravda*, December 22, 1989).
18. *Voprosy ekonomiki*, 1990, No. 8, p. 7.

2 The National Competitiveness Paradigm

Theories are reflections of the reality in the minds of the people analyzing this reality. Fashion in a theory may be just a fashion, or it might be a manifestation of the general recognition of a new reality. Recently there has been a notable surge of interest in national competitiveness. At first it looked predominantly like an American phenomenon, a demonstration on the part of American politicians, businessmen and academics of preoccupations with the declining role of American industry in the world. However, the scale of the discussion has been increasing, also in geographical terms. Having started across the Atlantic (M. Porter, R. Reich, P. Drucker, P. Krugman), it later benefited from the contribution of Europeans (J. Dunning, A. Francis, H.-P. Frölich, C. Carr). Quite soon the notion of competitiveness became something more than an issue of the business theory alone and developed into an important analytical key to the explanation of the modern process of internationalisation.

2.1 THE FORMATION OF A BI-POLAR MODEL

Historically, the first theoretical reflections on this process may be traced back to the beginning of the nineteenth-century. Internationalisation initially asserted itself through a vigorous increase in international trade, following the rise in production and consumption in a number of European states based on capitalist entrepreneurship and the fruits of the First Industrial Revolution. It was only logical, in this early stage, that the attention of theorists, when directed to the realm of the international economy, was drawn almost exclusively to foreign trade and its consequences.

Two major approaches emerged. These pioneering insights were so powerful that, in fact, they have defined the scope of the discussion ever since and, hence, cannot be left out in this analysis. Very much contrasting on the surface, they marked the two poles in explaining international trade and international economic relations in general.

The relationship of the two in the historical perspective is very suggestive. The first, free-trade theory, seemed to have all the necessary credentials to be presented as a powerful example of a victorious teaching, revealing to the benefit of the thankful world the hidden mechanics of international economics. The record of the other, the protectionist doctrine, might invite many to regret once again the pitiful human weakness of persisting in one's delusions. Indeed, as much as the free-trade theory looks to be logical, rational, democratic and progressive by claiming that any trading country would gain from international trade provided nothing impedes market forces to disclose its comparative advantage, protectionism seems to be nationalistic, discriminative and politically biased when defending the right of the nation state to correct the 'invisible hand' of the market. In the realm of theory, the free-trade concept could boast the contribution of such giants of economic thought as Adam Smith and David Ricardo, politically it was backed by the authority of one of the oldest democracies of the world – the British. By contrast, in many minds protectionism was strongly associated with dictatorial regimes and war preparations. Protectionism is related to mercantilism which is based on the premise that, in international economic relations, the gains of one of the sides signal losses for the other. This is particularly irrelevant nowadays.

In decades of uneasy coexistence of the two doctrines, free-traders more than once announced a crushing theoretical defeat of protectionism. As early as 1923 John Maynard Keynes was writing that free trade was based on fundamental truths:

> which, stated with their due qualifications, no one can dispute who is capable of understanding the meaning of the words. (Keynes, vol. xix, p. 147)

However, the remarkable viability of protectionist heresy perplexed many minds in the free-traders' camp. As early as at the begining of this century a question was raised by liberal-minded economists, which still has not lost its significance: If the protectionist theory is so incompatible with the nature of things and contradicts itself, how does it manage then, after so many years of discussion, to enjoy such powerful support?

This question cannot be answered as long as one is willing to discuss the international economy exclusively in terms of pure economic rationality. Under certain conditions, national states cannot abstain from intervening in the economy. The free-trade conception implicitly suggests the willingness or ability of the states to pay the social and political costs of the adaptation period necessary to reveal their 'comparative advantage'. It is not by chance that this theory was developed in nineteenth century Britain, the country which had no doubts as to where its comparative advantages lay. The economic strength of Britain added to the persuasiveness of free trade postulates. As a result, a particular case was developed into a general (or generalised) theory. However, in more than one respect it was an idealistic concept built on a belief in the feasibility of the optimal international division of labour, and in the possibility of putting the world's resources and abilities to the best uses of all nations without discrimination.

This idealism was excusable at a time when international economic relations had not yet revealed their complexity. Even today the belief that market impulses may be efficiently corrected only by the market itself has influential advocates. But, it seems, this idea has never worked in practice. Attempts to correct the play of market forces are both numerous and never ending. This is especially true of national reaction to external changes. This may be attributed, *inter alia,* to the following three reasons.

First, the international market is far from being a structure in which market power is diffused to such a degree that all participants have the chance to be equally affected by its developments. On the contrary, the market of today is associated, in the first place, with the activities of transnational banks and corporations. Despite their sometimes accentuated supranational image, these are seen in countries other than their home-countries as serving foreign interests rather than the conductors of the impulses of a national-neutral international market. From this perspective, to speak in simplified terms, for a country to be exposed to the world market is very much the same as to be exposed to the transnational corporations and, eventually, to the policies of external power centres. Susan Strange (1988a) in *States and Markets* reveals the importance of what she calls 'structural power' ('the power to shape and determine the structures of the global political economy within other states...' [Strange, 1988a, p. 24]) in international relations, i.e., a power based upon control over key world 'structures' (production, credit, knowledge, and also transport systems, trade, energy, welfare) by big corporations headquartered and owned in a few industrialised countries, rather than on a capacity to exert political or military pressure by one state over another.

Second, there still remains the central problem of the cost of the market self-balancing in terms of material losses, the wastage of time and the growth of social tension. It stays in close relation to the fact that, *third*, national government cannot submit to speculative economic rationality only. Politics, ideology, defence, ecology are just a few of the priorities which would not be neglected. This is where the state steps in. It tries to equilibrate these priorities by reacting to the interplay of a variety of factors, with the balance of power between main social groups having a decisive vote. Although, as an abstraction, it is possible to imagine a certain optimum, in reality this equilibrium is most likely to be reached at some other point as there is no scarcity in historical precedents. Nationalism, for example, might overwhelm ideological belief, or political ambitions might subordinate economic common sense. In this respect Paul Kennedy's *The Rise and Fall of the Great Powers* (1988) is extremely helpful in supplying a historical record of cases where the economy fell victim to military expansion and political ambitions. The record reveals a striking regularity in the fate of great powers: at a certain moment their economy breaks down following an imbalance on the 'matrix' of state priorities.

2.2 INTEGRATING THE POLITICAL DIMENSION

Hence, any theoretical concept describing international economic relations, if it hopes to be of pratical use, should not omit the political factor. The perception of the ruling elite of what is good for the country translates into a set of laws, acts and regulations. By issuing them and by securing their observance by all the persons and agencies under its jurisdiction, the state implements its sovereignty. The state cannot allow itself to be indifferent to the character and the intensity of impulses transmitted through the channels of international economic interconnectedness. The question is whether it is in a position to cut off these channels, or at least dilute the exposure to external influences. The answer depends on two parameters: the degree of economic openness and the relative power of a state to handle the matter.

It is appropriate to address this set of problems as a structural phenomenon. Such an approach suggests that an economy may be profoundly involved in internationalisation without being overexposed to the world market in any particular field. The fact that no country – great or small – can resist the forces that impose these structures supports the thesis that, taking into consideration the present level of the development of productive forces, no country is big enough anymore, either as a market or as a production base.

For many, a protectionist doctrine is synonymous with tariffs and its critique is often confined to evaluating if tariffs and other impediments to international trade are good or bad for the development of national industry and the economy in general.[1] But, we can overcome this narrow approach to this doctrine as a specialised trade theory and put the controversy between protectionism and free trade in the wider context of the opposition between *laissez-faire* and what is now commonly known as the Keynesian school in economic thinking. This gives it a broader relevance.

By allocating expressively a particular role to the state, protectionist theory adds, in a sense, a new, political, dimension to the one-dimensional picture of the world dominated by economic rationality alone. In methodological terms this constitutes its cognitive value. It also explains why its appeal increases every time that the world economy enters the troubled waters of recession. Furthermore, as world trade was supplemented by the flows of foreign direct investment and 'hot money' as well as technology, labour, information, the protectionist idea understood, in a broad sense, as a bias on preserving the national economic (and not only economic) identity has gained ground. Keynes was probably among the first to recognise that the international economy had been entering a new phase when foreign economic relations were no longer the extension of the national economy but, rather, this latter was developing into a subordinate part of a new supranational whole. This made him write, in 1933, only ten years after his essay on free trade cited above:

> [T]he policy of an increased national self-sufficiency is to be considered not as an ideal in itself but as directed to the creation of an environment in which other ideals can be safely and conveniently pursued. (Keynes, vol. xxi, p. 240)

2.3   A FIRST STEP TO SYNTHESIS

The argumentation presented by Keynes in his article 'National Self-Sufficiency' anticipated many of the theses of modern open economy theories. At first glance this similarity may be puzzling: the latter seem to be more related to free trade thinking since they do not really dispute the merits of intensive transnational exchange of goods, capital, labour, etc. and accept them as an objective necessity.

Yet it is not difficult to notice that these theories are genetically linked to protectionism, although reflecting the realities of a different time. There is a strong tradition, especially in econometric literature, of viewing the problem of openness from the point of view of neutralising unfavourable outside influence,[2] that is exactly the approach followed by Keynes in 'National Self-Sufficiency'. This proves in a remarkable way that protectionist doctrine as a current of thought had never actually led to a deadlock. Rather it gave a shape to natural concerns of a world divided by national borders. At the same time, the open economy theories have principal distinctions in comparison with their forerunner: the task of how to stay free of the external impact has given way to that of how to cushion this impact whilst employing in full the advantages of the international division of labour.[3]

The open economy theories reflect a specific stage in the development of the international political economy and economics when the eminence of the process of internationalisation had been acknowledged by theorists, but its true scale and force had not been yet realised. Unlike the inter-war period, in postwar years the great majority of scholars have held the opinion that participation in international economic relations is not a matter of free choice but, in fact, has no alternative. Indeed, the twentieth century has brought about the unprecedented expansion of world trade and transnational capital flow which represent two major channels connecting numerous economies in a contradictory bunch. In recent decades they have been coupled with the cross-frontier streams of technology, labour, expertise and know-how. Together with the worldwide exchange of information and culture which provides the groundwork for a powerful demonstration effect apt to generate additional currents of goods, services and capital across national borders,[4] these new channels have pushed the process of internationalisation of national economies to the degree where it has become one of the most important factors of national development and world politics.

At the same time, it is widely recognised that the process of internationalisation has increased the number of challenges facing national policy-makers as well as entrepreneurs, added to the unpredictability of market developments. All in all, it seems, it has made the actors of international economic relations pay greater costs incurred by multiplied uncertainties. Therefore it is not surprising that the literature on the open economy and economic interdependence first concentrated on revealing the destabilising effects of internationalisation on the national business environment, and especially on the ability of government agencies to carry out the regulative strategy they conceived to be necessary for national interests or, more precisely, their ability to acquire the results they had in mind when launching it.[5]

2.4   THE CRISIS OF THE 'MACROECONOMIC AXIOM'

The important developments in the international economic sphere and the consequences that followed have driven an increasing number of students to the conclusion that economic dynamics have decisively shifted from the national economy to the world economy. Stephen Hymer, whose *monopolistic advantage* FDI theory (1960, published in 1976) is praised by many as the most weighty contribution in this field, writes about 'an interlocking system of cross-penetration' that changes the world:

When a corporation invests abroad, it not only sends capital and management out, but also establishes a system for drawing foreign capital and labour into an integrated world network. When many firms from many countries do this together on an expanded scale, as has been true over the last decade and will be increasingly true in the next, they are forming a new world system. They are unifying world capital and world labour into an interlocking system of cross-penetration that completely changes the system of national economies that has characterized world capitalism for the past three hundred years. (1979, p. 76)

The *interlock* hypothesis is a challenge to conventional theory. As Drucker (1986, p. 791) puts it:

Prevailing economic theory – whether Keynesian, monetarist or supply-side – considered the national economy, especially that of the large developed countries, to be autonomous and the unit of both economic analysis and economic policy. The international economy may be a restraint and a limitation, but it is not central, let alone determining. This 'macroeconomic axiom' of the modern economist has become increasingly shaky.

Drucker's criticism of the 'macroeconomic axiom' stresses that it poorly, if at all, accounts for the reciprocity of national economies. Open economy theory seems to be a tool to combine a traditional macroeconomic approach with the realities of the interconnected world. However, in the final analysis, the open economy theories speculate on how to cope with strong foreign influence on the national economy in order to achieve a desired macroeconomic equilibrium on a national scale, i.e., practically, on how to reduce a dynamic multicountry approach to a more static and, hence, particular case.

Specialised theories dwelling on important phenomena of the international economy, such as foreign portfolio investment theory, foreign direct investment theory, foreign trade theory and so on, are often instrumental in explaining why this or that phenomenon occurs but they tend to treat their subject as a separate event bearing in itself the mystery of its origin. International portfolio investments are usually explained on the basis of interest rates; direct investments, at one time, were put in relation to managerial resources (Penrose, 1959), monopolistic advantages of a firm (Hymer, 1960[1976]), a product life-cycle (Vernon, 1972), intangible assets (Caves, 1982) and net ownership advantages (Dunning, 1979). The example of FDI theories is particularly significant since they address the most important development in the world economy over the last two decades. Although very inventive in revealing the inner springs of transnational direct investment flows, these theories are often only very discreet in what regards the consequences of FDI for national economies and national politics in recipient countries.

It is hardly against the truth to claim that, in the post-war period, the first serious attempt to scrutinise the intensification and diversification of international economic ties not only at a firm level but also in the context of the interaction of the national and the international economies, long before the internationalisation process took its present scope, were made by development economists.[6] Raul Prebisch (1950; 1978) and other noted writers such as Hans Singer, Gunnar Myrdal, Albert Hirschman, Francois Perroux elaborated on a centre-periphery concept. They frequently demonstrated that foreign investment and exposure to the international market might bring about some progress to a restricted group of economic activities (mainly export-oriented), while actually conserving obsolescence in other spheres. Prebisch also showed that reliance on foreign capital is not enough for transferring the innovative capitalism of the industrial core to the stagnant developing periphery. Later Prebisch and his colleagues were heavily criticised for opposing the pattern of outward-oriented development, with the newly industrialised countries being invoked to support the rightfulness of this pattern. Still, the dependency theory cannot be so easily dismissed. Leaving aside its other implications, it is relevant to point out here that, by stressing the importance of structural changes and industrialisation in the developing countries, it, in fact, linked the economic progress in these countries with their ability to increase their competitiveness in the world market by eliminating their specialisation on producing and exporting raw materials. As for the newly industrialised countries, their experience is no less valid as an argument in favour of Prebisch's position as against it in as much as their success had been prepared (at least this is true of South Korea, Singapore, Taiwan, and Malaysia) by import substituting industrialisation while their economies in general had been subject to large-scale interventions on the part of government. What may really make a difference in the case of these latter is the fact that the performance in international markets was eventually chosen as a yardstick for measuring the efficiency of this policy.

In the industrialised world the need for a broader – nation-to-nation rather than firm-to-firm – approach to economic internationalisation was first realised by non-economists. Jean-Jacques Servan-Schreiber opened his *Le défi américain* (1967) with a claim which fully exposes the militant and provocative spirit of his book:

La troisiéme puissance industrielle mondiale, après les Etats-Unis et l'U.R.S.S. pourrait bien être dans quinze ans, non pas L'Europe mais *l'Industrie américaine en Europe.* (p. 19)

Servan-Schreiber happened to be wrong in many of his predictions. His book is important none the less because it has drawn wide attention to two major issues which became focal points of prolonged discussions. One was the issue of power exerted through FDI and, in wider terms, of new dimensions of power in the interrelated world. The other – how foreign are foreign companies and what could serve as a criterion for defining the nationality of transnational corporations and whether the nationality really matters.

Since the time of *Le défi américain* our perception of these problems has become much more sophisticated. Political economists have traced modern sources of power where they were not looked for before.[7] As for the firms' nationality debate, the main finding probably has been the conclusion that the prosperity of country-owned firms and the prosperity of the country itself is not necessarily one and the same thing (see, for instance, Reich, 1989; 1990a). As we have seen, the interaction (i) of national economies with one another and (ii) of national economies with the world market (which, due to the formation of supranational structures of TNCs, is larger than an arithmetical sum of national economies) has been winning increased attention from different sciences. The diversity of interpretations reflects the immensity and versatility of the internationalisation process itself. For practical purposes of policy-making it is crucial, however, to single out a key notion (supported by a relevant theoretical insight) to serve as a strategic pivot for policy-making.

2.5 TRANSLATING INTERDEPENDENCE IN ECONOMIC TERMS: NATIONAL COMPETITIVENESS

Summarising recent important facts and concepts pertaining to the international sphere, it is legitimate to suggest that they lead to a notion of *interdependence.* Increasing numbers of political scientists analyzing the sources of power in international affairs are willing to attribute to the interdependence the role of the most influential single factor behind the changing profile of international relations, both political and economic (Keohane and Nye, 1977, 1987; Nye, 1990; Strange, 1988a, 1988b; Vernon and Spar, 1988; Waltz, 1979). Traditional economics, as follows from Drucker's remark, is slow to recognise this development. For the aim of economic policy-making, however, the general notion of interdependence is too wide to be sufficient and there is still a need for an appropriate equivalent specifying this term for economic relations to be found. A *national competitiveness* concept suits best for this purpose.

2.5.1 Why National Competitiveness?

The competitiveness theory first emerged as a firm competitiveness theory and for a long time it was monopolised by management specialists. There has been little debate as to the capacity of the firm to generate real income above a certain return ('a competitive floor') to be chosen for estimating relative competitiveness. When firms became global, the same approach was expanded to define international competitiveness:

> Competitiveness is the capacity of a firm under free and fair market conditions to produce goods and services that meet the test of international markets while, at the same time, maintaining or expanding its real income. (de Woot, 1990, p. 8)

As incomes rise through the sale of products and services, the market share of the firm or, to be more precise, the change of the market share over time, with some approximation, may be regarded as an indication of its competitive position. Such analysis proved especially relevant for international comparisons in which the direct confrontation of revenues is difficult owing to differences in accounting practice, in fiscal legislation, in the currency composition of sales and so on. Hence, when the nation's competitiveness is taken as equal to the ability of firms flying its flag to improve their international sales, then national competitiveness can be defined as the power of the nation 'to capture and expand a share of the world market' (Cox, 1987, p. 303) or to achieve a trade balance surplus or a balance-of-payments surplus.

This approach, which could be identified as traditional, has been widely criticised recently. One group of critics, whilst not questioning the underlying assumption of the essential similarity of national and firm competitiveness, insists however that the market share as a measure of national performance is legitimate only with some due qualifications to account for such developments as the shift of traditional industries to developing countries,[8] the growing importance of so-called intangible assets (technology, know-how, managerial skill, etc.) as well as the exchange of services and information.

The other group challenges the traditional approach on more serious grounds claiming that it is impossible to identify nations with corporations.

This claim contradicts a longstanding and quite widely spread belief (cultivated, *inter alia*, by those interpretations of a popular *managerial revolution* theory that tend to link the performance of big firms to the will of the 'captains' of big business to act in the 'best-balanced interests' of 'stakeholders' (shareholders, customers, employees, suppliers, and plant community cities) or to maximise the 'wealth-producing capacity' of their enterprise[9] – that what is good for big companies is good for the nation.

The globalisation of firms itself has probably given the hardest blow to this assumption as transnational companies proved to be quick in relocating to remote countries with less demanding social standards or in other ways showed that national loyalty was not their guiding motivation. As Robert Reich puts it, commenting on the predisposition of US firms to expand employment, investment and R & D abroad:

> American competitiveness is not the profitability or market share of American-owned corporations. In fact, because the American-owned corporation is coming to have no special relationship with Americans, it makes no sense to Americans to entrust our national competitiveness to it. The interests of American-owned corporations may or may not coincide with those of American people. (Reich, 1990a, p. 59)

One is likely to find this assertion somewhat premature as regards the characteristic of relationships between American-owned firms and Americans; none the less, it is extraordinarily instrumental in marking an important modern trend of great consequences.

If the claim 'nations compete' is accepted, two major questions – (i) what kind of a relationship is this competition? and (ii) what makes the core of national competitiveness? – become most challenging and significant.

2.5.2   Competition as a Relationship

Earlier we tried to specify the narrowness of some popular approaches to international economic interdependence: the idealism and the negligence of the national-political component of free trade ideology; the 'zero-sum' philosophy implicit to mercantilist and neomercantilist postulates; the partiality of specialised theories and the static character of macroeconomic inroads. Still mankind is indebted, though to varying degrees, to all of them for stimulative insights. What could a national competitiveness approach offer? It does not pretend to be a new original explanation of the international economy. Nevertheless, it has the potential to update our perception of the world and to be helpful as an intellectual tool for strategists.

Competition divides as much as it unites. It is always an interaction. To use an analogy from physics, namely, from a field theory, competition is an environment built of and filled with mutually attracting and repelling elements (or agents). Hence national competitiveness is generally about interaction and interdependence and more specifically about the trajectory of an economy across an economic environment, and factors defining this trajectory. For the national state it is about measuring and optimising the trajectory of its economy against other economies, keeping in mind that such an optimisation is possible insofar as any national economy is an active part of the world economy; otherwise the trajectory will be shaped by independent factors alone.

This approach implies the abandoning of national-centric ideas of the world (i.e., the shift from a 'we *and* the world' philosophy to 'we *in* the world' philosophy); the necessity of conceiving and following certain general rules of the game; and the rejection of a 'zero-sum' approach to international economic relations.

Drawing on exact sciences for another analogy, economies are not like planets whose galactic routes are defined once and for ever. They are more like man-made space objects equipped to change their orbits, but the amount of fuel is limited so that the moment when the engine can be started as well as the time-length of its action should be calculated very thoroughly.

When put in the terms of competitiveness, the interrelation between the international performance of a country and its economic growth, unlike in the open economy theory, focuses on the constructive side of interconnectedness. The existence of this 'positive' side follows from the premise that no economic progress is possible unless sufficient competitive space is available to stipulate *productive destruction*, the term introduced by Joseph Schumpeter to describe a competition propelled evolution.

The prominence of competitive space is readily deducible from the Schumpetrian theory of innovation driven growth in which he stresses that competition is not all about prices. His theory has received much attention of late owing to the attention it pays to technical progress and innovation – the two big issues that cannot be overestimated nowadays. Schumpeter contrasted a dynamic model of innovation-driven evolution with a classical model of static reserve allocation. Schumpeter's emphasis on innovation arises from his theory of monopolist capitalism. It made him look for explanations for the successes of capitalism other than the ability of market forces to secure the efficient utilisation of resources. He tends to stress the role of the non-price competition; eventually he came to the conclusion that:

the fundamental impulse that acts and keeps the capitalist engine in motion comes from the new consumer goods, the new methods of production or transportation, the new markets, the new forms of industrial organisation that capitalist enterprise creates. (Schumpeter, 1943, p. 83 in the 1976 edition)

What matters for our purpose is the fact that major new tendencies in technology, methods of production, storing, transporting, management, etc. which eventually conquer the whole world and determine the economic development and, indirectly, social development for a considerable period of time, first declare themselves on the national scale and only gradually filter into other countries. Mass production methods, for instance, were initially introduced in the United States; in the 1930s they were adopted in the Soviet Union and, since World War II, mass production spread worldwide to revolutionise not only the production itself, but the consumption pattern and the living standards of billions of people.

The *competitive space* postulate suggests that countries with an open economy are better placed for absorbing world trends as they are more sensitive to external signals. Their exposure to the world market would also demand more prompt reaction to external 'irritants'. The importance of this factor is stressed by Porter (1990): nations succeed, he maintains, where local circumstances provide an impetus for firms to pursue new strategies for competing in an industry early and aggressively:

Nations fail where firms do not receive the right signals, are not subject to the right pressures, and do not have the right capabilities. (Porter, 1990, p. 68)

Therefore, in principle, economic openness theoretically provides an advantage, especially if the process of internationalisation has such a scope as it has gained lately. It is a great problem to utilise this advantage: the task of fishing out 'positive' (or right) impulses (those carrying information on progressive mainstream changes) alone poses tremendous problems. Nevertheless, closed economies, or closed industries within generally open economies, are considerably less responsive and take the risk of being forced to pay a high price for being late in following the tendency of the world economy.

One of the most significant examples is the history of the decline of the American automotive industry. The oligopoly of the 'big three' made it very inert to the world trend in automotive design and production. According to J. DeLorean, for many years one of the top General Motors executives:

> there hadn't been an important product innovation in the industry since the automatic transmission and power steering in 1949... In place of product innovation, the [American] automobile industry went on a two decade marketing binge which generally offered up the same old product under the guise of something new and useful. (quoted in Flink, 1988, p. 293)

In the 1960s, for the first time in its history, Detroit was forced to consider competition on the part of Japanese and European manufacturers; the moment of truth came with the first shock of the oil crisis. The years 1980s the 'big three' met amidst a desperate struggle for staying afloat. When finally the industry had overcome its decay by the middle of the decade, it emerged profoundly renovated; not only were the products superior, but the business strategy itself had changed: research and development were promoted to a key position, a lot of emphasis was put on internationalisation (including co-operation with competitors – Japanese and Europeans). Examined in retrospect, the core of the crisis of the American automotive industry appears to be not so much the conflict of choosing between small and bigger cars as the struggle between two tendencies, old and new. The latter anticipated a modern 'state-of-the-art' product: sophisticated, functional, energy- and material-efficient, technologically intensive. The former represented a dated mass production approach in which economy of scale was the first major priority as much as the second and the third, and styling was substituting for technological progress. Had the industry been less inward-looking, it could have participated in developing the new trend rather than catching up with it in a later stage.

The above story highlights the argument that under certain circumstances the size of a national market alone is not a sufficient condition to secure innovation. Schumpeter defined the modern non-price competition as 'not that kind of competition that counts' but as an ever-present threat. Obviously, in quite a few cases the 'threat' is not big enough to result in a pronounced effect when national companies are left to themselves. Therefore, it is little wonder that recently free trade has received a lot of lipservice as a means of encouraging innovation and strengthening national competitiveness. And yet, as the failure of the Uruguay Round has demonstrated once again, action falls far behind rhetoric. This is not surprising either. Vital economic, political and social interests are at stake, the price of a mistake may be high.

The statement that a better competitive position of a nation could be secured only in the course of competitive struggle itself or, in other words, that no form of isolationism is consistent with striving for economic progress might look, on the first glance at least, quite obvious. In reality, it is far from being so. On the one hand, there is a long tradition in economic thinking to give priority to internal economic problems; on the other hand, there is a deep-rooted mentality characteristic of different social layers (including quite often, as numerous examples demonstrate, a ruling elite) to favour a defensive approach to the alleged and real influences of foreign markets.

One of the most notorious cases is, of course, the Soviet Union in which a new and 'superior' economy was intended to be built in a situation of almost total insulation from those economies which it was allegedly to overwhelm and, thus, with which it was actually competing. However, symptoms of this mentality can also be easily found in advanced capitalist countries. 'Buy American' campaigns in the United States are just a small example. How much this mentality is still spread in the country is indicated by the fact that the *Business Week* magazine (December 17, 1990, p. 34), in a special report on why the United States is failing in the international competitive race, found it necessary to address its American readers with a reminder which, despite its pathetic intonation, amply conveys the essence of competitive thinking: 'Success will come by embracing the world economy – not trying to escape it'.

The outlook on the international economy from the point of view of competitiveness denies trench psychology but it recognises the legitimacy of concerns over national interests. A national competitiveness approach assumes that people sharing territory, language, culture and traditions on top of economic activities cannot but have certain common interests distinguishing them from the rest of the world. At the same time, it equally suggests that these interests can be better pursued in co-ordination with other nations through the adaptation to tendencies forming across international economic space.

Action presumes counteraction. Among other things, competition is always a struggle for one's own interests. The success of this struggle depends on two instances: how amply and correctly these interests are defined and how well the instruments for implementing them into life are chosen. Even, in Porter's terminology, 'positive' impulses have to be adapted to country's particular circumstances. With international competition having developed into a major force prompting the progress of productive forces, impulses transmitted through the world market become too important for the national economy as a whole for separate firms to be left alone to cope with them. For instance, America's two most successful export industries – aerospace and electronics – have been continuously slashing jobs even though orders from abroad keep increasing.

This performance follows a more general trend, even more pronounced in Japan, according to which the success of an industry does not translate any more in additional manufacturing employment but rather leads to the further substitution of capital for labour. In the United States, in R & D-intensive industries as well as in traditional sectors such as automobile production, international competition has produced a decline in blue-collar employment. Those firms with the most international exposure are in the forefront of 'deindustrialisation' of America: they use foreign production bases for labour-intensive production, and introduce capital-intensive production, cutting blue-collar jobs in their home-country.

The challenge presented by this trend is too great for separate firms and industries. It is a national challenge as, according to experts, the occupational profile of the United States together with other industrialised countries is going to undergo radical changes within the next twenty-five years. Given the importance of the change and its social, cultural and political consequences, it is hardly possible that it will not provoke a governmental reaction. With the growth of interdependence the responsibility of the government increases. Under the Labour Party, Britain was trying to resist the trend described above. Because of governmental policy, the number of blue-collar workers per unit of manufacturing production had been going down far more slowly than in other developed countries. As a result, the comparative industrial power of the country declined while the unemployment rate eventually soared.

2.5.3 Competitiveness and National Interests

By summarising what has been said previously, the term *national competitiveness* for the purpose of this research may be defined as *the ability to protect or pursue national economic interests in the situation of profound international interdependence.*[10] This formula meets the request, present implicitly or explicitly in many publications on the subject, for a broader definition of national competitiveness breaking away from the conventional mind set:

> which imprisons industrial strategy to narrowly based concepts of manufacturing productivity and export market share. (Rugman, 1987, pp. 95–6)

This definition offers certain advantages in comparison to those proceeding from the premise that the competitiveness of a country essentially is the competitiveness of its business by expressively stressing several important points.

a) National competitiveness is not a value in itself, nor is it exclusively about firms. In the last analysis, it is about people. What the reference to national interests is particularly designed to point at is the welfare effect of national development. Talk about the competitiveness of a nation is meaningless if it is not related to the welfare of the nation. By accentuating the well-being of the people this definition downplays the traditional measures of competitiveness such as export quotas and emphasises per capita national income, the level of employment and quality-of-life indexes.

b) This definition underlines the relativeness of national competitiveness not only in the sense that, for a country, it can be measured only vis-à-vis another country, but also that it should be related to the stage of development of the country in question and its 'priorities list' corresponding to this stage. For instance, industrialised and developing countries compete inasmuch as they are actors in the world market. However, the former compete on the basis of leading-edge technologies whilst the latter can reciprocate only by relying on cheaper labour. The situation is far from being equal: technological innovation, unlike the exploitation of cheap labour, is an inexhaustible source of competitive advantage.

c) By stressing the aspect of pursuing national economic interests, the definition above raises the point that international competition of nations is not a perpetual game of catch-up with more advanced countries through imitating these countries. Competitive issues should be addressed more directly, without relying too much on policy panaceas derived from generalised theories.

Most successful in competitive struggle have been those newcomers, such as the South-Asian 'Young Tigers', which managed to leap-frog several stages of development having taken advantage of a particular combination of economic, political and social circumstances. Such an approach demands realism in assessments and openness to non-conformist decisions. An example of this approach is provided by Japanese industrial policy. Christopher Carr (1990, p. 26) cites Mr Y. Ojima, Vice-Minister for International Trade and Industry, as stating that it was decided:

> to establish in Japan industries which required intensive employment of capital and technology, industries that in consideration of comparative costs of production should be the most inappropriate for Japan... From a short-run static viewpoint, encouragement of such industries would

seem to conflict with economic rationalism. But from a long range viewpoint, these are precisely the industries where ... demand is high, technological progress is rapid, and labour productivity rises fast.

d) The stress on interdependence warns against taking traditional theoretical models too far and puts weight on creating a long-range vision of where the international economy is going. As 'new' economics maintains, an obsession with short-term disequilibrium problems such as inflation and budget deficits, however important these problems are, is not enough to prevent the decline of national competitiveness. Even more important may be detecting longer-term tendencies characterising the general direction of the growth of the international economy and encouraging them on national soil.

The stress on interdependence, furthermore, is helpful for placing into the limelight the important insight of the open economy theory, namely, that extensive exposure to international markets is advantageous to strong economies while creating additional problems when the economy is out of balance. Hence, the organisation of an internal economic structure could be more important in terms of the results produced rather than the speedy opening of the economy, inasmuch as openness only gives results to the extent that the structure is properly adjusted.

The proposed definition fails to highlight any single critical element which, like the philosopher's stone in ancient alchemy, would be a key to transforming any national economy into a supercompetitive one. In economics, as in chemistry, this key element hardly exists, but there are many, according to economists, which can claim to play a particular role in forming national competitiveness. Adam Smith and later classical and neo-classical economists put in the centre of the growth of 'the wealth of nations' the accumulation of capital, Marx gave priority to labour productivity, and Keynes, while accepting in large part the classical equilibrium model, singled out the importance of the demand side. More recently, Porter and Frölich emphasise the prominence of efficiency and productivity of major firms and businesses; Reich argues in favour of the quality of the labour force; Rugman considers that nations should concentrate on utilising in full the comparative advantages their businesses possess, and Krugman (as well as Reich and Dunning) points out that in a modern economy created competitive advantages are much more important than those endowed by nature. However, Christopher Carr probably came closest to the essence of the confusion about the mystery of competitiveness when remarking that the principles behind achieving competitiveness are straightforward, but easily neglected. They do not diverge from those well known as determining economic growth though seen in a much broader context of the international economy and expanded interconnectedness between nations.

2.6 COMPETITIVENESS AND SCENARIOS OF REFORM

2.6.1 Cyclops Regains the Sight

Judging from press reports from Moscow and the capitals of other CIS member-countries, one might conclude that the only type of competition these countries could be involved in is that for a place on the charity list of international aid agencies. But, under closer examination, this conclusion appears premature. An attentive reader would be able to pick up in the current of alarming reports some valuable tips that would not let him forget that, in fact, the CIS used to be one of the most industrialised powers of the world only a very short time ago.

The dismissive approach to the economic potential of the CIS, quite tangible in the modern western literature on the issue, stems, in part, from the observation of the actual state of the ex-Soviet economy and the generalisation of the results of detailed examination by western experts of industries in Central European countries. On the other hand, to some degree, it follows a certain tradition in sovietology depicting the Soviet Union as a kind of economic Cyclops. Zbigniew Brzezinski's verdict[11] presents this line of thinking in its most refined form:

> The Soviet Union is a world power of a new type in that its might is one-dimensional ... the Soviet Union is a global power only in military dimension.

This evaluation is not groundless but, at the same time, it is not completely correct. It is biased by the Cold War logic according to which the industrial capacity of a nation belonging to the opposite block was estimated in terms of how much it could contribute to the military build-up. This was almost the only context in which the Soviet economy was regarded as competing with western industries. The market competition, due to the reasons outlined earlier, was practically nonexistent, which left many analysts the right to an unshaken belief in the superiority of western industries. Post-Communist revelations about the comparative technological level of socialist production and its many deficiencies only seemed to have reinforced this view. But the situation is more complex. The command system could make the economy as a whole inefficient, but this does not mean that in any particular case the products manufactured within the frame of this economy are hopelessly inferior to western standards.

The *International Herald Tribune* (January 8, 1991) reported that the United States was completing a deal to buy an advanced type of a nuclear reactor built by Russia in order to leapfrog a development stage, to start from operational hardware and make a variation; some of the alloys used in the structure are virtually unknown in the West. *Time* magazine informed its readers of the test of a Soviet battle aircraft undertaken by German military experts whereby it was found superior to all models currently in service in the Bundeswehr. *Izvestia* (May 8, 1992) wrote that the price on the French fighter Mirage in the world market had halved after the announcement of the Russian government that arms producers would be allowed to effect the direct sale of their products. These examples may be found too insignificant to turn the tide. The truth is, however, that owing to the gigantic scope of the Russian economy 'particular cases' may accumulate on such a scale that they may destabilise whole branches of the world economy. The example of the aluminium industry is very much to the point. In 1991, the flow of this metal to the West increased dramatically and equalled one million tons. Coming on top of a recession in main markets, it caused the price of aluminium to fall to its lowest level in real terms and the western industry to shut down about 10 per cent of its capacity.[12]

Earlier I wrote about the problems posed for the economy of the CIS by its forthcoming integration in international markets. The above examples demonstrate that the CIS is also a challenge to the established structures of these markets. This implies that, from the first steps towards an open economy on, the CIS member-states should contemplate their strategy in terms of national competitiveness taking into account that for the West they are not just lost sheep returning to the herd but potential competitors and a threat to the existing international economic regime.

The West does not hesitate to take preventive measures against exports from the CIS. A trade war between Russia and other member-countries of the CIS on the one side and the US on the other side is a reality. The United States actively withstands the intention of Russia to increase its quota in the international market of enriched uranium from seven to 25 per cent. The conflict has progressed according to a standard scenario. The Association of American Producers of Uranium accused the producers from the CIS of price dumping and excessive production as imports had soared to 110 million dollars in 1991 from just two million dollars in 1986. The Association has proposed a punitive import tariff that would more than double the price. The exporters denied these charges. None the less, the Association received support from the US administration. The Commerce Department introduced a 116 per cent tariff on the uranium from the CIS effective from the autumn of 1992 proceeding from the assumption that the republics' costs were comparable to those in Britain, Canada and Namibia.[13] The obvious duality of the official policy did not embarrass the administration which, criticising Western Europe for excluding goods from Eastern Europe, itself have taken measures causing damage to export trade of some of the most impoverished of the ex-Soviet republics.

Another precedent is even more instructive as it shows the pattern of Western response to the entry of Russia in the high-tech sector of the international market. Washington exerted great pressure on Russia and India in order to force them to cancel a deal involving the shipment of three Russian-made rocket engines to India. According to the official version, the United States was concerned by the military–strategic implications of this sale since the engines might have been installed in mid-range ballistic missiles. Indians and Russians put forward a different version of events. The official intervention of Washington followed when the Indian Organisation of Space Research had turned down the offer of an American corporation which asked a three and a half times higher price than that set by Russia's Glavkosmos for its products. Experts claimed, however, that the true reason for the American *démarche* should be looked for beyond a particular deal. The objective was to force the Russian space industry away from its largest foreign market, the only one in this region not yet controlled by American producers. As the lever the US used the threat of taking away their support for the G-7 plan to provide the CIS with 24 billion dollars in financial loans. This threat was not realised, but Washington has put a two year embargo on Glavkosmos. This is a hard blow for one of the few competitive industries in Russia. Furthermore, it is a blow at plans of converting Russia's military-industrial complex and, allowing for the share of this complex in total national output, at the restructuring of Russian industry on the whole.

To take what lies on the surface, the message of the competitiveness theory to post-Communist reformers is that integration in the world market and foreign investments will increase competition, which in turn will increase efficiency, which in turn will increase competitiveness. However, at a closer examination the chain of causation does not appear to be so simple.

Theoretically at least, different scenarios of integration are possible. The one advocated (and imposed) by international financial agencies and the Group of Seven puts the whole burden of the transition on the shoulders of ex-socialist countries. They are urged to accept the western model as the absolute truth without being given time to rethink their own heritage. More than that, while there is room for discussion as concerns the longer-term outcomes of shock therapy, in the short term they are devastating for the national productive forces especially in the case of the CIS in which they exist in the form of huge enterprises and manufacturing complexes. This impedes privatisation, slows down reorganisation according to market principles and, therefore, frustrates one of the main arguments in favour of abrupt actions, namely, that reforms must proceed simultaneously in all directions. The 'big-bang logic' has pushed national industry to the line where hundreds of enterprises are to be either closed down or sold out to foreign investors. Nor necessarily inefficient ones since there was no possibility to measure their efficiency according to world standards. The analyzing scenario, hence, allows transnational corporations to *internalise* potential competitors in an early stage and, most likely, at a low cost. International markets will expand but this will have no or little effect on national producers if, because of the lack of resources, experience and competitive advantage, they fail to penetrate the oligopolistic structures of these markets.

2.6.2   The Alternative Scenario

The alternative scenario would be to increase the national bargaining power by concentrating efforts on disclosing, preserving and reinforcing existing competitive advantages, and creating new ones already in the early stages of reforms in order to countervail asymmetrical interdependence leading to one-sided dependence. It does not put in question the ultimate goals of reforms, but provides for amending obsession with relatively short-term equilibrium problems with a vision of the international competitive situation. The competitive advantages should be looked for in national industry, the skill of the labour force, plus the size of the national market. Respectively, in relation to foreign investment this approach envisages pursual of a policy aimed at avoiding the eventual transference of most competitive enterprises, branches and industries into a foreign-controlled enclave-type sector of the economy, shortening the period when national competitiveness will be anchored to such a hopeless factor as cheap labour. In addition, it will be counteracting the centrifugal tendency of the new division of labour bringing about the concentration of high-tech industries in core countries.

As general points of reference, this scenario should provide for the preservation of national industry and especially for the protection of living standards because the deterioration of the latter will have as its very next consequence a decline in the capacity of the nation not only to increase the educational level of its workers, equally blue-collar and white-collar, but even to reproduce the highly trained and highly motivated labour force at a previous scale. This goal may be achieved in the course of a fundamental restructuring of the economy according to the new forms of ownership and the demands advanced by the international environment. Foreign capital must be given an important role in this process but in such a manner that the judgement of international investors, though an important factor within the framework of any open economy, could not prevail in deciding the fate of the national economy.

Realistically speaking, the countries of the CIS, facing severe economic, national, ecological and, in some republics, political crises, have a weak standing at bilateral and international levels, and the second scenario may appear utopian. Is it really so? A closer look at the potential of Russia, the core republic of the former Soviet Union, gives grounds for optimism.

The *territory* of Russia is 1.5 times bigger than that of the United States, England, Germany, France, Italy and Japan taken together. The *population* of Russia is equal to the combined population of England, France and Italy. It is ethnically homogenous (82 per cent are Russians) and very well educated – 70 per cent have degrees at the level of higher and further education. Russia possesses almost all natural resources necessary for modern industrial development plus it is particularly rich in forests (five hectares of forest per head against 0.8 hectares in the US).

The *industrial potential* of Russia can be characterised by the following figures. Its share in the world production of oil is 19 per cent, of gas – 32 per cent, of coal – nine per cent, of steel and mineral fertilisers – about 12 per cent, of cement – 8 per cent. By the cumulative amount of GNP, in 1990, it occupied the fifth position in the world-league table after the United States, China, Japan and united Germany. The per capita GNP figure (5867 dollars) puts it in the middle of the scale together with Greece, South Korea, Czechoslovakia, Hungary and Venezuela. Russia has an extensive and diversified machine-building industry, though this is oriented mainly to military purposes and has serious innovation and quality problems.

The country has a potentially enormous *internal market* and a considerable *export capacity*. It is one the world's most important suppliers of gas, non-ferrous metals, timber, some other resources and arms. Technologies and know-how may become one more important export item as about one million engineers and scientists are involved in *research and development* activities.

The aforesaid implies that Russia remains a world-class power with out-standing prospects for development. Now everything depends on the strategies chosen and decisions taken. Starting from 1985, the economy has suffered a sequence of heavy blows each causing serious damage. The Chernobyl catastrophe, a sharp decline in oil prices and the earthquake in Armenia each swept away hundreds of billions of dollars.[14] No less disastrous in financial terms were the consequences of the 'antialcohol campaign' and more recent chaotic liberalisation experiments, let alone the disintegration of the former USSR. 'I do not think that any western economies would have sustained even a fraction of these calamities for more than a year', writes a renowned Russian economist Yurii Ol'sevich (1992, p. 29). As it was in the years of the Second World War, the Russian economy has demonstrated once again an incredible capacity to resist shocks. This leads to the question of how to combine the introduction of the new principles of ownership and management with the strengths of the crumbling system.

This is, of course, a very challenging question. Finding ways towards the implementation of what I have called the 'alternative scenario' would mean to give at least a partial answer to it. This implies if not a revision then a revaluation of the aims of the 'big bang' approach in the national context. It also implies that the government should show more commitment towards shaping an active strategy towards foreign investment.

Notes

1. In fact, besides the *welfare* approach to protectionism as described above, there is a *positive* theory of protection which is not concerned with assessing the desirability of interventions affecting trade or resource allocation (see W. Corden, 1979[1971]).

2. In one of the recent macroeconomic textbooks the author writes about his subject in the following words: 'Each country is capable of generating its own economic problems but most are also effective in creating problems for others. [A] change of government is followed by a short period of attempting to implement policies which focus on domestic problems but which are thwarted by the reaction of the rest of the world.' (R. Morley, *The Macroeconomics of Opened Economies* Aldershot: Edward Elgar, 1988, p. ix).

3. Modern protectionists, who are sometimes called 'new protectionists', have long abandoned militant intonation when expressing their views and at most can allow themselves to warn the public against some extremities of open regimes (see P. Krugman 'Protectionism: Try It, You'll Like It' in *The International Economy*, June/July 1990, p. 35–9).

4. US movies, music, TV programming, and home video together now account for an annual trade surplus of some $8 billion. Sales of US television

programming to Europe alone gross at about $600 million a year. Only aerospace outranks pop culture as an export ('America's Hottest Export: Pop Culture' in *Fortune, December* 31, 1990, p. 28).

5. Some of the significant books on the matter are: R. Cooper *The Economics of Interdependence,* (London: McGraw-Hill, 1968); P. Buomberger *Theorie und Strategie der Geldpolitik in einer kleinen, offenen Volkswirtschaft* (Zürich, 1979); R. Dornbusch *Open Economy Macroeconomics* (New York: Basic Books, 1980); R. Keohane, J. Nye *Power and Interdependence. World Politics in Transition,* (Boston: Little, Brown & Co., 1977).

6. Dudley Seers acknowledged this debt when he stood out to recommend adoption of the insights of development theories into the concepts addressing the problems of developed countries inasmuch as these problems are raised by 'powerful external forces, especially the policies of transnational corporations, and [by] the strains of absorbing modern technology' (*Development and Change,* Vol. 10, 1979, p. 714).

7. For example, Susan Strange (1988a, p. 133) stresses the importance of knowledge and the language as the means of communication: 'The American language has become the *lingua franca* of the global economy and of transnational social and professional groups ... American universities come to dominate learning and the major professions not only because they have numbers and resources of libraries and finance, but also because their work is conducted in English. By comparison with this predominance in the knowledge structure, any loss of American capability in industrial manufacturing is trivial and unimportant.'

8. How really misleading market share figures could be is demonstrated by a Mexican case: half of the value of Mexico's manufactured exports is made up by the supply of so-called 'maquiladoras' (border plants belonging to foreign corporations engaged in assembling products for the US market) while the average use of Mexican input in maquiladoras' production is a mere 1.5 per cent of final value. In other words, the actual competitiveness of Mexico is different from what is suggested by export share calculations alone if they do not allow for the special role played by American and other foreign corporations in the export sector of Mexican economy.

9. See *Harvard Business Review,* March–April 1991, pp. 106–14.

10. A somewhat similar definition may be found in the Report of the President's Commission on Industrial Competitiveness: 'The definition of competitiveness for a nation must ... be tied to its ability to generate the resources required to meet the nations needs' (*The Report of the President's Commission...,* Vol. II: Global Competition: The New Reality Washington, 1985, p. 6).

11. *Encounter,* December 1983, p. 12.

12. *Izvestia,* March 21, 1991; *Financial Times,* April 2, 1992, p. 26.

13. *The New York Times,* May 29, 1992.

14. See *Soviet Economy,* 1990, Vol. 6, No. 1, pp. 21–2.

3 Russia's Previous Experience as a Capital-Importing Country

3.1 WHEN THE 'BEAR' BEHAVED LIKE A 'YOUNG TIGER'

A profound restructuring of industry and agriculture has been one of the main objectives of recent social and economic reforms in the Russian Federation. The introduction of new forms of ownership is expected to trigger off serious technological and organisational shifts affecting the size of enterprises, the pattern of the division of labour, the occupational profile of the population, the comparative importance of different industries and sectors of the economy and so on. It is not the first time in its modern history that the Russian economy has gone through a period of drastic change. Both capitalist industrialisation in pre-war Imperial Russia and socialist-accelerated industrialisation of the 1930s provide a precedent for the 1990s. Both intended, in one major effort, to transform Russian industry to an updated technological basis. Much the same ambition lies behind the current reforms.

The two Russian industrialisations share many features. They were state-led, had the development of heavy large-scale industry as their prime objective and were carried out mainly at the expense of the country's rural population. If, in the 1930s, the international economic situation and the investment climate in the country had been different, they could have had still another similarity – the extensive usage of foreign capital, technique and entrepreneurial skill. However, all in all Russia possesses rich and diverse experience as a capital importer worth examining. It can reveal some country-specific characteristics which might be important to consider also in the framework of the current debate.

The first external loan was placed by a Russian tsarina in Amsterdam in 1769 while the first foreign-owned company in Russia received the Imperial authorisation in 1855 (Dongarov, 1990, p. 8, p. 15). The scope of capital inflow and its impact on the national economy, as well as the types of capital entry policy pursued by the government, varied over time. It is logical to split the history of foreign investment in Russia into two major periods divided by the October Revolution. Neither of these periods is completely homogeneous regarding the economic and political situation,

51

business conditions or regulations applied. But, for the purpose of this research, such classification is relevant as factors determining the investment climate formation and governmental capital entry strategy remained quite stable during each of the singled-out periods.

It has been quite common in recent years that lessons drawn from the experience of newly industrialised countries were evaluated by academics as most relevant to post-Communist economic transition. However, as was shown before, this experience can be interpreted in more than one way. Some authors praise it as a triumph of economic liberalism, others treat it as a pattern of sophisticated *étatisme*. The achievements of the Asian 'young tigers', the four most successful of newly industrialised countries, may be unique for the last few decades but they are certainly not without precedence in a broader historical prospect. Imperial Russia at the turn of the century in terms of economic development did something very similar to what South Korea and Taiwan did in the 1970s and 1980s. Within only twenty years it effected a great leap forward to become a major industrialised country. Allowing for all the difference between the conditions then and now, Imperial Russia's case appears to be valuable as a historical test for modern economic and political doctrines. Furthermore, as yet another story of a successful transition, it may help to disclose some regularities pertaining to this phenomenon and help to overcome conflicting explanations of other cases.

The last two and a half decades of tsarist Russia provide an example, maybe unique in its scale, when a huge influx of foreign capital had fertilised previously underutilised or idle national labour and natural resources to produce a tremendous outbreak of economic activity which, within the life-span of only one generation, had transformed stagnant rural Russia into a dynamic industrial power. The rise of the Russian economy was outstanding by any standard. In the last ten years of the nineteenth century, Russian industry showed a remarkable yearly increase in production equal to eight per cent. At the beginning of the twentieth century, after the stagnation of 1900–6, another booming decade followed with an average increment of over six per cent per year (Falkus, 1972, p. 45). Between 1890 and 1913, the production of textile grew 3.2 times, of iron and steel in 5.99 times and of oil 2.48 times (Haumann, 1980, p. 27). To a certain extent the record rate of growth can be explained by the general backwardness of the country's economy at the moment when, in Rostow's terminology, its industrial 'take-off' started. None the less, in absolute figures the results achieved were equally impressive. Russia joined the league of world superpowers in all the major industries (for comparative data see Wood, 1984, p. 222–3). It outranked France as a steel producer, was second only to the USA in oil production and by the overall length of railroads was third in Europe. At the same time, the Russian Empire remained a country of a double standard: it was roughly on par with other European industrialised countries if measured by gross production figures and lagged behind drastically whenever per person figures were compared. According to these latter figures Russia, in fact, rested among the poorest nations of Europe.[1]

Later this duality was inherited by the Soviet economy. It retained its intrinsic weakness during the entire period of its existence. It was the cost paid by the economy for the political ambitions of its leaders, first Russian and later Soviet, who were determined to preserve and even reinforce the status of a great power that Russia first acquired in the eighteenth century. In pursuing this goal, the leadership of the country was tempted to subordinate the living standard of the people to other priorities such as capital accumulation, the development of heavy industries and the escalation of a military potential. Historically the disparity between political aims and economic means emerged as probably the main challenge to Russian and Soviet policy-makers.

3.2 IMPERIAL RUSSIA: FOREIGN CAPITAL IN THE COUNTRY OF ECONOMIC NATIONALISM

3.2.1 Preparing the Grounds

The policy towards foreign capital adopted in tsarist Russia on the eve of this century was designed initially as primarily a sort of response to the aforesaid challenge. The defeat in the Crimean War, in 1856, by its consequences was a watershed in the history of pre-revolutionary Russia: it made clear to the tsarist government that without radical social and economic changes the country would be inevitably pushed aside to the periphery of world politics and exploited economically (see Kennedy, 1988, pp. 170–7). The existence of serfdom impeded the development of a modern industrial economy by depriving Russia of its most basic precondition – a free labour market. In this respect the abolition of serfdom, in 1861, was a major breakthrough towards capitalist production. However, even after the reform which was incomplete in many ways, social and economic conditions in the country did not favour rapid industrialisation. Capitalism in Russia was developing, though at a pace vastly inadequate to other European countries.

This inadequacy was once again demonstrated in the course of an arms race in Europe which accelerated dramatically towards the end of the nineteenth century. The Imperial government had found itself unable to rearm its military forces as often and as quickly as its major rivals. This discovery prompted the government to seek to expand the industrial basis for military production. Domestic industry was incapable of meeting this requirement. By the 1870s, within two generations, Russia had lost its position as Europe's largest producer and exporter of iron and had turned into a country increasingly dependent upon imports of western manufacturers. Russian industrialisation needed a catalyst. It appeared in the form of a symbiosis of efficient governmental interventionism and the invasion of foreign capital.

3.2.2   The Role of the State

Even before the liberation of serfs the state in Russia was very deeply involved in the national economy. Nevertheless, for the most part of the nineteenth century, there was neither consistent economic policy nor an accepted view even on central economic issues – whether factories were good or bad, what tariff policy should be, or how agriculture ought to be improved. Public revenues presented the main focus of government concern. It showed in Russian tariffs: during the whole period they were rather high fetching a substantial contribution to the state budget yet not high enough to give a solid protection to national industries. In the 1860s and 1870s, Russian import of industrial products was huge and included not only sophisticated items but also very basic commodities such as nails and hessian.

After the liberation of the serfs in 1861, government economic policy underwent an important qualitative evolution. It started to reflect certain theoretical content, became more logical and coherent. However, the concept itself had changed profoundly within only a few years. In the two decades that followed 1861, it was based on the ideas of free trade and *laissez-faire*. Private initiative and unregulated markets came to be seen as the best prerequisites for the accelerated development of the Russian economy. As it happened, Russian capitalism was too weak to take advantage of this governmental philosophy and to respond to it with higher rates of growth.

Starting from 1882, governmental economic policy took a new direction which it never abandoned thereafter. In its most elaborate and complete version this new strategy was embodied in what became known as 'Witte's system' – an economic programme named after its inspirator, an outstanding tsarist statesmen. It never existed as a detailed and comprehensive plan. Sergei Witte was very much a pragmatist, and in his activities of Finance Minister (1892–1903) relied heavily on improvisation. Nevertheless, his actions were never chaotic. They were based on a clear general economic outlook having as its hard core the principles of economic nationalism and *étatisme* whose most prominent propagandist at the time was Friedrich List. In the long run, it was these principles that constituted a framework for Witte's reforming effort.

3.2.3 Witte's System

The interplay of three elements characterised Witte's system.

The first element was a belief that railroad construction was to play a crucial role in precipitating the large-scale industrialisation of Russia. According to Witte's plan, railroad orders were to serve as a catalyst for the rapid expansion of heavy industries, while railroads themselves should provide previously missing means to unite different economic regions of the country in a common market big enough to provide an outlet for capitalist mass production. Light industries and agriculture were expected to benefit as well, but in a later stage, thanks to such secondary outcomes of the railway boom as the increasing personal demand of millions of workers and employees engaged in the railroad construction.

The second element was an emphasis on state intervention as a driving force, at least until a certain moment, behind industrialisation. Government spending and initiative were to back private capital in those spheres where it was active and to substitute for it where it was missing. State orders for heavy industry products, mainly railroad equipment, were chosen as the principal lever of state intervention. How powerful that lever was may be concluded from the fact that, by the beginning of the First World War, state demand for iron and steel products made up 23 per cent of the overall demand for these products (Haumann, 1980, p. 36).

The third element reflected the assumption that national capital resources were insufficient to provide for the requirements of accelerated industrialisation. Hence, tapping foreign sources of investment capital and encouraging foreign assistance in technique and equipment were to occupy the central place among the concerns of governmental economic regulations.

In many respects the implementation of the 'Witte's system' proved to be a success. As was mentioned earlier, at the turn of the century Russia went through a period of unprecedented growth. The contribution of foreign investors and entrepreneurs to this process can hardly be overvalued. Cumulative foreign capital in Russia increased from 0.5 billion rubles in 1861 to 2.7 billion rubles in 1881, to 4.7 billion rubles in 1900 and to 7.6 billion rubles in 1914 (Jones and Gerenstein, 1983, p. xiv). Of this total, in

1913, 74.3 per cent was in state bonds and state guaranteed railway loans, and 25.7 per cent in joint stock companies. Imported direct and portfolio investment was heavily concentrated in just a handful of key industries where foreign capital share was indeed overwhelming or immense. Thus, in mining enterprises foreign capital represented 91 per cent of all joint stock and bond capital, in chemical industry 50 per cent, in metal processing 42 per cent, in timber and wood processing 37 per cent and in the textile industry 28 per cent (Liaschenko, 1948, p. 378).

3.2.4   Technology Transfer

Impressive as they are, these figures do not reveal in full the significance of the foreign contribution. The inflow of capital was accompanied by the transfer of technology which literally revolutionised Russian industry. Russia had received many technologies and products which were either unknown in the country or superior in the quality to those traditionally employed. Olga Crisp, a noted student of Russian economic history, points out that the 'newness' of much of the country's industry was a real advantage: many foreign-financed plants were, from the technical point of view, superior to those of the country from which the capital originated. In some industries the gap in labour productivity at all-Russian and foreign-financed enterprises was absolutely notorious: thus in the Ural one minor extracted 6100 puds[2] of iron ore per year against 16 400 puds per minor in Krivoi Rog (Crisp, 1976, p. 166, p. 250). At the same time it is noteworthy that foreign capital was very selective in introducing modern technologies. The main beneficiary was metallurgy while in industries where easy access to natural resources or market monopoly compensated for low labour productivity archaic technologies were still widely employed (Gatrell, 1986, pp. 159–60).

3.2.5   The Making of an Investment Climate

What made Russian bonds and stocks so popular with foreign investors? This phenomenon cannot be attributed to any single reason alone. It emerged as a product of the interplay of factors originating in Russia as well as in capital exporting countries themselves. Nevertheless, as will be shown below, governmental regulations provided a pivot for this success.

Not all the change was owing to Witte. Some of the prerequisites favouring foreign investment in Russia existed before 'Witte's system'. Others were independent from it.

First of all, Russia historically enjoyed an excellent reputation with international creditors. In France, for instance, Russian loans had been placed since 1830 and there had never been a single case of default. The government had almost a pathological concern for its credit standing abroad. Foreign debt was not only meticulously served and honoured, but the Russian financial ministry was known to organise interventions in foreign credit markets in support of Russian bonds. Internal monetary policy was also aimed, to a certain extent, at reinforcing the appeal of state loans to foreign creditors. The latter consideration was one of the motives behind anti-inflationary measures of the 1820s and also later in the nineteenth century.

Of no less importance was the political situation in Europe in the second half of the nineteenth century. Russia happened to have as its most important political allies two major creditor-countries – France and Great Britain. Close political co-operation between the three states encouraged private investors in France and Britain. On top of that, European superpowers competed for economic and political influence over Russia and considered credit relations instrumental to this end. For political reasons, Germany closed down its money market for Russian loans in 1887, whilst Paris and London for the same reason actively favoured Russian borrowing.

The geographical position of the Russian Empire also had played its role. Russia seemed to be a natural choice for cautious rentiers who were many in Western Europe in general and in France in particular. They were not inclined to risk their capital in exotic ventures in exchange for the promise of fabulous return but preferred Russia because it was nearby and its economy and politics could be monitored with a certain degree of accuracy. At the same time, investing in Russia inspired interest in more adventure-minded capitalists as well, as having business in Russia was instrumental for approaching Turkey, Persia and Manchuria which, at the time, were economically tied to the Russian Empire.

Last but not least, Russia benefited from the fact that, by the end of the nineteenth century, the industrialised countries of Western Europe had entered a particular stage of their development which, after having been first examined, in 1902, by J. A. Hobson in his *Imperialism*, became widely acknowledged as imperialistic. Among other features it was characterised by the hyper-accumulation of investment capital in economically most advanced countries and by a strong trend towards substituting capital export for the export of commodities or for investing in the enhancement of the productive capacity of national industry. The outflow of capital became constant and huge, boosting the search for new promising outlets for investment (see for detail Kenwood and Lougheed, 1977, pp. 38–56).

3.2.6   Capital Entry Management Strategy

This was the background against which the Russian government developed its capital entry strategy. It essentially rested on four pillars.

The first was a ruble stabilisation policy which climaxed in the achievement of a state of convertibility of Russian currency into gold at a fixed price in August 1897. That was an explicitly outward oriented campaign designed to provide foreign investors with yet another argument in favour of Russia as an investment outlet. This move was to confirm once again the soundness of Russia's finance and the country's general creditworthiness. Simultaneously Witte introduced another novelty serving the same aim: some items of governmental expenditures were transferred to a so-called 'extraordinary' account so that net losses from the operations of state railways and some other expenses were not allowed to affect the picture of budgetary health. This simple window-dressing operation proved to be exceptionally efficient: since after this step (and until Witte's resignation) the state budget never showed any deficit.[3]

The introduction of a gold standard was warmly received by investors and quickly translated into better terms for Russian loans (see Crisp, 1976, chapter 8). But the cost of this operation was high, in the opinion of some historians, even unjustifiably high (see, for example, Kahan, 1989, pp. 103–5). It was not confined to the price of abandoning the previously existing silver standard and accumulating gold reserves in the sum of 1095 million rubles by 1897. Millions of Russian grain exporters had paid for it by the loss of the export premium existing in the form of a disparity between the external and internal rates of ruble. Moreover, striving to give Russia's currency the most solid image, the authorities arranged regulations that required a very high ratio between gold reserves and bank notes in circulation, thus incurring extra costs and exerting a constant deflationary impact on the economy.

A change in tariff regulations was another new feature in Russian economic policy during the period of industrialisation. The relatively liberal statute of 1868 gave way, in 1891, to a new one prescribing practically prohibitive duties on the majority of imports. Russia stepped into the era of import-substituting growth. The new tariff's impact on foreign producers were twofold: on the one hand, establishing production operations in Russia had turned into the most appropriate way to tap the Russian market; on the other hand, the new tariffs boosted domestic prices[4] and increased return on the productive capital.

The implication of the new tariff was much wider than just to isolate Russian markets from foreign-made products. It also supplied the government with new instruments (though quite crude) to regulate the process of industrialisation. The tariff system was selective – it was biased in favour of high value-to-weight equipment and discouraged importing simple and labour intensive equipment (Dohan, 1990, p. 217). Maybe even more important, by granting tariff allowances and exemptions, the government managed to offer an incentive which hardly any foreign firm could have ignored, while the threat of abolishing a particular duty altogether was the instrument the government could always resort to exert downward pressure on prices.

State subsidies to heavy industries were also seen as a means to attach foreign capital to the industrialisation effort. Two types of subsidies were practiced most frequently. The first was incorporated into the mechanism of state orders for equipment (mainly railway). They were normally given for three years in advance at constant prices which noticeably exceeded what the free market could offer. Hence winning a state order brought to a firm liberation from market uncertainties together with guaranteed income. The profitability of the state orders was so enormous that there were cases when a possession of just one such order was enough justification for constructing an all new plant to carry it out (Liaschenko, 1948, p. 317). The other form of indirect subsidy was a state guarantee for corporate loans. The following figures may give the idea of its significance: on January 1st 1914, government guaranteed bonds accounted for 22 per cent of all French investment in Russia (Crisp, 1976, p. 198).

Finally, the Russian government made every effort to stabilise the balance of payments and the balance of trade of the country regarding a sound balance of payments as yet another important prerequisite for the unimpeded inflow of capital resources. An emphasis was put on facilitating the export of grain and oil. Authorities never tired of inventing new incentives for agricultural export. For instance, railroad tariffs (the railroads were mainly state-owned) were structured in such a way that it was cheaper for the grain producer to transport his harvest to a sea port for export than to supply it to a nearby city. In combination with import impeding tariffs exports promotion helped keep the Russian trade balance in the black and compensate at its account for deficit items in the balance of payments.

Despite certain effort on the part of the government the investment environment in Russia was far from being perfect. Foreign entrepreneurs were quick to discover that their Russian ventures tended to be a great deal less profitable than one could have expected them to be.

The Russian labour force was cheaper than that in Western Europe but this was neutralised to a great extent by the lack of skill and lower productivity (Gatrell and Davis, 1990, p. 140). Another negative factor was the absence of industrial and social infrastructure. Therefore bigger than usual overhead expenses were inevitable. The foreign entrepreneurs discovered that it was customary in Russia to place upon plant owners responsibility for various services, which elsewhere fell within the scope of the munici- pality or the state, i.e., for laying roads and building bridges, establishing water supplies, building houses, hospitals, communal baths, etc., for the workers and their families. How great the costs of this type could be is evi- dent from the balance sheet of a French company which was forced in 1894 to make an outlay of about 60 million rubles for the construction of houses for workers and employees (Crisp, 1976, p. 252).

In the 1890s, industrial returns were also undermined by fierce competi- tion among foreign firms in the Russian market. Widely advertised success of first foreign ventures provoked a true investment fever. The word 'Russia' had acquired magic force to mobilise money at call. Conse- quently, many foreign-owned firms in Russia were overcapitalised and overproducing. Another result of the feverish haste were mistakes and mis- calculations made by foreign entrepreneurs in the exploratory stage of their projects when preparatory examinations were executed. In a few cases these errors caused a prompt close-down of newly constructed enterprises, in many others – additional investment and soaring costs.

Furthermore, foreign entrepreneurs in Russia had to cope with obsolete commercial laws, arbitrariness on the part of state officials, enormous red tape and the existence of 'informal' relations between civil servants involv- ing bribes and favoritism. Every foreign company needed an Imperial Ordinance to incorporate and later special permission to make any major change in its structure, such as increasing capital, floating loans or entering a new line of business. Foreign companies were prohibited from engaging in certain branches of industry. The Imperial government could withdraw its authorisation at will. The attitude to legality of Finance Minister Witte himself tells much about the business climate in the country: in the opinion of the minister, in a contract between the government and a private firm only the latter was bound by the law if a conflict arose (Van Laue, 1974, p. 208; see also McKay, 1970, pp. 277–8).

The analysis of the investment climate in Russia at the turn of the twen- tieth century and during pre-war years would not be complete without mentioning that public opinion was generally very strongly biased against foreign capital. There was a widespread notion that foreign capital was destroying Russian agriculture, had seized natural resources of the country, was exploiting its population and transferring colossal profit abroad. For- eign firms would be accused of being responsible for an excessive increase in the price of oil, coal, iron, etc. (McKay, 1970, pp. 290–3). Economic backwardness helped encourage a national inferiority complex which manifested itself now and then in furious anti-foreign campaigns. After the Russo-Japanese War in particular, it seemed advisable to many companies not to stress their foreign character. The government itself was busy inspiring, through its agents, chauvinistic sentiments in the people as an antidote to rising class consciousness.

Responding to these circumstances, foreign capitalists preferred to use a Russian registry for new firms, or to take over Russian companies. The share of companies operating with foreign status declined since the turn of the century from 22.4 per cent in 1904 to 8.1 per cent in 1913, although in reality foreign participation in the Russian industry was on the increase (Jones and Gerenstain, 1983, p. x). Many foreign entrepreneurs active in Russian business had chosen to change their nationality and eventually to 'Russify'. In the main foreign capital had entered Russia in the form of participation in share capital; thus the real magnitude of its intrusion remained disguised.

3.2.7   Behind the Mystery of the Second El Dorado

If average returns were not extraordinary and, on the whole, the investment environment was not particularly friendly, what could account for the readiness with which foreign investors were supplying their capital? One of the factors not to be overlooked was the specific composition of creditors and investors themselves. Big firms eager to open a Russian branch to preserve Russian markets as an outlet for their products were rather few. Most ventures were financed by thousands of small investors who bought stocks and debentures offered to them by founders, promoters and underwriters – a parent firm, an individual or a bank. The profit of the latter was a multiple of the shareholders' return and, what was even more important, it did not depend directly on dividend payments or on the economic performance of the venture altogether. All sorts of commissions, bonuses, fees and other income-generating opportunities, open to insiders only, were the prime source of enrichment of this category of investors. An official investigation disclosed cases in which 70–80 per cent of mobilised stock capital had found its way into the pockets of founders and promoters (Liaschenko, 1948, p. 232).

Russian loans had opened one more profit opportunity to a restricted league of powerful market operators. The issue of Russian governmental and railroad bonds poured golden rain on French banks. Within only ten years seventeen major loans were placed at a nominal value of 3.7 billion rubles. At the net bank commission of less than 2 per cent the net earning of French banks may be estimated at approximately 189 million francs. In addition, banking houses earned a commission on the service of Russian loans and had other related sources of income. Because of the mammoth amount of operations (and remuneration) involved, Russian loans were more attractive to banks than Turkish, Bulgarian or South American issues despite the higher rate of profit of the latter (Crisp, 1976, p. 212).

In the light of this data it is little wonder that many prominent industrialists, financiers and bankers in Europe had a vested interest in channelling rentier money to Russia. Success stories, such as that of the South Russian Dniepr Metallurgical Company paying its shareholders 40 per cent on initial investment, were widely publicised, helping to establish for Russia the reputation of being the new El Dorado. The names of Le Creuset, Hartmann, Châtillon, Cockerill gave weight to new projects and opened the rentier's wallet. Banks were particularly active in forwarding reports on investment opportunities in Russia. On some occasions it was a well-paid job: Crédit Lyonnais, for example, dispatched reports on a functioning coal mine which its Russian proprietor was anxious to sell in exchange for a commission of 10 per cent of the shares of any subsequent company (McKay, 1970, p. 89). As for ordinary subscribers, under the particularly depressive conditions of the capital market in major creditor countries, they normally showed stoic adhesion to Russian bonds and stocks which appealed to the conservative notion of a secure investment.

3.2.8 Foreign Capital and Monopolisation of Russian Market

As was mentioned earlier, foreign-owned firms made a considerable contribution to the technological progress of Russian heavy industry. It is no less important that they accelerated tremendously the process of concentration of capital and production in the country. Foreign ventures, unlike their Russian counterparts, knew no shortage of capital. They had constant recourse to borrowed money. Russian firms, on the contrary, were chronically short of capital. On the Russian credit market money was 2.5 times more expensive than in France. Even leading industrial firms, regardless of the special patronage of the tsarist government, were compelled to use equipment a generation old. Foreign-owned plants instead were equipped according to modern standards from the start.

Consequently, the position of foreign-owned companies on the Russian market was exceptionally strong. Big firms went to great lengths to enforce it even further. Foreign capital initiated the monopolistic division of Russian markets. Upon French initiative and under French leadership two mammoth syndicates, Prodameta and Produgol, controlling the production and sale of iron and coal respectively, were organised in 1902–4. By 1907–9, syndicates had absorbed the majority of enterprises in all main industries.

The market power of the syndicates was enormous. For example, the biggest one, Prodameta, the association of thirty metallurgical enterprises (a mere 17 per cent of their total number in Russia), by 1911 had put under its control 90 per cent of the sales of assorted and sheet iron, 96 per cent of girders and pipes and 74 per cent of pig-iron products (Gatrell, 1986, p. 179). Produgol in its turn accounted for 60 per cent of the country's coal output. The consequences of monopolisation for consumers were disastrous: not only did prices soar but, in 1911–12, the country was hit by a pig-iron and coal 'famine' when members of Prodameta and Produgol held back a large proportion of output instead of supplying the growing needs of metal-working, engineering and other industrial customers. For the consumers the burden of tariff-protected prices augmented owing to monopolistic pricing: the price of coal from 1912 to 1913 rocketed by 40 per cent, the price of quality iron by 26 per cent from 1908–9 (Haumann, 1980, p. 35).

The creation of syndicates may be judged as having been a major attempt on the part of foreign capital to improve the investment climate in Russia during the period of the 1900–6 depression. As was shown before, the tsarist government did a lot to attract foreign investors. In their turn, foreign firms and banks, using their market force, were quite persistent in their effort to make the most of the situation and adjust business conditions in their favour even further. Although the Russian government was extremely authoritarian, foreign capital proved to be a force not easily disposed of. Foreign entrepreneurs used various methods to exert pressure on the government. Close 'informal' relations with mighty ministry officials and local administrators were instrumental in pursuing this end. Many top-level officials, after resigning from the civil service, landed up in the boardrooms of big foreign-owned firms and banks. Their expertise and even more so their connections seem to have been indispensable in making business run smoothly. It was a normal practice that a multimillion state order would be placed with a handful of plants – 'favourites'. Thus, among several dozen metallurgical plants, there were six such privileged producers, all foreign-owned, to whom winning a state order meant, in 1902 alone, to get a factual subsidy of eight million rubles (Liaschenko, 1948, p. 317; McKay, 1970, p. 272).

Another way of bringing pressure to bear was based on the exploitation of the tsarist government's pathological fear of losing its credit standing in foreign capital markets, especially Paris. Government steps conflicting with the interests of big foreign firms in Russia would immediately entail an inspired press campaign in major creditor countries. As the Russian government cut down orders for railway equipment, speculations started to circulate that foreign investment was being expropriated gradually as the state consciously made the foreigner's position untenable (Crisp, 1976, p. 178; McKay, 1970, p. 281). The message of this defamation campaign and a few others that followed was that the government should not deprive foreign firms of its active support. However, shortly after the turn of the century, the conditions of state finances could not afford to continue the substitution policy at its previous scale. Under these circumstances the government's consent to syndicates – they were given a free hand despite the public protest – may be interpreted as a compromise: the government did not make new material obligations but left open a possibility for big firms to improve their standing by themselves although at the expense of the Russian public.

As the Russian government did not dare displease foreign banks, so their appetites grew. By 1910, the government had to face the repeated attempts of foreign bankers and industrialists to take over some of the important levers of governmental economic regulations. In 1907, in Paris the main Paris and St Petersburg banks formed a company to which the Russian banks handed over all new operations entrusted to them and in particular all government concessions. As Crisp (1976, p. 186) rightly points out:

> the implementation of this arrangement would have deprived Kokovtsov [Russian Finance Minister after Witte] of the possibility of maneuvering between competing firms and of his right ... of entrusting particularly profitable operations to Russian banks alone

as the French part had stipulated that the majority of the orders for industrial products, arising out of the transactions carried out by the new company, should be placed with French firms. It is symptomatic that the Russian government, when addressing itself to this case, had to cope with only slightly veiled blackmail. Indeed, the new company had as its initiator a French official in whose power it was to veto the admission of securities to the Paris Bourse. A few years later, in 1909, two eminent Paris bankers put forward a project to establish a bank in Russia to administer the allocation of railway orders to industry (Crisp, 1976, ibidem).

Having found itself on the defensive, the Russian government amended its strategy towards foreign capital. On the whole, its attitude to monopolistic market structures remained ambiguous. After all, its policy of 'favoured' firms had prepared the groundwork for syndicates. None the less, in 1910, it effectively blocked the formation of a foreign-led American-type trust in the metallurgical industry. In other steps to check the syndicates it had frustrated the attempts of French banks to put under control the distribution of state orders; introduced competitive bidding on railway equipment; opened court proceedings against Produgol, and warned Prodameta that if market needs were not satisfied the government would increase production of state-owned enterprises and suspend import duties on metallurgical products and coal.

3.3 EVALUATING RUSSIAN EXPERIENCE

The events of the industrialisation epoch in Russia have been extensively covered in the literature on economic history. Nevertheless, two important questions are still open to discussion. One concerns the appraisal of the contribution of the foreign capital to Russian economic development. The other deals with the efficiency of governmental economic policy towards foreign investment. In the publications on the subject one comes across quite contrasting views. Two examples illustrate the diversity of opinion. John McKay (1970) pays great tribute to foreign entrepreneurs but denies the constructive role of the Government on the ground that many government incentives were of long standing and less efficient that is usually believed. On the contrary, George Carson (1959) stresses the importance of government regulations but puts in question the contribution of foreign capital to Russia's development by confronting the relatively modest amount of foreign investment[5] to the enormous sum of total public investment in the economy.

In this book I share the view of those scholars such as Olga Crisp who consider it pointless, in the particular circumstances of Russian industrialisation, to try to ascribe the merit of relatively successful industrialisation to the activities of either the state or foreign capital. What happened was the result of a combined effort from both sides given that existed general prerequisites in the country and abroad necessary to make this effort fruitful. The following considerations make the basis for this conclusion.

3.3.1 The Role of the State

The notably authoritarian political organisation made the state the chief economic agent in the country. No major economic development could have taken place without the state being involved. Under these conditions the absence of counteraction to foreign capital could already be seen as a form of regulation. In reality, the Russian government did more than that by explicitly favouring foreign capital.

Indeed, the incentives proposed by the government were not new. Speaking in broader terms, the liberation of serfs was the most significant incentive making any capital investment, those originating abroad included, possible. It was not each separate incentive that mattered, but rather a particular atmosphere which they helped to create together. Because of huge state investment in railway construction and protective tariffs, foreign investors found in Russia the prospect of earning a higher rate of return than at home and the growing capacity to absorb capital. This winning combination made Russia an extremely promising and attractive outlet for foreign capital.

3.3.2 The Role of Foreign Capital

Ever since the early 1890s, net capital investment in Russia amounted to over 11 per cent of national product which was quite comparable with the rate of other European industrialised countries. The net inflow of foreign investment rarely exceeded 12 per cent of net domestic investment. However, foreign capital impact on the Russian economy was more profound than these figures show:

(i) public investment apart, Russian sourced investment was split among millions of small, often family-owned, businesses heavily relying on self-financing; it was very difficult and time-consuming to organise the financing of a big project. The recourse to foreign capital markets eased the concentration of capital and hence paved the way for large-scale modern production in Russia. Without the stream of foreign capital the Russian industrialisation would have been inevitably stretched over time, as well as having a different configuration. Instead of parallel advance in all the major branches of the complex of heavy industries, as it was, there would have been probably consecutive increment of the industrial capacity;

(ii) the contribution of foreign investment should not be assessed in strictly financial terms alone. The technological and entrepreneurial aspects are at least equally important. The former has already been discussed. As for the latter, foreign businessmen brought with them not only their skill and experience, but also a new entrepreneurial culture, new approaches to decision-making in business, new relations among industry and banks, a new technique in marketing, etc. This spared Russia decades of accumulating experience and errors.

3.3.3   Some Conclusions

What possible lessons concerning the issues of the investment climate and the capital entry management system could one learn from the early Russian experience? The most instructive seem to be the following:

(i) *The long-term factors of the investment climate*. Economic circumstances in the country were not simple. The economy was in transition, structurally it presented a mixture of precapitalistic and more advanced capitalist-type elements, very much as it is now when it is a mixture of administrative–command and post-Communist elements. The coexistence of such controversial elements was not, on the whole, really 'peaceful'. A great disparity existed between various sectors of the economy, basically between industry and agriculture, constituting an intrinsic weakness of both the economy and the society. That gave a particular 'colour' to Russian capitalism: it was a victorious force but its capacity to expand was still restricted by external factors. The two dying classes – land nobility and commune-organised peasantry – were still strong. Also the state system did not correspond to the needs of the market economy.

Nevertheless, foreign capital showed quite extraordinary enthusiasm with respect to Russian investment opportunities. This can be attributed to two factors. The first was a generally positive evaluation on the part of investors of the growth potential of Russia and, hence, of the revenue-generating capacity of capital invested there. This estimate took into account the enormous natural and human resources of the country but even more so it was the recognition of the fact that, finally, these resources were becoming open for use according to the rules of the market economy. There were clear signs that the country had stepped on to the path of reforms promising a gigantic outbreak of economic activity. The direction and the guiding lines of these reforms – industrialisation, the consolidation of the market, the promotion of money and credit relations, etc. – were easily distinguishable and corresponded to the investors' interests.

Strong confidence in the stability, the continuity and the predictability of a political situation in Russia constituted the second incentive prompting the expansion of foreign investment. Indeed, French rentiers, legendary for their conservatism, caution and obsession with the security of their assets, had chosen Russia as a *client préféré*. This confidence, in its turn, seems to have rested on two circumstances. One, quite obviously, was the impression of solidity that the Russian political system made on contemporary outside observers. The other, more important for the argument of this research, was the relative openness of the Russian national economy. This claim could seem to be an overstatement. The export quota of Russia, in

1909–11, was only about six per cent as against 17.5 per cent in Great Britain, 15.3 per cent in France, 14.6 per cent in Germany and 11.0 per cent in Italy (Bairoch, 1976, p. 80).

But the 'openness' in question is the kind that cannot be measured in international trade figures alone. Rather it shows itself in various signs testifying a considerable degree of responsiveness of the national economy to exogenous factors. Russia's exposure to the international economy should be seen in the context of the problems and contradictions of a country in which economic backwardness was coupled with imperial political ambitions. In the long run, as the subsequent collapse of the Russian economy under the pressure of the First World War demonstrated, the two proved to be incompatible. This contradiction remained a factor exerting great pressure on the economy as well as on the government, especially as the Industrial Revolution of the nineteenth century had given as its offspring a military–industrial revolution which diminished the importance of territory and population as power elements (see, for example, Holsti, 1991, pp. 156–8). To resist this pressure Russia was in need of constant recourse to international commercial and credit markets. Such a dependence emerged initially during the first years after the Crimean War under the influence of the policy that Russia should remain agricultural and import manufactured goods. This soon led to the situation which Witte, in one of his secret memoranda to the Tsar, described in the following words:

> The economic relations of Russia with western Europe are fully comparable to the relations of colonial countries with their metropolis. (cited in Carson, 1959, p. 120)

The success of industrialisation had helped Russia to become self-sufficient in some industrial products but it was not enough to alter the situation in principle. Although not necessarily big in volume and absolute figures, supply from abroad, together with ready access to foreign credit, remained strategically important. This accounts for many nuances in Russia's conduct in the realm of international economic relations. Government's concern for Russia's credit standing abroad, a persistent effort to balance Russian foreign trade with a substantial surplus, as well as an obstinate tariff war with Germany at the turn of the century are just a few examples which illustrate this point. European bankers and industrialists were well aware of this particular sensibility of Russia and were right in regarding it as a partner which could not afford to take reckless steps. If the political obligations of Russia as a party to several important international treaties are added, it becomes quite clear that the foreign creditors of the country thought they had every reason to have faith in their debtor.

Overall, the general favourable appraisal of the Russian investment climate, based on the evaluation of long term factors, seemed to influence the investor's decisions to a greater extent than the individual defects of Russian business conditions. The legal status of foreign firms (in particular in the early years of industrialisation) had disadvantages by comparison with local firms; business traditions in Russia differed significantly from what was the norm in Western Europe; the infrastructure was insufficient; the quality of the labour force was generally low, etc. And still foreign investors were willing to overcome or circumvent these obstacles once the general situation was seen as sound and promising. This behaviour fits well with recent findings concerning motivations behind the foreign investment policy of big firms, which will be examined at length in the next chapter of this thesis. As it turned out, international investors appear to be more sensitive to general business environment in the host country than to specifically designed incentive packages.

(ii) *The efficacy of state regulations.* The example of Russia brightly illuminates the advantages and limitations of import-substitution as a concept of national development. The inflow of foreign capital and quick industrialisation may be securely attributed, to a great extent, to the introduction of a new trade tariff and state subsidies to heavy industries. As the indirect indication of the efficacy of the state policy one may point to the fact that foreign capital was active in those industries in which it was channeled with the help of government regulations but was only marginally involved in other sectors of the economy. This evidence, however, may be interpreted as a sign of the potential feebleness of government tactics. In sectors lacking tariff protection foreign capital tended to expand by means of commodity import rather than by direct or portfolio investment; modern technology was installed on a wide scale only in a few privileged industries while in others foreign firms adhered to obsolete local techniques; despite the implementation, in some cases, of really modern equipment and processes, local production by foreign firms was not competitive in international markets. The government's reckoning that the inflow of foreign capital would increase competition and deflate prices, thus compensating for the upward pressure on a price level exerted by protectionist tariffs, was also frustrated as soon as foreign entrepreneurs initiated syndication.

In the particular case of Russian pre-war industrialisation, these developments may hardly be assessed as the failure of government policy inasmuch as it did not address many of them directly. In more general terms they point rather clearly to at least two conclusions. First, import-substitution strategy tends to result in bringing about only a 'closed economy'; second, there always exists a contradiction between business rationality and state regulation.

Two further observations are also noteworthy. First, shortly after having been allowed to operate in Russia, foreign capital made quite a successful attempt to counterpose their own power structures and pressure centres to governmental structures and governmental pressure. Second, foreign participation never opened external markets to Russian products and Russian integration in the world economy remained a one-way street.

3.4　SOCIALIST RUSSIA: A TRANSPLANTATION EXPERIMENT

3.4.1　The Thrust of Industrialisation

The October revolution caused radical changes in every major area with maybe one exception: the revolutionary authority proved to be equally captivated, though for different reasons, by the idea of accelerated industrialisation. Moreover, quite soon the Soviet government followed in the tracks of its overthrown predecessor by contemplating plans to use foreign investment as a foundation for large-scale industrialisation. A governmental concessional programme was announced as early as May 1918, only a very short time after the nationalisation of foreign property and the abrogation of foreign debt. The two policies, contradictory as they were, had a common platform: the desire to enforce the new rule economically and socially. Nationalisation was justified by the necessity to seize 'the commanding heights in the economy'; the plans to invite foreign capital – by the need to expand these 'commanding heights' and turn them into the stronghold of the socialist state.

For the new regime the increase of industrial production was of paramount importance both in the short and long term. First, the enhancement of industry (or merely the restoration of the industrial potential of tsarist Russia devastated in the years of the World War and revolutions) was a necessary prerequisite for expanding the material basis of those social forces whose support constituted the main strength of the Soviet regime. Second, large-scale modern industry with its higher degree of concentration, of economic, financial and labour discipline, of accountability, and better adaptability for monitoring and planning was seen as a vitally important counterforce to the anarchy of small producers, carpetbaggers and smart traders dominating the ailing economy of post-revolutionary Russia. They were considered by the Bolsheviks to be the greatest threat to the Soviet system now that the influence of big capitalist firms and banks had been undermined by nationalisation. It was even more important, however, that, in the long run, industrialisation was regarded not only as the guarantee of the survival of the new state surrounded by capitalist enemies but as a main path towards a prosperous Communist society.

The necessity in the restoration and subsequent expansion of industry was more than self-evident. However, by 1920, when the Bolsheviks finally achieved victory in the Civil War, after the years of 'War Communism', the troubles of military campaigns and foreign military intervention, after economic blockades and disastrous harvests, the capacity of Soviet Russia's government to pursue the policy of industrialisation seemed to be even more restricted than that of the tsarist government at the turn of the century. The economy lay in ruins. Large-scale industries had suffered most. In 1920, the production of iron ore was only 2.4 per cent of the output of 1913; of pig iron – 2.4 per cent; of steel – 4 per cent; of cotton manufactures – 5 per cent and of sugar – 5.8 per cent. Total industrial output had declined to less than one third of 1913 volume, total agricultural output was only half of the pre-war quantity. The value of manufactured consumer goods sold to the population had decreased by nine tenths (Hutchings, 1982, p. 31; Baykov, 1950, p. 8). The use of money and the velocity of monetary circulation became very limited, having given way to barter and rationing; owing to hyperinflation, any substantial accumulation in a monetary form by private persons and firms, as well as by public bodies, became pointless.

Two possibilities for raising resources for industrialisation had been discussed within the Bolshevik party at the beginning of the 1920s. Both possibilities had influential supporters. The one advocated by Trotsky was to transform the country into a military camp and mobilise resources through the expropriation of the peasantry and the utilisation of forced labour ('labour armies' in Trotsky's discourse). This was a path towards autarky and isolationism. The other, seemingly less radical and revolutionary, was to bring back economic incentives for production and to turn to foreign capital as a supplier of financing, technique and know-how. This plan was backed with Lenin's authority. He put great weight on Russia regaining its position in the international economy. He insisted that Russia should fully enjoy the advantages of the international division of labour and repeatedly claimed that foreign private capital invested under the control of the government in large-scale industries ('the state capitalism' in Lenin's terminology) was in fact an ally of the socialist regime in its struggle against the element of unorganised petty bourgeois production. The bias given by Lenin to the policy of attracting foreign investment is fully evident from the following examples. Explaining the origins of the famous New Economic Policy, he mentioned in the first place the necessity to restore a favourable economic climate for foreign investment:

> [T]he practical purpose was always important to me. And the practical purpose of our New Economic Policy was to lease out concessions. (Lenin, 1923, p. 472)

Moreover, the pioneering 'Goerlo' plan (the State Plan for the Electrification of Russia), projected under Lenin's supervision in the yearly 1920s, envisaged that out of 17 billion rubles of total investment six billion should be attracted from abroad in the form of long-term credits (Dongarov, 1990, p. 46).

3.4.2 Concessions

In Soviet Russia the development policy of relying on active foreign participation never progressed beyond a very initial preparatory stage. After Lenin's death, the strategy towards foreign capital participation in the Soviet economy had been repeatedly addressed at Party congresses, each new discussion revealing growing hostility to this idea. Finally, in 1928, the victory of Stalin's doctrine of 'Socialism in One Country' put an end to this line of thinking altogether. This doctrine, in a different, Lenin-like phraseology, was a reprint of Trotsky's plan of economic restoration put forward at the time of 'War Communism', condemning the country to isolation and enormous hardship. Paradoxically, by this time Trotsky himself had turned into a convinced supporter of what he called 'external New Economic Policy' (i.e., the policy of attracting foreign capital for the purpose of diminishing the strain of domestic accumulation) and, in 1925, he took the post of Chairman of the Chief Concessions Department of the Council of People's Commissars (Government) of the USSR.

For the greater part of the 1920s, however, the impulse given by Lenin to the concessional policy was still bearing results. A necessary legal framework was established and organisational steps were made to enrol foreign capital in the concessionary undertakings in the territory of the USSR. Yet, the role of foreign concessions and joint ventures in the economy of the country remained negligible indeed. Their share in the gross capital investment reached only 0.57 per cent in 1927–8; in the gross output of Soviet big industry 0.4 per cent (1925–6); in the sales of industrial products 1.0 per cent (1928–9)[6] (Dongarov, 1990, p. 118; Baykov, 1950, p. 126). According to an authoritative account, state revenue from the concessions amounted to only 14 million rubles in 1923–4 (E. H. Carr, 1978, p. 455). These modest levels are not surprising. What does surprise in fact is the evidence of considerable interest showed by foreign investors in Soviet ventures. All in all, from1921 to 34, several thousand offers were received by Soviet Concessions Commissions in Germany, Great Britain, the United States and France of which over two thousand were passed over to the Chief Concessions Department for further examination. However, only 163 concessions were sanctioned.

3.4.3 Against All Odds

The general positive response of foreign investors to the Soviet concessional initiative remains quite an intriguing feature of international economic relations of the 1920s and 1930s, especially if it is projected against the state of the investment climate in the country. The conditions were generally discouraging. The proprietors of Russian ventures faced numerous difficulties inside the country as well as beyond its borders. Soviet Russia was the object of a credit, transport and trade blockade set by its creditors – the major European banks and non-financial companies – and supported by their governments. This was their response to the nationalisation of foreign property and the default on foreign debt. This impediment alone considerably increased the costs and risks of financing investment in Russia and hampered the sale on the world market of products originating within the country. As a result, many industrial sites formerly owned by foreigners which the government would be eager to lease never found a concessioner despite their obvious revenue-generating potential.

Far more frustrating were conditions in the country itself.[7]

a) Excessive red tape. As early as the 1920s Soviet Russia gained the features of a bureaucratic state. A concessional agreement usually required years of negotiations. Thus, the concessioner had to wait at least six months for the government's formal authorisation of the negotiated contract.

b) Unsatisfactory legal protection of foreign ventures. The concessional agreement was the only legal document defining the rights of the concessioner. There was no legislation regulating property rights, the repatriation of capital and income, etc. The agreements were often compiled at the government's bidding and included discriminating clauses. On top of that the government and local authorities were free to issue laws and orders imposing further restrictions on the concessioner, such as the Decree of September 10,1926 committing concessional enterprises to buy government bonds for the sum of 60 per cent of their reserve capital.

c) The systemic inadequacy of the economic environment. The concessioner had to cope with such deficiencies as low productive though relatively expensive labour, the scarcity of material supplies, the unreliable transportation system, etc. Still more important concessionary enterprises, being like any capitalist venture a market-oriented profit-seeking entities, had found themselves transplanted into the economy in which market values were neglected for the sake of the political–administrative control of the economy. In the course of a concentration process the internal market had been monopolised by state-owned trusts. They were as much political as economic organisation in the sense that the state order had more weight for them than all the objective economic indicators. State trusts could afford to be badly managed because, unlike the concessionary enterprises, they could not go bankrupt. As a result, the market mechanism, archaic and inefficient as it was after the black-out during the period of 'War Communism', was even further distorted by non-compromising state administration. It was quite common that the concessioner would find it impossible to induce local suppliers to provide for necessary components as all their output had been already allocated according to state orders. In practice, the concession could survive only until the state lost interest in its existence. As soon as that happened, the concession was rejected by the environment as a 'stranger' and an unwanted competitor. It is no wonder, therefore, that over 90 per cent of all the concessions were sold out before the term of the contract.

d) Isolation from the outer world. The state monopoly of foreign trade and currency payments was responsible for another hard blow at the efficiency of foreign concessions. It restricted, or even made impossible, the usage of such traditional means of optimisation of the economic performance of multinational firms as intrafirm trade and credit, high manoeuverability of resources, easy and quick access to international markets, etc. The state monopoly of trade implied that all the foreign trade was to be carried out through state foreign trade organisations (V/O) only. The latter, entrusted to protect state interests against the interests of individual firms, would place the order of the concessioner on their own will. As many of the concessions had to rely quite heavily on supplies from abroad, they were extensively exposed to the arbitrariness of the V/Os and, eventually, to state administration. Furthermore, when, as early as 1926, the government started to take measures to insulate the Russian convertable currency, *chervonets*, from the foreign market and to cut its link with gold, problems with expatriating profit and capital arose, gradually eroding the *raiason d'être* of the existence of foreign investment in the Soviet Union.

e) General public hostility. Within the Soviet society foreign ventures were treated with suspicion, enmity and prejudice. This was the conclusion of a special investigation on the investment climate in Soviet Russia undertaken at the request of the Politburo of the Bolshevik party in the early 1920s. The cases of sabotage were frequent, foreign concessions used to be maltreated by local authorities and their Soviet partners. However, if at the beginning of the decade this attitude caused concern on the part of the government, only a few years later it contributed to the tension itself by putting on trial the employees of a number of foreign concession on a fabricated charge of high treason. This created a social vacuum around foreign ventures and forced some of them, including a most successful Lena Goldfields, to close down.

If the investment climate was so discouraging, what could explain the anxiety of many foreign firms to establish business in Soviet Russia? In order to answer this question it is necessary, first of all, to have a more detailed look at the composition of concession-seekers in the 1920s. Mostly they were small firms interested in organising either commercial ventures or small-scale enterprises producing simple consumer goods. As for bigger firms, apart from the proposals of some major automobile firms to construct car assembling plants in Russia, they generally abstained both from vast investments as well as from investing in machine-tool industry and some other industries to which the Soviet government gave priority,[8] while showing some interest in mining and timber industries. In the latter case former owners were active in recuperating their business in the form of a concession. Both patterns look logical. Small investors were eager to capitalise on the poor state of a Russian internal market suffering from both the scarcity of goods and the inefficiency of state trade organisations. Russia's was a strong seller market. To enterprises with a short period of capital turnover involved in the production of basic goods (such as pencils and matches) it promised, at least in a short prospect, a quick and lofty return big enough to compensate for the inconveniences of doing business in Soviet Russia. And indeed, the Russian market was ready to accept prices securing producers one rouble of revenue on every rouble of costs (Os'mova and Stulov, 1990, p. 53). In the case of large-scale industries where big foreign firms could be engaged the very same characteristics of the Russian market, in the isolation from the world markets, had quite an opposite effect: its underdeveloped state did not correspond to the requirements of modern capital-intensive mass production, presuming the extensive usage of numerous sub-contractors and the relative stability of economic environment necessary to justify a long-term investment.

3.4.4　The Chance Missed

The exception made by foreign capital for extracting and timber industries should be explained by the vacuum which emerged in international trade when Russia was forced to withdraw from its traditional export markets. Relative export strength in certain commodity sectors gained by pre-war Russia gave the Soviet economy a historical chance to retain its position within the contemporary system of international economic relations. In fact, when Lenin counted foreign capital among the sources of Soviet industrialisation, he reckoned upon the indispensability of Russia in the framework of the international economic system as it emerged in the first decade and a half of the twentieth century. In reality this chance was missed. A new economic system, in which the USSR was to play only a marginal role, started to take shape at a very rapid pace already in the inter-war period. These structural changes occurred because of the shock given to international trade and investment by the Great Depression at the beginning of the 1930s as much as to the purposefully autarkic policy of the Soviet government.

Foreign ventures were extinguished because they did not fit the system – this was probably the main lesson of the Soviet experiment with transplanting capitalism. The system as objective reality was rejecting foreign investment despite officially proclamations and (half-hearted) actions. Also none of the declared ends were achieved because Bolsheviks were soon forced to abandon their illusions that foreign ventures would prefer the ideal of harmonic development of the host country to other more pragmatic interests. The authorities could not submit to the reality that foreign investors were consciously using to their advantage the hardships of the country, miserable state of its economy and its markets, and was anxious to curtail this possibility. Soon, however, both the elite and the society developed a sort of idiosyncrasy to the very possibility that *profit* could be extracted at all by foreign capital in the territory of the country in whatever reasonable amount. By trying to put this perception into life, they cut the tree of foreign entrepreneurship in Soviet Russia.

Notes

1.　According to the calculations of Paul Bairoch, in 1910, in Europe Russian GNP was second only to German while on a per capita scale it was superior only to that of Serbia and Bulgaria (Bairoch, 1976, pp. 154–5). According to the estimates made by Russian economist S. Prokopovich, the national income of Russia Empire (excluding Finland) calculated for the industrial sector only was equivalent to 37 per cent of that of the United States which means that allowing for bigger population Russia had a per capita income of only 20.4 per cent of American level.

2. The pud is a traditional Russian measure of weight equal to about 16 kilograms.

3. The 'extraordinary' account deficit during the same period amounted to over 2.5 billion rubles (Liaschenko, 1948, p. 195).

4. In 1913, Russian wholesale industrial prices were on average 39 per cent above the world level (Davis, 1990, p. 15).

5. In fact, the estimation by Paul Gregory of net foreign investment in Russia suggests that, for many decades before the October revolution, there had been no net transfer of resources from abroad in the Russian Empire as foreign debt payments exceeded net foreign investment (see Gregory, 1982, pp. 95–8 and Appendix M).

6. In special branches of production some concessions occupied quite an important place: Lena Goldfields in 1926 extracted one third of all the gold produced in the country while the Harriman concession supplied one fourth of the world output of manganese (Dongarov, 1990, pp. 96–7).

7. The summary below follows the documents and reports published and commented on by A. Dongarov in Chapter IV of his *Foreign Capital in Russia and the USSR* (1990) and by M. Os'mova and O. Stulov in their article 'Foreign capital in our country: something new or long-for gotten old?' in *Kommunist*, No. 18, 1990, p. 51–8.

8. As late as 1929 the Chief Concession Committee of the USSR was seeking to interest foreign investors in building such important projects as the Magnitogorsk and Taganrog metallurgical works (Schwartz, 1951, p. 129). Owing to insufficient home production, in 1932, for example, 78 per cent of all machine-tools installed were imported (Nove, 1989, p. 220).

4 Investment Climate and Investment Risk

4.1 CONCEPTUALISING THE INVESTMENT CLIMATE

In section 1.2 the following definition of the investment climate was proposed: investment climate is a multiple category encompassing everything that the foreign investor takes into consideration when evaluating how well conditions in a particular country favour capital investment, including the economy and culture, ideology and politics. Defined in this manner, the investment climate becomes, rather unexpectedly, in a considerable degree a complex matter for conceptualisation.

This results, first of all, from the fact that, thus defined, the category of the investment climate appears to comprise quite a strong investor specific element inasmuch as the investment climate represents business conditions as they are evaluated, in every separate case, by a particular investor through the prism of his specific interests, strategies and advantages. So, unlike meteorology, strictly speaking, the same economic territory, in the terms of the above definition, may comprise as many investment 'climates' as is the number of foreign investors.[1] A similar point has been made by Kobrin (1978) who wrote that political instability is clearly a property of the environment, while risk is a property of the firm. Such an approach explains why countries which, according to conventional wisdom, are least appropriate for foreign ventures manage, none the less, to attract foreign capital, as was the case of Soviet Russia in the 1920s and 1930s.

Further, the notion of the investment climate tends to be unmanageably extensive. It may be analyzed at macro and micro levels, in terms of economics, political science or, for instance, sociology.

Thus, at a macro level, it includes the economic and political situation in the country, as well as public sentiments and the national cultural background. Several parameters are usually referred to in this context, including the following.

Politics – the official attitude towards foreign ventures; the tradition of observing international agreements; the participation in the system of international agreements and agencies providing the infrastructure of the world economic regime; the strength of public institutions; the continuity of political rule; the degree of pragmatism (or, conversely, idealisation) of state politics; the efficacy of state apparatus, etc.

The economy – the general economic situation (crisis, stagnation, boom); the exchange regime; the rate of inflation; the state of development of the capital market and the banking system; the tariffs and non-tariff barriers; the budget deficit and the balance of payments; the conditions on the labour market. In particular, foreign investors are sensitive to regulations and conditions putting limits on the freedom of the movement of capital and to factors determining the costs of production – the cost and quality of labour, and the development of the transport infrastructure in the first place.

The social and cultural sphere – the public attitude towards private property in general and to foreign property in particular; the degree of the cohesion of the society on the essential strategies of economic and social development of the country; party and trade-union mobilisation; the tradition of business ethics; management culture; the educational level of the population; traditions influencing consumption pattern, etc.

At a micro level, the investment climate shows itself in bilateral relations between the foreign investor and various state agencies, the foreign investor and local economic agents: suppliers and buyers, banks, trade-unions, and others. This level is very important. It is there the general estimates of business conditions by investors, based on the analysis of macro level data and other summarised input, takes the form of concrete relations between a foreign venture and a local environment.

The two levels interrelate. It is their combination that constitutes the investment climate since, for example, the effort of the central power to attract foreign capital may be undermined by the absence of motivation on the part of local authorities or paralyzed because of low executive culture. On the other hand, local initiative and involvement, especially in large countries, are essential to the success of the policy of central authorities as they may compensate for the defaults in regulation on a national scale.

To cope with the broad range of factors forming the notion of the investment climate one needs to introduce a model which, at the cost of abstracting from certain aspects of the subject, would permit to focus on its principle features. This book dwells on the problem of how to optimise strategy towards foreign capital (direct investment mainly) under the particular conditions of the transitional economy. This implies concentrating on two of the major broad categories of risks faced by international business in such an economy: political risk and policy risk.

The two types of risk are interdependent. It is not always easy to make a straightforward distinction between them. First, for the foreign investor any country's sovereign risk is the risk of change. Second, in both cases the issue in question is control by national authorities over the activities of foreign-owned ventures and the resulting constraints for the foreign investor. *Political risk* stems from political change. Respective theory mainly deals with those situations when the authorities decide on breaking the existing regime for foreign capital by administrative measures in order to achieve a radical and decisive change in control in their favour. Expropriation, understood both as formal public expropriation and as a cluster of government actions resulted in establishing a political environment urging forced divestment of foreign ownership, is one of the principal objects of research here. The *policy risk* literature, in turn, usually refers to those uncertainties affecting international investment which are related to the economic regulation options of the host-government within the continuing regime for foreign capital, i.e., exchange control, local contents, fiscal payments, licensing of foreign trade, etc.

4.2   A FRAMEWORK FOR ANALYZING POLITICAL RISK

4.2.1   Theories of Political Risk

In brief, the main contributions to the political risk theory[2] may be summarised along the following lines.

The host government may wish to extend its control over the local subsidiary of a multinational corporation to a degree which cannot be secured by traditional instruments of economic policy. Expropriation is the most radical and far reaching method leading to fulfilling this goal. Such a development is usually associated with drastic changes in the political regimes of host-countries, including wars, revolutions and other political turmoil. Hence, political stability at the grassroots level in the periphery of society and government political stability are among major concerns of the political risk theory. Though ideologically-motivated expropriation is possible, normally forced divestment is a means rather than an end. This implies that expropriation is not necessarily a by-product of political regime discontinuity. The host government may be determined to make this step as a result of a rational decision-making.

Political risk is too amorphous a subject to be easily adapted to a systemic quantitative analysis. To overcome this difficulty, the mainstream of theory follows the assumption that recipient countries have governments that pursue a consistent set of objectives and that the people of this countries have observable and stable attitudes towards foreigners, private property, and contracts. However, the theory allows for several departures from this assumption. The concept of 'crazy state' accounts for a situation when the behaviour of the representative citizens is irrational (e.g. the example of Iran after the Islam revolution). This and other 'paradox' cases confront the investor with a political environment bearing risks which are particularly difficult to identify and foresee. For obvious reasons such cases strongly resist any generalisation or formalisation. The most the literature can offer the business is a recommendation to be especially prudent in approaching them.

Rational governments can decide on expropriation on the basis of some rational cost-benefit calculus. Yet motivations may be different. Some governments aim at maximising a country's welfare. Others pursue the goal of retaining power or increasing their popularity with the people (a self-interest concept). Restraints on foreign capital may serve to divert attention from pressing problems by merely giving the appearance of effective action.

According to a *public-interest* hypothesis on expropriation, the rational government will only expropriate firms if it believes it is able to run them reasonably well on its own. Hence, the ability of a foreign firm to avoid hostile actions on the part of the government depends on the quality of technology and managerial skill it has transferred to the host country while the propensity of the authorities to nationalise a foreign venture is almost entirely dependent on the managerial and technical capacity to run the enterprise. From this viewpoint, extractive investment is more exposed to expropriation risk because basic technologies are easily accepted in the market. In recent years, owing to the globalisation of economy, foreign ventures of transnational corporations have become protected not only by internalised technology but also by being deeply integrated into the international production structures of their parent companies. Their value as a property plunges down dramatically if they are pulled out of this international context.

A *social-political* hypothesis seeks to explain expropriations that do not show a sectoral concentration. This concept hinges on such factors as national sovereignty and national identity, national aspirations and national frustration as key determinants of expropriation, with the host government using foreign ventures as a scapegoat for the country's problems (the propensity to expropriate model). This approach does not regard the host government as the only or even the most important initiator of political risk but rather considers the risk to be a product of the host-country social-economic environment as a whole while the government passes on this risk to transnational corporations in an attempt to diminish its own exposure to internal pressure.

The recommendations of the political risk theory to the managers of firms planning to internationalise (apart from those built on pure common sense such as insure yourself, or pass the risk to someone else, or hide the fact that you are foreign, or make your investment short-time) rely heavily on the postulates of the rational concept of public policy, i.e., the theory extrapolates on the premise that the government policy is correctly designed to secure net value achievement – a positive ratio between the values it achieves and the values it sacrifices. Quite predictably, the strategic line of defence it proposes to investors is to make provisions to maximise the cost of expropriation and minimise its benefits for the authorities.

The theory is less explicit when dealing with risks originating from a broader social-political environment in the host-country. Concepts worked out under the assumption that the national propensity to expropriate depends on the frustration of a nation's aspirations related to economic development imply that political risk is higher in countries in which welfare and economic expectations are low in comparison with the level of aspirations. However, the obvious scarcity of applicable results has entailed, in recent years, a noticeable shift of emphasis from political risk assessment towards research on conflict management.

4.2.2   Choosing an Approach

Political risk analysis ranges from political science oriented approaches to empirical-based forecasting services. The latter seek to provide quantitative measures for political risk. None the less, they are still very subjective as the matter itself is hardly appropriate for quantification. The former instead, remaining at a broad conceptual level, provide some very useful insights opening possibilities for general observations on business conditions in a particular country.

As follows from the definition of the investment climate accepted in this thesis, for the authorities of the host-country to model political risk as it is perceived by the foreign investor would mean to place themselves into the references system of the investor and, on this basis, to extrapolate his decisions. We assume, therefore, a hypothetical investor who relies in his conclusions on the methodology of the political risk theory outlined above and, of many types of political risk analysis, gives preference to *scenario creation* as an instrument to forecast political disturbances.

Such an investor, contemplating starting business in Russia, will immediately face the situation, in political science terminology, of low political performance. Spontaneous resorts to violence (or acts in which violence is threatened or for other reasons is very likely); weak legitimacy of the polity (very substantial amount of citizens does not consider it worth of support), and consequent uncertainty about the persistence of the polity over time;

plus crippled decision and executive efficacy of the state – these are only some of its features. In other words, it is exactly the situation of government disturbances and mass political disturbances which both the theory and common sense treat as expressly inappropriate for the realisation of an investment project.[3]

The analysis, however, cannot be terminated at this point. International competition urges TNCs to take risks. As Jeffrey Hertzfeld[4] claims:

> global companies cannot hedge their bets by holding back from the [ex]-Soviet market and waiting for the picture to clear... Five years from now, conditions may be somewhat more predictable, but by then first movers will have established advantageous positions both with [ex]-Soviet customers and with [ex]-Soviet partners.[5]

In fact, political stability in a society does not mean the absence of any disturbances altogether; political continuity is not equal to unchangeable policy. Hence, the importance of diagnosing the nature, depth and endurance of the disturbance, based on a premise that relations between the foreign firm and the host-authorities are hardly ever without a conflict. As was once observed, it is not the conflict itself that is dangerous, but rather its mismanagement.

4.3 THE SOURCES OF POLITICAL RISK IN RUSSIA

4.3.1 Government Risk

Since, by definition, political risk represents itself in administrative actions, understanding the motivation behind government actions is essential for scenario creation. Of course, this does not diminish the risk itself but allows the investor to pass from the state of *uncertainty* about government actions to the state of prognosticated (or calculated) *probability* associated with a particular action. According to modern decision theory (see, for example, Harsanyi, 1977; Elster, 1986), the possibility to apply the principle of mutually expected rationality is central to make the above passage feasible. The concept of rationality initially was about a choice of the most appropriate means to a given end. However, a more general concept of rationality has proved to be more appropriate for political forecasting in the circumstances of profound socio-economic changes. It accentuates *ends* rather than *means* and treats choices among alternative ends as rational if they are based on clear and consistent priorities or preferences.

Hence, the evaluation of government risk takes the form of a comparative analysis of the alternative ends facing the government in confrontation with its actual choice in terms of the rational concept of public policy (see above). If the priority or the set of priorities chosen by the government meet the criteria of the latter, one may expect to find a certain degree of longevity and continuity, as well as necessary public support, as characteristic features of the national economic policy. Otherwise, the most probable scenario will be an inconsistent and chaotic policy multiplying pressures on the government and eventual scapegoating.

On the face of it, post-Communist governments in Russia have shown distinctive qualities of pragmatic and technocratic rule. They have proclaimed devotion to the cause of profound renovation and restructuring of the national economy according to market economic principles and indeed have been pursuing internationally recognised economic reform policy. The authorities obviously expected that such an approach would acquire them a good reputation with the international business community and favourably influence political risk assessments by foreign investors inasmuch as rigorous pursuit of a predetermined economic pattern made the policy more cohesive, transparent and predictable.

The accentuated devotion to technocratic rationality demonstrated by the first of these governments led by President Boris Yeltsin and Vice-Prime Minister Yegor Gaidar, i.e., the attachment to what is presented as the policy dictated by pure economic common sense alone, was, to an extent, a legitimate reaction to the excessive emphasis on ideology of the previous regime. At the same time, in a sense, it was a *forced* technocratism. Governments which assent to power as a result of social upheaval are doomed to reforms, real or illusory, in order to demonstrate that they differ from the regime they took over and, thus, to justify the change and reinforce their own legitimacy. All the revolutions, and *perestroika* and the events that followed *were* a revolution, try to follow this pattern. The initial success of the Bolshevik revolution was later consolidated owing to the enormous transformation pressure evoked by this event in the society. The major fault of Gorbachev's management of *perestroika* was that, having initiated a revolution, he failed, at a certain moment, to come up with initiatives radical enough to correspond with its dynamics.

There is little doubt that the post-Gorbachev leadership of Russia has drawn lessons from this experience. From the outset it was keen not to lose reforming momentum in its politics. However, from the very first moment, it found itself in a very difficult situation. The breaking up of the 'real socialism' doctrine which, in the absence of any constructive alternative, had been one of the main reasons for the seeming stability of the society, has left a tremendous ideological and conceptual gap. The resulting vacuum has not so far been filled. What emerged was a society without a sustaining ideology and a polity without a ruling party or a party block. The primary legitimacy of the government relied basically on two pillars: the personal authority of the head of the state (the authority based on the negation of the past rather than on a positive idea of the future) and the belief that this government is important as a symbol and, in a sense, a guarantor of a democratic process in the country.

Under these conditions the selection of the 'big-bang' doctrine was a self-evident step prompted by the instinct of self-preservation.[6] Under Gorbachev, economists were trying to work out an economic programme that would have accounted for the specificities of the domestic economy and would have led towards a welfare society. Under Yeltsin, for political reasons mainly, the task has been simplified. The government has set an objective of establishing a capitalist society and, in order to fulfil it, has borrowed its economic philosophy ready-made from conservative Western experts. By doing this, the government has chosen to neglect some important facts. First, that monetarist economic concepts were elaborated in conditions utterly different from those now confronting Russia. Second, that standard recipes for overcoming economic backwardness are non-existent: otherwise there would be no poor and backward countries left in the world. Third, that the IMF orthodoxy implicitly hinges on constructing premises for foreign investment expansion irrespective of a country's own interests.

The Yeltsin/Gaidar government took over when the country was facing one of the deepest crises in its history threatening to undermine the basics of national survival. However, it did not opt for an anti-crisis strategy but rushed to price liberalisation instead in the hope that foreign investment would pour in as production fell. This choice has wiped out savings, wages and pensions, and reinforced chaos in the economy, mounting hardships over hardships for the people, without clear economic or social benefits.[7]

Yet the regime enjoyed tangible political dividends:

(i) by laying claim to public support on the grounds that it was a government of action ready to take responsibility when others had failed. Exploiting public fears concerning the threat of the restoration of totalitarianism, it sought to consolidate its legitimacy, insisting that the survival of the government was equal to the survival of democracy and vice versa. The message carried by the pro-government press was easy to read: 'Maybe you do not like what we do, but we are *the* democrats. If you do not want the come-back of Bolshevism, support us whatever we do, otherwise you are reactionary'. The democratic credentials of the government was one of the reasons why a mass revolt did not follow the introduction of drastic economic measures as many had forecasted. Another reason was linked to the fact that the government was in a position to shift the responsibility for the hardships accompanying its politics to the former regime.

(ii) by providing himself with international backing. Gorbachev paved the way by extensively relying on international public opinion and, even more so, on official and semi-official support and solidarity from the West to compensate for the failures of his internal policies. Gorbachev owed his international popularity to his bold disarmament policy and to the new political thinking he introduced. The first post-Communist Russian government had accepted the rules of the game offered by the IMF. In exchange it had received more leverage on his political opponents who, as follows from the intrigue of the Parliament–government confrontation during the sixth Congress of People's Deputies in April 1992, were forced to submit to the reality that they could not remove the government without risking being deprived of the foreign currency from the IMF.

(iii) by creating an atmosphere which helped to neutralise, at least for a while, the resistance of former Soviet and Party *nomenklatura* still retaining, under various camouflages, their influential positions. They boycotted *perestroika* as endangering their privileges. Hastily prepared and inconsistently implemented reforms have prepared the ground for wildcat privatisation which appears to give *nomenklatura* exceptional chances to keep for themselves their privileged position, now as first generation capitalists.[8]

The example of current Russian politics has shown that between demonstrative technocratism and realism may lay an abyss. Speaking in terms of the business climate for foreign investors, government risk in Russia appears to be not so much the threat that the cabinet may easily fall owing to the unpopularity of its policy. After all, reform-minded governments have never been particularly stable. More important is the damage a dogmatic policy may cause to the reputations of the market as an institution. In turn, this will substantially restrict the prospects for foreign investors. It is mass disillusionment in 'market democracy' that could cause discontinuity in policy. The official propaganda goes to great lengths to explain to the public that illegal business, sharp dealing, the grabbing and looting of state property, the expropriation of wage-earners through hyperinflation, racketeering and organised criminality are not typical of a market-based economy, but it refuses to accept that all these are consequences of a one-sided economic strategy. Judging from press publications, more and more people need to be persuaded that the actual chaos in the country was not the intended result of government reforms. In the presence of certain prerequisites, generalised belief may become specific fears, antagonisms and hopes, leading to a hostile outburst which may not only sweep away the regime but devastate (at least for some time) nuclei of a market economy in Russia.

Under these conditions it would be erroneous to estimate government risk on the evidence of how much the administration seems to be determined to be rigorous in pursuing a once announced strategy. The result, in terms of policy continuity, can be the opposite. The ability of the government to correct its macroeconomic policy according to the constantly changing conditions of the volatile Russian economy has acquired the importance of the main precondition for providing continuity of a democratic pro-market policy in the country.

The corrections in question are not of the type which a defaulting government feels obliged to adopt in order to win back some of the declining public support. Flexibility is often confused with weakness. In reality, more adaptability would mean that reforms (and reformers) have entered the state of maturity. The frontal attack on the bastions of planned economy has failed. This proves once again that in economics, first, there are no simple straightforward dependencies at the macro level; second, belief in the automatism of the process of accommodation at the micro level are false. Flexibility in politics, though to such a degree which does not result in the oblivion of the ultimate end, coupled with a prompt reaction to the specific challenges of every particular phase of transition emerge as two major qualities distinguishing a successful government in Russia.

Clearly, a new interpretation should be given to the relationship between the nation-state and international financial agencies. Normally, private business regards it as positive for the investment climate if nation-states actively co-operate with the latter and enjoy their blessing and financing. However, if the International Monetary Fund persists in its dogmatism as the further decline in output – as is likely – will urge Russia's government to ease off its shock-therapy grip, the conventional approach is going to lose its point. The IMF will undermine its own aim of promoting foreign investment if it remains under the delusion that in an enormous country such as Russia one may concentrate on one set of problems and forget about twenty others no less important.

4.3.2 Post-Communist Nationalism and Regionalism

From the point of view of investment risk, nationalism and regional separatism are of particular importance. First, ethnic tension is often a cause of persistent political instability fraught with very serious conflicts up to mass violent action. Second, foreign property is a 'natural' victim of nationalistic wrath.

Taking into consideration that the USSR was a country of over one hundred nationalities, it is precarious to generalise on the nature of nationalism there. But, on having examined a variety of causes, one cannot overlook the fact that across the territory of the former Soviet Union this phenomenon has certain common characteristics which are particularly relevant to the investment climate: these are the development of particular economic interests and the role of local bureaucracy in shaping them as important factors behind the escalation of nationalism and separatism.

Often nationalistic sentiment was inspired and manipulated from above by a significant section of the local Party and managerial apparatus striving to gain greater autonomy from the central authorities in Moscow.[9] Klaus von Beyme claims:[10]

> The main problem of ethnic strife is that large parts of the elites in the non-Russian republics *have ceased to look upon the Soviet Union as a vehicle of [sic!] career mobility.* (1991, p. 107)

Boris Kagarlitsky, a prominent activist of the Russian democratic movement, in the book *Farewell Perestroika* made the following eye-witness account of the political events in Estonia in the late 1980s:

> [T]he P[opular] F[ront] became the major factor in the intra-Party struggle for power; it advanced demands which had the total backing of local apparatchiks but which for the time being they had decided not to proclaim in their own name... The support for the PF of many of high-ranking members of the Party's leadership ... was a secret to no one. (Kagarlitsky, 1990, p. 40)

Such a situation was typical of many parts of the USSR. Still now, already in independent republics, many leaders with a *nomenklatura* background continue to play vigorously the nationalistic card in a search for mass support.

Within nationally homogenous territories the aspiration of local leading bodies to reinforce their position by transferring to them rights which previously belonged to Moscow has given an impulse to regionalism. It is particularly pronounced in territories rich in natural resources, such as Western Siberia, or enjoying specific geographical advantages potentially transferable in an economic strength, such as Kalinigradskaia *oblast'* (ex-Eastern Prussia) or the island of Sakhalin in the Sea of Japan.

National-bureaucratic and regional-bureaucratic trends cannot be explained by ambitions of the local elite alone. They have their roots in profound disillusionment in administrative–command economic management which alienated both individuals from the results of their activity and peoples from their habitat. However, this congenital deficiency of the Soviet economic mechanism itself was often interpreted in such a manner as to present its devastating consequences, equally affected all the regions and peoples of the country, as the result of a deliberate 'hegemonic' and 'imperialistic' policy of the centre pointed against national republics and peripheral districts. In the years of perestroika, this brought to life numerous concepts of 'independent development' advocating safeguarding local economies from the all-Union market and reducing economic ties with other republics to a minimum while relying on alleged success in the external (Western) market.

These concepts gained a positive response in the part of the society and made those who did not bother about the national question before more nationalist-minded. Observers have taken notice of the awakening of a particular type of rational, composed nationalism in all the ex-socialist states. Josef Joffe, foreign editor of the *Süddeutsche Zeitung*, wrote in the *International Herald Tribune* (March 22, 1990):[11]

The ... most important lesson of the East German voting [in favor of one Germany] is this: Economics is more important than nationalism or ideology ... [T]he East Germans behaved like any normal 'democratic' electorate: They voted with their pocketbook. ... [N]ot so much 'Deutschland über alles' as 'Deutsche Mark über alles'.

Joffe is echoed by the prominent Estonian economist, Mikhail Bronstein, who wrote in an analysis on economic nationalism in the Soviet Union (*EKO*, 1988, No. 12, p. 92):

It is a reaction to the 'piracy' of all-Union departments, to the persistent shortage of good quality production and to the impossibility of obtaining modern technique and technology.

4.4   CONSEQUENCES FOR THE INVESTMENT CLIMATE

4.4.1   Chances and Threats

Conventional belief is that militant or aggressive nationalism is always a threat to international business. The case of the ex-Soviet Union, however, on the face of it at least, may seem to be different.[12] *Post-Communist economic nationalism*, at the level of decision-making elites at least, does not look similar to the bellicose, xenophobic nationalism characteristic of the nineteenth and early twentieth centuries; nor to that of former colonial countries that, having obtained political independence, sought to achieve economic independence through protection and the pursuit of inward oriented development policies; nor to the 'new' economic nationalism of developed countries which emerged as a reaction to the process of globalisation. The nationalism in question involves a strong dose of economic materialism, combined with noticeable indifference towards ideological nuances, along with a belief that ex-socialist countries should be quickly integrated into the modern industrialised world. Formerly in the Soviet Union and now in the Russian Federation, the indispensable component of all independent national and regional development programmes was and still is a demand for freedom to participate more actively and more directly in the international market.

Inasmuch as national aspiration for economic welfare is linked to an export-led growth doctrine, post-Communist nationalism may provide certain opportunities to foreign investors. Indeed, having gained sovereignty, most ex-Soviet republics undertook prompt measures, mainly legislative, to attract capital from abroad. However, in the long run, this type of nationalism is likely to prove to be as much a destabilising factor as any other type by contributing to what Harald Knudsen called the 'national frustration' level determining the nation's propensity to expropriate.

Bureaucratically-inspired nationalism and regionalism developed first as a weapon in political struggle within the Soviet elite in the years of the eclipse of *perestroika*. As such the two were aimed explicitly against the centre and, implicitly, against other Union republics and the existing economic integration within the Soviet system. Vigorous attacks on co-operational ties and the division of labour within this system, on the one hand, and the propaganda of accelerated internationalisation, on the other hand, were the twin facets of the same political strategy. As a result, the negative consequences of the disintegration of the economic complex of the USSR, especially for large-scale enterprises, were downplayed while the capacity of local economies to enter external markets and to attract international investors was exaggerated. Had the Soviet economy operated successfully, the cost for republics and regions going off on their own would have been so self-evident that this sort of propaganda would not have been readily accepted. However, the growing economic chaos, fuelled not least by separatist pressure, reduced the public estimates of the loss involved in breaking away.

Economic reality quickly correct speculative schemes. The enormous, almost insupportable cost of hasty disintegration has already become evident: according to academician Abel Aganbegyan, 85 per cent of the production decline of the CIS states after 1988 resulted from the severing of economic ties and the contraction of inter-republic trade by the former republics of the USSR.[13] Consequently, this has raised expectations towards internationalisation and foreign investment. These are the expectations of economic growth and increase of living standards, improvement in the quality of life, reducing pollution, etc. They may prove to be ill-founded. Professor Bronstein is quite explicit on this point:

[L]et us come down to earth. The West gives nothing away for free. In order to buy goods and technology from them, we must sell our goods in Western markets. But what is there to sell? ... [W]ith our current production methods and the quality of our output we have, to put it mildly, very modest opportunities for competing in external markets.[14]

Realising this is certain to bring disillusionment both to elites and to the people, and to result in policy changes. In terms of the rational theory of public policy, such changes could provide net value achievement only on condition that all relevant values in the society are known. The politically biased estimation of relevant values causes distortions that make the policy short-lived. Sooner or later governments come to the point at which they have to convince their citizens that national well-being is protected and enhanced by their actions. For post-Communist countries this presents the challenge to move from the stage of monetarist experiments, the so-called 'stabilisation phase' in the vocabulary of the IMF, to the stage of growth in domestic production. Frustrated hopes for international support, even though from the beginning unjustifiably exaggerated for political reasons, will backfire, forcing the government to implement a more restrictive approach to foreign trade and foreign capital.

Frustrated expectations concerning foreign capital inflow can lead to the deterioration of the investment climate as nationalistic agitation makes it difficult to estimate realistically the actual capacity of the national economy to attract investments. The governments of the newly independent republics and local authorities in Russia have only recently taken the burden of responsibility for the fate of their peoples and their territories. Before, the central government in Moscow was a customary target for criticism with regard to its alleged incompetence and negligence when managing local resources and industry. At present the new regimes are willing to get the most of direct relations with foreign investors. If the evidence from the negotiations concerning the first two large-scale foreign investment projects in the territory of the Commonwealth of Independent States – the development of the Tengis oil field in Kazakhstan and shelf oil around the island of Sakhalin – may be viewed as indicative of the prevailing attitude, making deals with the new regimes will not be an easy task for foreign investors. Foreign observers have noted two characteristics in the host-side approach: distrust with respect to commercial partners and a lack of realism in evaluating proper bargaining strength.

4.4.2   The Time-bomb of a Multipower Regime

As was already mentioned, militant nationalism and regionalism were key weapons in the hands of the opposition to Gorbachev and his *perestroika*. They were widely used for tactical ends, in Russia as much as in other Republics, to achieve immediate results in undermining Moscow's central authority and loosening traditional power structures. Later these circumstances have given ambiguity to regionalism in post-Communist Russia. On the one hand, the shift towards recognising the right of localities to take more responsibility on their own was progressive and democratic. In a vast country such as Russia, it is the only way to bring revival to many remote places which had never succeeded in drawing the attention of central departments to their problems or were mismanaged by them. On the other hand, at the state level the initiatives in this sphere were strongly biased by ongoing political considerations. As the political situation has changed following the collapse of the centralist federal state, the new regime in Russia has failed to be consistent in its regional policy and to meet duly the increasing pressure 'from below' inspired largely by its own declarations. The regime lacks a political infrastructure to impose its will in the provinces. In the meantime, the introduction of local democratic elections has radically changed the orientation of local bosses. They have become dependent upon their voters and could not be removed by a directive from Moscow any more. As a result, economically-prompted regionalism does not find any counterbalance on the political side. From the point of view of consequences for the investment climate, however, the described inconsistency may have the effect of a time-bomb.

First of all, it is necessary to mention the dangers following from the precedent of *mnogovlastie* [multipower] which was one of the most notable marks of the crisis of *perestroika*. In the context of the situation, the term described the collision of power triggered by the decision of some Soviet republics to give republican laws priority over union laws contrary to the Soviet Constitution. The Baltic republics, Moldavia and Georgia paved the way. However, it was the willingness of the Russian Parliament to follow suit that had given a critical impulse to the unfolding crisis of the federal system in the USSR. The logic of the current historical moment urged Russian legislators to close their eyes to the fact that their own state was also multinational. By doing so, the Parliament has set an example of a *non*-constitutional action to local authorities in the territory of the Russian Federation (not only in national regions) which they did not fail to follow.

As a result, a situation of many levels of government have emerged. It is far from being unique. Surveys on investment possibilities in quite a few countries (for instance, Brazil, India) report that foreign investors who have to deal with different levels of power (central, state and regional) sometimes find it difficult to understand which one really controls the decision-making. Such a situation is never estimated as favouring the inflow of capital. What makes it especially adverse in the Russian Federation is the fact that the division of power has been still continuing. Moreover, often it takes the form of a disorderly process revealing, in some instances, all the characteristics of an economic war. This is especially true of the situation at the local level as regional bodies take actions bearing patently negative implications for other territories without warning other regions in advance or even without considering their full effect against a broader, rather than strictly local, background.

The desire to fence in the local market has come to dominate regional politics.[15] Some districts have adopted legislation regulating the export of industrial products and food, including shipments to the neighbouring territories of the Russian Federation, and have given it precedence over respective federal laws. As for the nation-state level, the clear signs of confusion and indecision have been noticeable over the principles and instruments of territorial and sectoral management. What makes the situation even more complicated is that lacunae in the governing structure leave place for new powers. One of them is 'producing associations' organised by highly positioned officials and managers and closely resembling the functions of traditional Soviet ministries. On the other hand, there are rumours of 'spontaneous privatisation' meaning that some productive units no longer take orders from anybody.

According to these indications, *mnogovlastie* is very much different from a conventional process of redefining authority between the central state and local governments. In Russia the latter seek to redistribute wealth across the country in a revolutionary manner by unilateral measures whereby rights are not endowed but captured.[16] This raises legitimate questions about the relationship between national and local policies towards foreign capital, as well as about the capacity of the nation-state to be representative in relations with foreign business.[17] Local authorities, especially those in republics, insist on oversight of agreements and contracts at least and more often on the right to choose and to veto.

4.4.3   Conflicts over Natural Resources and Special Economic Zones

Quite a number of important legislative acts regulating the modern Russian economy had their origin in the effects of the political struggle of the last months of the agony of the Soviet state. This only naturally leads to doubts concerning their durability, which no investor can ignore. Now that the political conditions have changed, the major weak point of these regulations becomes ever more evident. They bear the stamp of separatist logic and, at the moment of adoption, were designed to attract local elites on the side of the partisans of sovereign Russia in their struggle against the attempts of President Gorbachev to create a new federal state with a strong centre. As Russia gained independence, these acts and regulations have come to contradict the objective of preserving common market space within the Russian Federation. Clearly, in perspective, such regulations are likely to form a basis for tensions in relations between the central power and local authorities.

This danger deteriorates the political environment for the foreign capital in general and at least in two cases it may have a direct impact on foreign investors.

The question of control over natural resources is one such case. The extractive sector, at least during some initial period, promises to become a major target of international investors and thus has enormous strategic importance.[18] Many deposits are located in the autonomous republics or other territorial formations in Siberia and the north-east of the European part of Russia. The second Congress of People's Deputies of the Russian Federation, in 1990, endorsed a programme providing for the transfer of full powers of control over resources to the localities; but it envisaged also the sale by the Federation of oil, gas and other raw materials to other Union republics and in the world market. The programme implied that Russia would be able to join the ranks of the world's most prosperous nations as soon as it jettisoned the 'burden' of the rest of the USSR. The authors of the programme preferred not to elaborate on the possibility that extracting regions might choose to jettison the 'burden' of the rest of the Russian Federation at a certain point.

Although, in May 1992, a new Federal Treaty was initialled by 14 of the 16 autonomous republics, the document raised strong objections in all such republics rich in natural resources which did not want to share control over their mineral wealth with Moscow. Thus, the Republic of Bashkortostan, a major supplier of oil, in a special supplement to the treaty proclaimed land, minerals, natural and other resources in its territory the property of its population. Issues related to the utilisation of this property will be regulated by Bashkir laws and agreements with federal government. The republic has also proclaimed itself an 'independent participant in international and foreign economic relations, except areas it has voluntarily delegated to Russian Federation'. The former autonomous republic will independently establish principles of taxation and payment of duties to the federal budget. Such unilateral actions and the reaction they provoked on the part of the central authorities have pushed forward the spiral of confrontation. This only delays the moment when the inevitable division of power and control can be settled to the satisfaction of all parties involved increasing uncertainty costs for investors.

The second case deals with the creation of free economic, or enterprise, zones.[19] In September 1990, the Russian Parliament passed a bill giving freedom to local authorities to establish such zones within their territories. The decision was taken without a serious preliminary examination of the complex nature of this form of international investment promotion. The concept of the zone economy as well as the role of the zones in reforming the national economy were not altogether clear. However, this did not hamper the parliamentary decision because it perfectly fitted the logic of the unfolding 'war of sovereignties'. For the Russian leadership the free zone ideology was instrumental in taking whole vast regions out of the direct control of federal economic bodies. Vice-governor of Chita *oblast'* recalls in his interview to *Rossiiskaia gazeta* (July 18, 1992) the time when 'for purely political reasons the then Chairman of the Supreme Soviet of the Russian Federation, at present its President, was signing heaps of orders affording the status of the free economic zone to various territories'.

Local authorities were enthusiastic about the new regulation as it provided them with legitimate grounds to evade certain fiscal obligations before the federal budget while putting forward claims for additional financing for infrastructure and construction projects. Moreover, since the allocation of investment resources remained one of the main levers of control in the hands of the central power, attracting foreign investment seemed to provide an opportunity to diminish this control. As regards the political motivation, it is tightly related to the general aspiration of local authorities to more independence from the centre. Finally, it is important to keep in mind that in a country with a monetary system in disarray and a chronic scarcity of all types of products, foreign currency and imported goods have always a special appeal to the public. Dozens of plans for organising free zones were announced within a very short time but few were carried beyond a very preliminary stage as the breakdown of the Union economy progressed.

In sovereign Russia the interest in developing free economic zones has revived. However, in the absence of what could have been a state pro- gramme, the wild-card principle of allocating zone privileges is likely to end in conflict. The problem is that, at least during an organisational period, the free zones demand a lot of initial investment which stipulates the redistribution of budget funds in their favour. Free economic zones belong to those regulation instruments that bring costs to all regions of a country while often benefiting only a few. Under present conditions this may have two outcomes. Either regions which do not plan zone expansion protest if their neigbours intend to establish theirs, or all regions will seek to get a zone status to parts or the whole of their territory however inappro- priate are local conditions. Eventually, the realisation of the idea of free economic zones will be blocked in both events.

4.4.4   The Consequences of the Living Standard Collapse

Yet another danger facing foreign investors relates to the formation of cer- tain features of the social environment in the country. Any nationalistic doctrine, including those according with bureaucratic rationality, carries a potential for xenophobic intolerance. This potential could develop into reality fuelled by discontent, demands, and mobilisation originated outside the realm of ethnic/nationalistic sentiment. As has been shown earlier, eco- nomically-motivated resentment directly provoked the surge of nationalism in the USSR in the late 1980s. This nationalism/regionalism gained support from the population not because the majority were living under miserable conditions, but because the people were told that their republic (region, dis- trict, etc.) had been robbed by other republics and the centre and that they would have been much better-off if they had stopped subsidising others and seceded from the federation. That was the controlled and quite selective nationalism of reasonably prosperous people anxious for more prosperity.

The economic catastrophe that followed the breakdown of the all-Union market has brought about the downfall of 'accustomed' absolute standards of living affecting millions of people in all the parts of the former Soviet Union (for data see section 5.2.1) and has led to related relative shifts in economic welfare among population groups within newly organised state entities. This changes the premises for economic nationalism: now it will focus on the defence of the livelihood of millions of common people and become much less controlled and selective. It will be directed against everything which is seen by them as ravaging their livelihood. As the traditional image of the 'enemy' – the central power in Moscow – cannot be used any more to channel public discontent, it will turn elsewhere. Since modernisation and competition tend to destroy the 'inefficient' life support system of the increasingly marginalised part of society, this latter starts to fight for protecting and conserving its basis of survival against the invasion of market forces referring not only to economic, but also to social, cultural, ethnical, religious and other means.

Ethnic and nationalistic demands together with regionalism represent specific political risk to foreign investors. But, in terms of strategic investment planning, it is important to recognise its genesis in the CIS as re-formulated economic resentment. This claim is especially relevant with respect to the Russian Federation. The nationalities sharing the Federation have had a common history for centuries. They existed in the framework of a single Russian state long before the establishment of the empire. Although, at a local level, there are social forces that see their task as being 'to rupture the course of history' and assert their national identity, which has disappeared under the pressure of Russification, but even more so under the pressure of modernisation, the stability of historical ties between the peoples of Russia over centuries indicates that cultural and religious differences alone cannot account for the recent ethnic tensions. In this context, risk evaluation of nationalism and regionalism in Russia has to be implemented through the prism of the development of economic reforms and related expectations.

Indeed, in the foreseeable future any serious political counteraction seems improbable. In a country in which over one hundred registered parties keep splintering, in which parties boasting four thousand card-holders are considered large while, according to public polls, only ten per cent of the electorate have a clear party loyalty, nationalistic and regionalistic slogans remain the most secure keys to mass support. The government in Moscow has tried to tackle this problem by installing a new centrally controlled apparatus in the place of the old. Under political pluralism, however, this tactic has no future. The only constructive response is to create an environment in which separatism will be explicitly counterproductive as it is known that a key to the political survival of new regimes is the ability to channel the energy of the masses away from politics into economic activity. A combined package aiming at strengthening the state and economic reform is needed. It is not clear that the correct approach has been found. The 1992 reforms have only increased the enormous disparities in initial economic conditions within the Russian Federation as well as in the CIS leading to the growth of inter-ethnic and regional tension.

4.5   POLICY RISK

4.5.1   The Concept of Policy Risk

Political risk apart, foreign investment is very likely to be exposed to what has come to be known as policy risk following the adoption by host-countries of formal industrial policies and the conscious and deliberate setting up of entry-control and management systems to deal with foreign investment and business (Ting, 1988). In recent years this type of risk, though less dramatic than political risk, has been regarded more and more by analysts as central to the strategy of transnational corporations, owing to its particular relevance to the challenges of the current stage of relations between exporters and importers of capital. This development has two distinguishing features. One is the growing acknowledgement by host-countries of the positive contribution of foreign investments to the development of the national economy.[20] Rapid industrialisation, dispersion of technology and managerial skills, and the inclusion of local producers in international selling networks are the consequences in terms of national development most often ascribed by the literature on export-led growth to foreign direct investments of transnational corporations. The other feature is the desire of host-governments to derive the maximum benefit from the presence of foreign capital in the country. Accordingly, foreign ventures have become subject to sometimes more and sometimes less sophisticated regulations aimed at shaping their performance in accordance with a certain design.

In order to increase technological and other benefits from foreign inves-tors, these regulations normally include various incentives but may also incorporate some disincentives in the form of tax provisions, production and marketing limitations on foreign investment projects, local content requests, indigenisation programmes, countertrade requirements, exchange control, foreign trade licensing and intellectual property rights restrictions, etc. These measures restrain the freedom of operation of transnational cor-porations but on their own they are not policy risks as is sometimes argued (see, for example, Ting, 1988, p. 45). It is the *dynamics* of these regulations and the *uncertainty* accompanying them which represent policy risk.

In contemplating a foreign venture, the investor would never fail to con-sider the benefits and risks of the project. Such an analysis, however, is necessarily tentative because it is normally based on the extrapolation of risks which are necessarily country-specific. In the case of policy risks this approach appears to be particularly precarious. Policy risks are established within the host-country's legal framework, which remains the sovereign domain of national legislators. Policy risks are tied to a subtle and latent process of day-to-day policy-making and, unlike political risks, need not be preceded or accompanied by explicit social confrontations. It is particularly difficult for foreign firms to foresee and 'manage' some seemingly minor corrections in regulations (such as a slight percentage point change in national component content) which, nevertheless, can have a very strong impact on the investor.

It is more feasible and practical to estimate the prevailing trend underlying the fluctuations in a host-country's capital entry management policy in order to determine whether or not it is moving towards liberalisation. Such an analysis should account for three sets of facts: (i) the economic philosophy of the nation-state as it is revealed in official programmes and declarations, and real action; (ii) the actual set of regulations concerning foreign investment and their efficiency in the context of stated goals; (iii) factors which may necessitate unexpected adjustments in the current official economic course.

Clearly, policy risk and political risk, i.e., discontinuities stemming from political change, are interrelated. The dynamics of the national capital entry management system (CEMS) is never determined solely by economic considerations. The government is a political and public body and its decisions necessarily depend on the configuration of the country's social landscape. Therefore, the most drastic changes constituting policy risks tend to have the same roots as political risks, with profound social instability in the first place. The replacement of a government of one political orientation with a government of a different political orientation is one of the most probable causes of policy risk. At the same time, political decisions are often made from economic necessity. As the dividing line is difficult to define, the relative artificiality of distinguishing between political risk analysis and policy risk analysis should always be kept in mind. This implies that, first, the two inevitably overlap; second, that policy risk conceptualisation is valid only with due reservations.

4.5.2   The Genesis of Russia's CEMS

The principle feature of Russia's capital entry management system is volatility. This is hardly surprising as the whole country is in a state of flux. The formation of the system began only recently, at the earliest in the second half of the 1980s, and since then has been implemented in very complicated conditions. The period in question should be split into three stages. The first corresponds to the creation of the foundations of the system. The second was characterised by the state of confrontation and strife between the central government and the republics, which resulted in the introduction of some radical amendments giving the system a more liberal and up-to-date stance. In the third and current period, against the background of a serious economic crisis, the CEMS has become increasingly controversial as short-term priorities tend to prevail over longer-term interests.

The First Stage (1987–1990): The making of the system. The foundation of the CEMS in the Commonwealth of Independent States was laid by an edict on joint ventures adopted by the Presidium of the Supreme Soviet of the USSR in January 1987. As the first law on foreign private property since the 1920s, it had principal importance as one of the milestones of *perestroika* in economic and political thinking. It was the factual recognition of realities which the Soviet leadership had preferred to ignore over decades, namely, that the socialist path of development leading to autarky had failed, that Soviet industry needed western assistance and that the efficiency of privately owned enterprises was not inferior to that of publicly owned as was postulated by the official teaching. However, the positive content of the 1987 joint venture law was less significant than its historical importance. It was revised in May 1989 and again in March 1990, but the amendments did not eliminate its inherent weaknesses.

The main problem with the joint venture law lay in its attempt to include foreign capital in a state property-based economic system, with only the smallest possible concessions to market principles. As a compromise between conservative (protective) and pragmatic approaches, it provided, despite all amendments, numerous loopholes for state intervention in the management and operation of foreign business (see Kozlov and Kuznetsov, 1989). Consequently, policy risk was very high. For a substantial period of time there was no foreign investment law as such, and also no property law, leasing law, land law, joint-stock company law, etc. Under these conditions joint venture and other foreign investment contracts provided, presumably on an *ad hoc* basis, only very limited protection. It would be incorrect to claim that the inconsistency of the joint venture regulations was not evident to legislators. Soviet law, inappropriate for a commercial system, was being rewritten to promote and protect market exchange among individuals and corporations. Simultaneously, bilateral investment agreements were concluded with a number of major industrialised countries in order to facilitate the activities of foreign investors in the Soviet Union. Characteristically, these agreements were ahead of national legislation as regards the degree of freedom and protection they guaranteed to investors. Bilateral investment agreements, prepared from 1988 to 1990, stipulated that host-governments would (i) afford foreign investors national (i.e., non-discriminatory) treatment; (ii) not engage in acts of expropriation without fair market compensation;[21] (iii) guarantee repatriation of profits; and (iv) submit any disputes to third country arbitration.

These efforts, however, were not free from the ambiguity so typical of *perestroika* in general. By introducing the concept of private property, entrepreneurship, private leasing, etc., the newly established legislation constituted a revolutionary step forward in the context of Soviet economic and social history. At the same time, the practical utility of these norms, especially from the point of view of protection of the investor, was marginal. Thus, the 1990 Law on Property did not acknowledge private property in the sense adopted in market economies. Rather, all property (other than some household and related items) was conceptually joined to the state or the people, and the rights of labour. Thus Article 1(6) of the Law on Property stated that the use of property must exclude the alienation of the worker from the 'means of production' and the exploitation of man by man. Article 1(2) provided that an owner may 'possess, use and dispose' of property; however, this phrase appeared in all socialist property laws, and in itself does not clarify the degree of investment protection. On the other hand, many progressive norms, such as the inviolability of private property, were formulated in a very general way, thus leaving space for bureaucratic bodies to impose arbitrary interpretations. As for the international treaties, their ratification was delayed.

The Second Stage (1990–1991): Radicalisation. The beginning of the 1990s saw a new situation concerning the development of the national capital entry management system. The central authorities were experiencing growing pressure to move towards greater policy liberalisation. On the economic side official policy-making was mostly affected by a rapidly progressing disruption of the national economy and, externally, by the exacerbation of the foreign debt problem. The Soviet Union had lost its once high standing as an international borrower. Interest rates on the Soviet debt were rapidly increasing forcing a search for alternative sources of foreign finance. Private portfolio and direct investment, and official aid could have become such sources. In order to tap them the harmonisation of the Soviet foreign investment control and management practice with internationally acknowledged standards was essential. This was both a requirement of private investors and a necessary prerequisite for obtaining access to an international aid-package.

In the sphere of politics some important new realities were also to be taken into consideration. The factual dissolution of the union state was gaining momentum. The Moscow government had to face the 'war of laws'. In many national republics legislators were far more radical than their colleagues in the Union Supreme Soviet. Central authorities soon found themselves no longer powerful enough to block or override local legislative initiatives. What emerged was a peculiar type of competition between parliaments which was, on the whole, conducive to better quality legislation. In addition, as the republics expressly ignored the task of maintaining co-ordination between the different levels of legislation, the desire to preserve a centralised state increasingly forced the centre to show flexibility in compiling Union laws.

The results of the aforementioned factors showed in the course of the elaboration of a Union law on foreign investment. The projects of the Union law and its Russian Federation counterpart were brought out practically simultaneously, in the autumn of 1990. The Russian law proved to contain more incentives and guarantees to foreign capital. In particular, it made provision for the foreign investor to obtain full market value compensation in foreign currency if his property had been nationalised. The compensation was to be paid at the expense of the republican department which had taken the decision to liquidate the foreign venture. This clause was intended as a precaution against bureaucratic arbitrariness. The debates that followed revealed more support for the approach expressed in the Russian draft. Shortly after, similar articles found their way into the text of the next Union law dealing with foreign property, the Fundamental Principles of Investment Activities in the USSR (effective from December 10, 1990).

On the whole, both the Soviet and Russian investment legislation of that period followed the principle that internationally accepted norms must be implemented also within the country. The most important innovations were the following. (i) The circle of investors was enlarged. In addition to foreign juridical bodies also foreign individuals, states and international agencies were allowed to invest in the Soviet Union. Furthermore, they were allowed to create 100 per cent foreign-owned companies. (ii) Foreign capital was granted the national (non-discriminatory) regime of investment. (iii) The law provided guarantees against expropriation and other actions leading to an equal result.

Predictably, the new norms were greeted enthusiastically abroad, but this did not result in any substantial increase in foreign investment coming into the country as the gap widened between the letter of the law and its real content as stipulated by the actual situation in the country. Thus, the law established a national regime of investment for foreign capital, which anywhere else in the world would be a substantial advantage. However, in the Soviet Union it meant little because the regime itself had yet to be created.

National enterprises worked under such uncertain, volatile and generally unfavourable conditions that this norm, as things stood, could not have acted as an incentive. In addition there was a lack of clarity concerning many other rights of foreign investors. Completely worthless beyond the country's borders, the rouble remained the greatest stumbling block. On the other hand, the controversial juridical status of land and natural resources was a further discouragement.

During this second stage the Soviet capital entry management system demonstrated the contradictory nature of the final period of *perestroika* as the leadership hesitated to make the ultimate choice between market and administrative models of economic management. This may also be traced in the legislation on foreign investment. The Fundamental Principles of Investment Activities in the USSR, for example, together with many progressive articles, contained a clause that permitted state bodies and officials to interfere in the management and operations of foreign-owned businesses 'within the limits of their competence' (see Art. 20:2). This was explicitly contrary to prevailing international practice which demanded, as was fixed in some republican laws, that all relations between foreign firms and state institutions should be regulated only by contract. Taking into consideration how strong the position of state bureaucracy still was in the economy and society in general, such loopholes in legislation left foreign entrepreneurs ultimately unprotected against administrative dictates. Furthermore, the regulations had not been worked out in detail. Many fundamental laws still remained on the books. Yet as fast as new laws had been adopted, events had consistently overtaken them. Outstanding problems had accumulated a critical mass making an explosion inevitable.

The Third Stage (1991–1992): One step forward, two steps back. Despite all the drawbacks in the formation of the CEMS, the impulse given by *perestroika* to the process of internationalisation of the Soviet economy was so powerful that the flow of foreign investment into the country increased throughout the whole period from 1987 till 1992. The dynamics of the registration of new joint ventures was as follows: 1987–23; 1988–1076; 1990–1584 (Evstratov *et al.*, 1991, p. 158). In 1991, the number of joint venture registered with the Finance Ministry of the Russian Federation was increasing steadily to reach one hundred registrations on a monthly basis. Although in reality only 42 per cent of registered businesses later really started operations, by the end of 1991 foreign investors had put about one billion dollars into the Russian economy.[22] Disappointingly, the following year, 1992, did not confirm the tendencies of the previous period. New registrations evened out, and within the first three months of 1992 twenty foreign firms announced plans to discontinue their business in

Russia. Up to this point no major company had withdrawn its activities. These developments provoked a very worried reaction on the part of officials and experts who feared them to be an early sign of forthcoming mass disinvestment from Russia. The restraint demonstrated by international investors was a response to the Soviet Union's crackdown and a further deterioration of the economic and political situation. The same factors had an impact on the CEMS.

On the one hand, after the collapse of the Soviet Union the situation ceased to exist, with the exception of the Russian Federation, in which investors had to cope with conflicting instructions from union, republican and even local regional authorities, all eager to establish control over enterprises in their territory. On the other hand, a variety of national regulating regimes had at this time already emerged within the Community of Independent States. At present, they are very close to one another though, of course, not totally identical.[23] One may expect that, if collaboration within the frame of the Commonwealth does not expand, republican capital entry management regulations are likely to become ground for competition between former Soviet republics for foreign capital, thus weakening their bargaining power.

In Russia, probably the most decisive feature of the third stage has been the degree of disorganisation of the capital entry management system, exceptionally high even by the standards of the country. The critical state of the budget and the balance of current payments led the authorities to embark on emergency measures which eliminated or depreciated many foreign investor incentives, privileges and guarantees. The foreign investment law as adopted by the Supreme Soviet in July 1991 turned out to be much less liberal than the draft published half a year before. Characteristically, in numerous cases the law was overridden by the instructions of executive bodies, which was expressly illegal. At first, foreign partners in Russian joint ventures (JV) found their current accounts with Vneshekonombank blocked. Then fiscal authorities began to 'interpret'(!) two year income tax holidays for the JV envisaged by the law as one year and to levy tax, with the exception of few priority industries, on reinvested income.[24] Soviet JV partners were called on to increase budget payments. The Central Bank of the Russian Federation obliged JVs with a foreign capital share of over 30 per cent to sell 50 per cent of foreign currency revenues to a rouble stabilisation fund and a foreign debt servicing fund contrary to the law's postulation that 'currency revenues of these enterprises resulting from the exportation of proper production are left completely at their disposal' (Law on foreign investment in the Russian Federation, Art. 25). Foreign exchange and trade regulations were tightened, preventing joint ventures from achieving the currency self-sufficiency required to transfer dividend payments abroad.

These events have demonstrated that despite all the publicity given to official plans to promote foreign capital inflow, this objective has actually remained low on the government's agenda. The government has concentrated on a current stabilisation programme, whereas long-term investment policy, the correction of structural dislocations and, closely related to them, foreign capital entry regulations have been left without due attention, if not sacrificed, for the sake of a balanced budget and other monetarist priorities. Second, these events have distinctly proved that, while there is foreign investment legislation in Russia, along with a state Committee on Foreign Investment, there is nothing like a state capital entry management system as yet in the form of a combination of interrelated policies. This is evident from the chaotic state of the regulations themselves, but if additional evidence were necessary it would be sufficient to compare three important laws, on foreign investment, on land, and on taxation, adopted by the Parliament one shortly after another. As regards foreign businesses, they appear to stem from three different conceptual approaches, the latter two laws substantially narrowing the effects of the former.

4.5.3 Policy Risk in Russia

The previous brief review of Russia's foreign investment regulations demonstrates that they have been extremely volatile, controversial, short-lived and incomplete, thus representing almost the whole spectrum of qualities characterising high policy risk. This finding is hardly surprising. Policy risk cannot be low when the economic and political situation in a country is generally so clearly unstable. As Russia, first as a Soviet republic and later as an independent state, was struggling through the most critical period in its post-war history, the succession of governments of different leanings could do little, at least in the short run, to influence the course of events once the relative equilibrium of a planned system had been destroyed in the absence of a clear design of a mechanism to replace it. Policy-makers were constantly overtaken by events, political or economic, or both. Therefore the decisions adopted always bore the stamp of emergency measures even when they were supposedly meant to provide a frame for long-term policies.

None the less, it would not be correct to conclude that the experience of recent years has been predominantly negative. In comparison to the situation before *perestroika* some really revolutionary steps have been taken leading to the construction of what may be considered as a good foundation for a CEMS in the future. One result appears to be particularly important from the point of view of the foreign investor: the acknowledgement of the principle that foreign investors deserve encouragement and remuneration for the risks they run in supplying their capital to a foreign country has penetrated the juridical system of the country and to an extent, through publicity given to discussions on foreign investment, the social mentality. Equally important has been the legal fixation of basic guarantees protecting foreign property and the right to expatriate profits. The apparent progress in the updating of other juridical norms dealing with different aspects of business and property relations in the country will undoubtedly also have a favourable effect on capital inflow. All this must eventually eliminate many of the contradictions which still erode the organisational structure of the Russian economy. Overall, it is important to see that despite all fluctuations, the principal line of development of foreign investment policy has been oriented towards a more liberal and open approach.

The positive changes have most of all affected what can conditionally be called the higher levels of policy. Lower levels, i.e., the way the government ideology is applied, have remained less affected. In the actions of the present government of Russia ostentatious liberalism has coexisted in a picturesque manner with unceremonious administration, leaving foreign experts wondering which of the two represented the authentic concept of government policy concept. In practical terms this inconsistency in regulation passes much of the actual decision-making power on to ministries and their substitutes, and other lower levels of economic authority. They played an important role in the previous system, but lately have been losing importance, and their prospects and future role are unclear. As a result they still retain some levers of control, although their formal responsibility for the performance of the economy has almost vanished. This transitional situation has created a climate of low executive morality and illegal actions. Corruption and the shadow economy have developed to such an extent that they have ceased to be simply events in a criminal chronicle. They have instead become so much a fact of investment climate and policy risk that only a rare domestic or international press publication on foreign investment in the CIS does not comment on this subject. Foreign investors complain that their projects falter because of excessive red-tape and unmotivated last-moment changes in contract conditions with Russian officials seeming to be more interested in new trips abroad than in the result of the talks.

Above it was argued that government ideology is an important part of investment policy. Evidently, it is no less important that central authorities have been able to impose their ideology throughout the whole bureaucratic hierarchy, especially in a country with a weak democratic tradition.

Liberal economic policy can bring results when it relies on an extensive market mechanism and the authority of law. Both are missing in modern Russia. It would not be right to claim that the Yeltsin/Gaidar government did not realise this. On the contrary, the importance of functioning market relations as a foundation for efficient state and civil society was repeatedly stressed by government spokesmen as a motivation for drastic reforms. Still, a conflict between liberalism and administrating represented one of the main problems of the regime. It was not only the question of imposing the freedom of enterprise by way of command. It is also characteristic that the accentuated liberalism of many important government decisions appeared good on paper, but in reality only gave more space for administrative arbitrariness.

The government privatisation programme is a typical example. With this reform the government tied its aspirations to massive capital inflow from abroad. A principal point here is the investment exchange rate of the rouble. The authorities, not in the least instance prompted by obligations imposed by the International Monetary Fund, decided against a special investment rate. It was a fair choice from the point of view of liberal economic theory. Given practical conditions prevailing in Russia, this has only brought about new actual and potential contradictions. Indeed, under the state voucher plan the value of fixed capital stock to be distributed among the population was determined at 1.400 billion rubles, at ten thousand rubles per voucher. In dollars, at the average exchange rate for December 1992 of one dollar for 560 rubles, this would be less than 20 dollars. However, according to official statements the implementation of a single exchange rate would not mean that foreign investors would be able to buy state property at bargain prices as the latter's acquisitions would be subject to special taxes, payments and licensing to be fixed in some cases on an individual basis (*Isvestia*, July 25, 1992). It is clear to see that in terms of policy risk the second decision cancels many of the advantages of the first as (i) a final judgement on the conditions of property sale is postponed; (ii) the method adopted assumes many further specifications still to come thus increasing the uncertainty and cost associated by a foreign investor with a venture in Russia; and last but not least, (iii) much decision-making is left to the discretion of lower-level administration. In other words, the main defect of government economic policy is that the government consciously takes decisions which it cannot then implement. Inevitably, it almost immediately finds itself compelled to make exclusions for different categories of businesses, regions, branches, etc., which eventually not only neutralise the regulation but also provide a basis for corruption and executive chaos.

The duality described follows directly from the gap between official policy, which is often designed as if a market mechanism already functioned in the Russian economy, and the actual state of affairs characterised by the agony of the administrative–command economy. Moreover, the problem is that this agony has not been the result of the assault of market forces but rather a product of the self-destruction of the system as the elimination of centralised management has led to a chaotic monopolistic–bureaucratic structure instead of the market. Until this situation is overcome, foreign investment policy risk will remain high. In order for it to decline it is necessary to introduce changes to the policy, i.e., to remove it from the one-sided pressure of neo-liberal ideology and to reorient it towards structural problems such as the creation of competitive and balanced markets. The realisation of this goal would give the economy the type of stability necessary to avoid the U-turns in current regulations so harmful to fruitful foreign investment strategy.

Notes

1. Of course, one may interpret the relationship 'investment conditions–investment decision' in a different way. This would be that the investment climate of a country is an independent variable equally affecting all would-be investors while what differs is an investor's capacity to adjust to this variable. This approach is certainly no less valid than that proposed in this thesis. However, it hardly offers tangible advantages since it does not make the task any simpler: each investor may enjoy a unique combination of factors determining his adjustment capacity. At the same time, such a shift in emphasis would deprive any definition of the investment climate of an important component: the stress on the participation of investors in forming a perception of the climate.

2. Literature on political risk of foreign investment is enormous. (For a thorough review of the discussion of the 70s see J. D. Simon, 'Political risk assessment: Past trends and future prospects', *Columbia Journal of World Business*, Fall 1982, pp. 62–71, and, for later discussion, W. Ting (1988), Chapter 1). This section mainly refers to the following publications: R. Vernon, *Sovereignty at Bay*, 1971, London, Longman; L. H. Thunell, *Political Risks*, 1977, New York, Praeger; S. J. Kobrin, 'When Does Political Instability Result in Increased Investment Risk?', *The Columbia Journal of World Business*, Fall 1978, pp. 113–22; S. J. Kobrin, 'Foreign enterprise and forced divestment in LDCs', *International Organization*, Winter 1980; J. Eaton and M. Gersovitz, 'Country risk: economic aspect' in R. J. Herring (ed.), *Managing International Risk*, 1983, Cambridge, Cambridge University Press; J. D. Simon, 'A theoretical perspective on political risk' *Journal of International Business Studies, Winter 1984, pp. 123–43; H. Siegwart et al., Global Political Risk: Dynamic Managerial Strategies*, 1989, Basel, Helbing & Lichtenhahn; H. Picht, V. Stüven, 'Expropriation of foreign direct

investments: Empirical evidence and implications for the debt crisis' *Public Choice*, 1991, Vol. 69, pp. 21–38; H. Cole, W. English, 'Expropriation and direct investment', *Journal of International Economics*, 1991, Vol. 30, pp. 201–12.

3. According to Dexter Baker, chairman of the U.S. National Association of Manufacturers, 'The risks in Russia are greater than in any other part of the world' (*The New York Times*, May 4, 1992).

4. *Harvard Business Review*, January–February 1991, p. 84.

5. Clearly, there is no unanimity as regards expert investment strategy recommendations. Harvard Professor Larry Sammers praises the value of the 'waiting option' for investors. Referring to the ex-Soviet Union, he points out that 'being the second one in is almost as good as being the first one in, and is a lot safer' (*The International Economy*, June/July 1990, p. 83).

6. Moshe Lewin, one the leading scholars of Soviet history in the United States, pointed also to the 'knee-jerk response' factor behind what he called the flood of simple-minded programmes in Russia: 'Since the previous system was bad, we must now do the opposite' (*Dissent*, Spring 1992, pp. 172–5).

7. According to official statistics, in the first calendar quarter of 1992 compared to the same period of 1991 the output in Russia decreased by the following amounts (per cent): GDP 15; oil 15; rolled metal 15; industrial wood and paper 27; machines and equipment 29; consumer durables 9–29; meat, cheese, margarine and cereal 23–35; whole milk 45; sausage 50. The reduction in production of separate items was even more dramatic. Thus, the production of long-haul locomotives decreased by 82.4 per cent (*Rossiiskaia gazeta*, April 6, 1992, p. 2; *Delovoi mir*, April 9, 1992, p. 7).

8. The following is the 'classical' example of '*nomenklatura* privatisation'. A state research institute, the Central Research Institute of Complex Automation of Light Industry, spun off a private company, installed the secretary of its former Communist Party organization as president (the director of the institute was a share-holder) and then sold the firm 100 IBM-clone computers at ridiculously low state-subsidized prices. The company, PICO Inc., then began selling off the computers at market prices, up to one hundred times the purchase price (*The International Herald Tribune*, May, 18, 1992).

9. Recent data on leadership in economic enterprises and economic institutions show that by 1989 the nationalities were fairly well represented in the leadership in their Republics (with the exception of Russia, Uzbekistan and Moldova). Contrary to common belief, the representation of natives in the leadership in the majority of republics exceeded their share in the population (*Sotsiologicheskie issledovaniia*, 1990, No. 7, p. 40).

10. A similar argument was put forward by Seweryn Bialer of Columbia University in *Foreign Affairs*, Winter/Spring 1992, p. 170.

11. See also on this topic Jürgen Habermans, 'Der DM-Nationalismus' in *Die Zeit*, March 30, 1990.

12. For example, President of a New York research firm, John W. Kiser III, claims: 'I think the nationality problems present investors with more an opportunity, not a threat ... those in the nationalities are very aggressive and anxious to do business with the West' (*The International Economy*, June/July 1990, p. 81).

13. *EKO*, 1992, No. 3, p. 68.
14. *EKO*, 1988, No. 12, p. 92.
15. How far the process of autonomization of regional markets has gone is clear from the degree of regionalization of prices. Thus, in March 1992, the same model of a household refrigerator in Izhevsk cost only 30 per cent of the Moscow price, in Briansk 45 per cent, and in Kemerovo 165 per cent (*Ekonomika i zhizn'*, No. 21, May 1992, p. 7).
16. Political blackmail has become a favourite means of protecting national and regional interests. Regions widely and often successfully use the threat of secession whenever there is a conflict with the central power. How precarious the situation is shown by the collision between the government in Moscow and the authorities of a tiny district of Severo-Eniseisk in the backwoods of Russia. The latter did not hesitate to proclaim the independent Severo-Eniseisk Republic to gain control of a potentially profitable gold mine on the territory of the region ignoring the Constitution and the Federal law on mineral resources. The *status quo* was re-established only after the personal interference of Vice Prime-Minister Yegor Gaidar who 'returned' the district to Russian jurisdiction after having paid off local authorities with a promise of 100 million rubles of subsidized state credit on the development of the mine (*Izvestia*, June 29, 1992).
17. The saga of a project for developing a 750-million-barrel oil field in Russian Far East is quite instructive. The exploration of the field near Sakhalin Island in the Pacific Ocean started in 1974 with the participation of a Japanese firm. In 1990, island authorities decided to boost up oil production as a part of a plan to secure Sakhalin's financial independence with the aim of transforming the island into a special economic zone. Moscow authorities claimed the oil. In order to get more freedom to pursue his plans, the governor of Sakhalin insisted on organizing an international competition for the development contract under conditions worked out by local experts. The Russian Republic's oil ministry in Moscow selected a consortium with major American interest, while the governor of Sakhalin Island, ten thousand kilometres from Moscow, gave the contract to a rival bidder, a consortium with significant Japanese participation. Moscow overruled him but that did not put an end to the struggle between local and central authorities. The conflict has been deepening, making the future for the project uncertain.
18. The CIS, particularly Russia which produces between 80 and 90 per cent of the region's oil, according to estimates, may have up to a quarter of the world's undiscovered oil and more gas than any other country. The CIS has 141 giant oil fields each holding more than 500 million barrels of oil. The Western Siberia basin alone contains 16 per cent of the world's discovered reserves, but less than a fifth of these are being exploited.
19. In more detail the economics of free enterprise zones is analyzed in Chapter 6.
20. It is useful in this respect to compare the results of two comprehensive surveys of national control of foreign business entry. One was carried out by Richard Robinson (1976) and included fifteen countries in South-East Asia, South America, Europe and Japan. His main finding was that, at the beginning of the 1970s, host-countries were typically striving for the control over foreign investment to pass to local capital. Conversely, a 1989 OECD

report on international direct investment revealed that reluctance to accept multinational enterprises as partners in the development process was by then largely a thing of the past.

21. The adoption of the notion of 'fair market compensation' implied the extension of investment protection beyond 'property' in the sense of tangible movables or immovables. For the first time in Soviet juridical practice, 'property' came to include the market value of the ongoing business once established, or alternatively, the capitalized value of its prospective income flows.

22. *Ekonomika i zhizn'*, No. 5, February 1992.

23. Differences mainly concern the list of industries where foreigners may invest only under license or special permission, as well as the list of industries in which foreign participation is particularly encouraged; regulations of foreign ventures in banking and insurance; the right of foreigners to lease/own and dispose of land; the freedom to participate in the management of joint-stock companies; the international trade regime of foreign and joint ventures.

24. *Ekonomika i zhizn'*, No. 5, February 1992, p. 13.

5 Setting Priorities for Capital Entry Regulations

5.1 THE FOREIGN CAPITAL SECTOR IN A NATIONAL ECONOMY

5.1.1 'Enclave' Investment versus 'Integral' Investment

In Russia the recent few years have been marked by an impressive progress in the spreading of a market philosophy. Influenced by the traumatic experience of their country, many Russian statesmen and scholars tend to oversimplify the relationship between state and market and put too much faith in the self-regulatory mechanism of the latter. In the realm of foreign economic relations the belief in the unrestrained superiority of the market may lead to a certain aberration in economic policy as it leads to the conclusion that foreign firms, as representing market forces, should be treated more favourably than national enterprises which clearly carry the legacy of an administrative–command system. This claim has rarely been explicitly articulated even by the most radically-minded reformers. None the less, a steady current of publications and statements promoting externally financed development and the civilising mission of foreign capital has been strong enough to provoke fears of the imminent 'sale' of Russia within a certain part of the population.

The comprehension of the commercial, profit-oriented nature of the modern export of capital is indispensable as a foundation for a functional capital entry management system. It would be wrong to deduce, however, that prompting of market relations and economic openness are enough to secure the inclusion of foreign capital in a national productive system. The national competitiveness approach outlined in the first part of this research leads us to make a distinction between the two possible variants of relationship between the foreign owned/controlled sector and the national economy: *enclave* and *integral*.

In extreme cases the difference between the two is clear-cut. Free export producing zones and their variations provide an example *par excellence* of the enclave-type variant inasmuch as they quite often have physical borders separating them from the rest of the country. In other circumstances the difference may be not so explicit. The relationship between the foreign venture and the national economy does not depend directly on the share and the forms of participation of foreign capital in the venture or on its juridical status. The distinction between enclave and integral investment is basically qualitative and is related to the strategy pursued by the investor with respect to the local affiliate.

Enclave-type investments are usually sensitive to a particular combination of conditions to be found in the host-country, namely, (relatively) cheap labour force and land, abundant mineral resources, advantageous geographical position or particularly favourable fiscal legislation. For such an investment the general state of the local economy is less important than changes in these conditions, whether they result from the dynamics of the internal economic situation or from shifts outside the host-country which none the less modify its relative attractiveness as an off-shore production platform.

It would be incorrect to claim that, opposite to integral investment, enclave-type foreign ventures are export-oriented and that their business policy is determined by the logic of profit optimisation at the level of transnational complexes. Integral-type foreign-owned firms may also supply across the border and they are definitely not autonomous in decision-making. The crucial point is that the latter constitute part of the national industrial-production complex of the host-country, while the former remain outside it. The criterion should be the contribution to the growth of the value-adding capacity of the national economy. Nowadays the value added is in the technology and knowledge, in the adaptability of the labour force, and in the production of the sophisticated parts and components rather than in the assembling of finished products. Those countries are richer that have that capability within their borders.

Foreign capital comes to the host-country for profit, but it is not indifferent to the future of the country the way in which the method of profit extraction will influence its value-adding capacity. It is reasonable to assume that the influence is likely to be more positive if investors bind their profit expectations to a general increase in the efficiency of the local economy and the growth of national welfare rather than to the availability of some fixed conditions. In the first case, foreign capital comes in to grow *with* the economy, in the second – to grow *despite* it.

Integral investment has become a prevailing form of foreign direct investment in relations between industrialised countries. There foreign affiliates are, on average, analogous to domestic firms in value-added per worker, compensation per worker, and R & D expenditures per worker. Thus, in the United States the American component of automobiles produced by Honda is fast approaching the American content of the automobiles made by Chrysler.[1] On the other hand, according to a recent study,[2] local content levels of US transnational corporations in the EC are high enough that their behaviour is, in many cases, indistinguishable from that of European-owned corporations. Since, under these conditions, foreign direct investments contribute to high-quality productive activities in the host-country, the presence of transnational corporations spills over into more and better jobs, higher productivity and improved products.

Integral investments are positive inasmuch as they add to the national capital base over a longer period of time thanks to reinvestment, as foreign capital, technology and know-how have an immediate impact on national productive forces. Moreover, foreign firms directly participate in developing the efficiency and competitiveness of the national market in terms of both supply and demand.

For economically backward areas and newcomers to the world market, the choice between the two variants of foreign capital inclusion cannot be left to a market structured mechanism alone. The incompatibility in efficacy between the local and modern productive systems inevitably leads to the concentration of value-adding activities in a few core countries and their enclaves and enclave-like sites in periphery countries. The latter on their own do not have enough capital, competence, skills and infrastructure to employ existing manpower in sufficiently competitive production. Corrective regulations are necessary to compensate for local market failures but also to resist competitive pressures existing in the international investment market.

5.1.2 The Constraints of Export-led Growth

The factor of competition is very important. Although integral investment promoting policy appears to be preferable from the point of view of the interests of the host-country, it is not always easy for the host-government to maintain it. First of all, the host-country's economy and the development of national production factors must achieve a certain minimal level of maturity and sophistication. Given these conditions, there is still such a situation as competition between industrialising and newly industrialised countries for external sources of financing. It undermines the bargaining power of capital importers in bilateral deals with transnational corporations, and makes them devalue their demands and soften conditions.

If a host-country, already suffering from an erratic domestic economic situation, becomes exposed to the influence of external competition this only naturally pushes decision-makers towards the enclave variant inasmuch as low production costs and appropriate exchange rate policy appear to be sufficient incentives for export-oriented foreign direct investment.

This has proved to be the case in Russia. The question 'What can we offer to attract foreign investment?' has increasingly been raised there. The response of a growing number of experts has been pessimistic: hardly anything more than cheap labour, inexpensive resources and a liberal fiscal legislation yet to be created. The experts generally agreed that Russia's industrial potential could not be a 'bait' for foreign capital after having been disabled by the severance of traditional integration links, the shortage of capital investment, the infrastructural collapse, price increase and the hegemony of producers over consumers. This potential might be revived only by way of capital injections which, within the country, have no sources. Hence the position formulated by Russian Vice Prime-Minister Anatolii Chubais: foreign investors may be attracted only by cheap manpower and low prices but certainly not by our fixed capital and even less so by the quality of products.[3] This statement logically introduces yet another question: 'In comparison to other countries trading in the same market of cheap production factors (the countries mentioned most often are Central European and South-East Asian states, Pakistan, Turkey and Mexico), what will be a niche for Russia?' The answer was *particularly* low prices. At least this was suggested by Chubais' criticism of the plans to increase domestic oil prices to a world market level as undermining Russia's position as an outlet for foreign investment.

There are at least two considerations that bring into question the possibility for Russia to enjoy the advantages that help smaller countries to profit by acting as off-shore export platforms for transnational corporations. The first has to do with the financial aspect of the export-oriented foreign capital sector. Russian authorities should be prepared to pay, directly or otherwise, by way of generous infrastructure and incentive provisions for every job created by foreign investors. The available evidence suggests that the price may be really high. In 1979, the British government gave the US-owned silicon manufacturer Dow Corning 34 million pounds sterling in Regional Development Grants and other assistance, thus bringing the cost per job to 272 000 pounds sterling (Grant, 1982, p. 61). In 1982, the American Hyster Company informed public officials in five US states and four nations where it had production capacity that some Hyster plants would close. Operations would be retained wherever they were most generously subsidised. Within six months Hyster had collected 72.5 million dollars in direct aid. Britain alone was reported to have offered 20 million dollars to save 1500 jobs in Scotland.[4] Taking into account the dimensions of the Russian economy, much bigger than that of any other pursuing export-led growth, one may rightfully assume that host-government expenses would be enormous unless foreign participation were limited to a restricted number of projects, which is in opposition to official plans for large-scale foreign capital enrolment.

The second consideration reflects some external restraints. It would be erroneous to expect that Russia will be permitted to disregard the rules of the existing international trade regime. The majority of economies with an extensive enclave-type sector are sufficiently small not to provoke retaliation if their policies break certain rules and conventions. If, for example, a large country provides particularly generous concessions to exporters while limiting imports, the reaction of other trading nations will be sharper than in the case of a small country. The export policy of Mauritius, which is actually a single huge export processing zone, has never attracted attention internationally. China is already too big and too important to pursue a similar policy without arousing concern in other countries. This was revealed by debates in the US Congress, in the spring of 1991, on renewing for another year the Most Favoured Nation status. They demonstrated US determination to put Chinese trade practice more in line with the existing international trade regime by means which the Chinese could not ignore. Within the frame of the European Community a somewhat similar reaction was provoked by an Irish Republic export-encouraging regulation: the EEC has directly intervened to end a generous 'tax holiday' concession on profits on exports.

As has already been argued in this book, attempts to base the competitiveness of a country like Russia on defects inherited from the previous system have limited prospects. There are a considerable number of developing countries in Asia, Africa and Latin America in which the adoption of an export-led growth model has entailed the development of a considerable enclave-type foreign-owned production sector, but only in a few of them has the 'magic' of the model worked and the national economy developed to such a degree that foreign manufacturers showed interest in co-operating with domestic manufacturers.[5] A closer analysis shows that all these successful cases, which are practically limited to the East Asian 'Four Tiger' NICs, have considerably less common features than it is generally accepted. At the same time, each case owes so much to particular circumstances, the roots of which are deeply planted in national culture, history and social tradition, that there is no convincing evidence that the 'model' itself has resulted in their success.

If there is anything common in the machinery behind the economic miracle of the 'Four Tigers', it is the fact that three of them – South Korea, Taiwan and Hong Kong – benefited enormously from American and other economic and political support as anti-Communist outposts during the Cold War. This, and the fact that American capital also tried to use them as its bastion outposts in trade wars with Japan, established a specific situation in relations between the nation-state and transnational corporations there. Local authorities found themselves in a position where they could be reasonably selective about foreign investment. Foreign investment proposals have been evaluated in terms of how much they open new markets, build new exports, transfer technology, intensify input-output links, and increase the value of their countries as foreign investment sites (see Wade, 1990). Against this background it no longer seems to be incidental that in Latin America, where countries did not enjoy equal economic and political consequences of the Cold War factor, export led development has never produced similar results.

Generally the West has demonstrated a cautious attitude towards post-Communist Russia. At the initial stage of reforms especially some of its actions left room for uncertainty as to whether they should be attributed to a remaining inertia in political thinking, with the former USSR still treated as a probable enemy, or whether they were signs of a recently developed tactic aimed at weakening further a newly emerged competitor in the world market.[6] Whatever the answer, it is clear that, precisely because of the size and economic potential of the country and the change in the international political environment, restructuring in Russia will never enjoy such a positive external contribution as that experienced by Western Europe, Japan and some South-East Asian countries in the post-war period, although it may benefit eventually from the competition between the biggest industrial nations – chiefly the United States and Germany – for influence over the CIS nations as they develop their rich natural resources and open their markets to the West. Therefore, it is necessary for Russia to search ever more insistently for internal resources for a successful transition.

With this in mind, it is important to realise that an enclave-type foreign-owned sector may be instrumental in employing labour and supporting the budget and the balance of payments, and this justifies its presence in many countries, but it is hardly possible to expect from it anything more.[7] Environment and incentives for integral-type investment (ITI) have to be created in a different way. *ITI incentives are largely identical with those that encourage domestic economic growth and rapid expansion of the private sector.* This claim is not altogether unusual or original. In fact, it follows directly from the concept of an open economy set out earlier in this thesis. Economic growth makes an open economy still more open as it enforces its standing in the world market and boosts its attractiveness for foreign capital at the same time. Consequently, regulations which are originally not focused on foreign capital none the less participate in forming an investment climate. That is why it is possible to speak about a narrowly defined and widely defined capital entry management system. It is the latter that is dealt with mainly in the present chapter.

5.1.3   The Market Size as a Competitive Strength

It is a fact that the greatest capital importers are not among the developing or newly industrialised countries. They are the United States and the European Community. Excluding intra-EC foreign direct investment, the stock of inward direct investment in these two regions constituted up to 79 per cent of total world figures in 1980 and 54 per cent in 1988.[8] Both regions acquired eminence as destinations for foreign investment because of their enormous markets. Owing to the outstanding absorbing capacity of the latter much of the FDI was geared to serve them, making the locational advantage of market size an important variable facilitating the high levels of foreign direct investment. Significant important was the impact of state regulations. Laura D'Andrea Tyson (1990) reached the following conclusion on the pattern of behaviour of foreign multinationals in the United States: 'Where they are most American, US policies have encouraged them to be so'. In fact, although the United States has no explicit federal policies for attracting foreign investment, it often does so through the back door by the threat or actual practice of import protection.

Much can be learnt in particular from the EEC. Something similar to the present situation in the former Soviet Union occurred in Western Europe after the Second World War. Economic structures had been destroyed; political instability, shortages of consumer goods and equipment, and fears of financial chaos were very substantial. After stagnating through much of 1947, European growth accelerated in 1948, coinciding with the release of Marshall Aid. However, the several decades of sustained high growth that followed were related to Europe's own effort. Fortunately for Western Europe, there were leaders in the 1950s who were wise enough to create the new integrated structures of a common European market out of the ruins of opposing disintegrated structures. The Common Market programme attracted foreign direct investment from many countries through the allure of projected market growth as well as the possibility (real or imagined) of future difficulties in exporting to the region from outside the EC. At a later stage, foreign direct investment flows intensified as transnational corporations sought to gain access to new technologies, to make alliances with firms with complementary technologies and to amortise their fixed expenditure by expanding their market share. Many transnational corporations in a wide range of industries have found it necessary to position themselves strategically in the EC in anticipation of demand growth resulting from the unification of the European Community.

The size of the internal market and favourable prospects for demand growth also lay behind the expansion of foreign investment in tsarist Russia. As was shown earlier, railroad construction was the fuse for an explosion of market activities in the country. Russia soon gained fame as a country in which one could sell almost anything in enormous quantities. Foreign companies rushed in to secure a local presence as they subscribed to the belief that the pay-off for early investors could be great as the market expanded and matured later on. The Russian government recognised the importance of the demand factor for encouraging foreign production investment. In order to sustain high cumulative demand for industrial products it stuck to a policy of forced redistribution of income from agriculture to industry and from country regions to cities. The cost of this policy, so many historians claim, was quite high. What is important for this analysis, however, is the fact that Russia, though relying heavily on foreign capital, managed to avoid colonial-type industrialisation and within a short period of time came to possess a diversified industrial complex.

Unlike newly industrialised countries, modern Russia comes to the world market as a major industrial power. Owing to this, and to Russia's huge territory and high population, the internal market of the country could in the near future become as important a component of the world economy as the US and the EC markets, and transnational corporations could be as motivated to enter it as they are in respect to the latter. Clearly, such a scenario will remain hypothetical until the deficiencies inherited from the administrative–command system and the shock caused by the collapse of the centralised union state are largely overcome. Host-country-oriented foreign investment projects could not be numerous as long as guarantees of conditions for profit repatriation are missing. Hence the importance of rouble convertability and the development of exports. However, monetary surgery has made sustaining export expansion even less plausible inasmuch as it has resulted in considerable damage to the real part of the economy, the major generator of export earnings, in the form of sizeable output and unemployment losses (according to official estimates, 25 per cent of the GNP and five million respectively by the end of 1992[9]). To an extent, these developments were the natural outcome of the institutional changes typical of a transition to a market economy. However, they have undoubtedly been exacerbated by policy neglect of important realities in terms of both supply and demand.

5.2   THE FATE OF RUSSIAN INDUSTRY

5.2.1   The 'Decapitalisation' of the Russian Market

The stabilisation programme implemented in Russia has hit hardest at the two essentials of the market: the purchasing power of the population and the capacity of enterprises to accumulate capital. Consequently, this has blocked the establishment of the private proprietor as a central figure in market relations.

Government measures followed a repressive approach with respect to accumulations and current income. First of all, the Government applied a confiscational price and fiscal policy to the population in an attempt to arrive at market clearance prices. At the beginning of 1991, private accumulations in the form of liquidity, bank deposits, state securities, etc. equalled more than 500 billion rubles. A twenty times price rise in the first trimester of 1992 reduced this sum to 20–25 billion rubles at January 1991 prices. Inflation shock provoked by the pseudo-liberalisation of prices (the monopoly of state enterprises in many sectors reduced the price reform to yet another administrative, though uncontrolled, correction of prices) brought them for some product groups to a level at which they were affordable to only 1 per cent of the population. In general, about 90 per cent of Russians found their monetary income to have fallen below the official poverty line.[10] The price reform was coupled with the introduction of new indirect taxes ranging from five to 28 per cent over the retail price. In January 1992, according to official data, the real income of the inhabitants of Russia was equal to only 40 per cent of what they had earned one month before. At the same time, the people were forced to spend 4.8 times more on their current needs than before while fiscal payments increased 5.5 times. Relating the cost of basic foods to pension and minimum wages, several analyses were projecting a decline of kilocalories for low-income consumers to a level which the World Health Organisation defines as starvation.

The price reforms resulted in the collapse of the living standard and mass impoverishment, but not only that. No less serious were the consequences in terms of the psychological component of the internal investment climate. The government failed to compensate the holders of the state debt, i.e., practically every adult in the country, or to introduce any safety-net such as the indexation of deposits in state savings banks, generating a deep crisis of confidence in the monetary and financial sphere. The expropriation of lifetime savings of Russians coincided with the Yeltsin government's confirmation of its obligations to foreign creditors. The government was concerned not to anger foreign creditors whose money they thought to be necessary to build capitalism in Russia, but they refused to recognise the rouble savings of the people as the foundation of new property relations in the country. In the second quarter of 1992 the share of savings in the monetary assets of the population fell to a rock-bottom level of 2 per cent. This impoverishment and the expropriation of private wealth taken together created a deeply inappropriate environment for mass privatisation of state property, regarded by the government as the hard core of the second phase of transition which had to bring about the revitalisation of the Russian economy.

The impoverishment of the population was paralleled by the erosion of the financial self-sustenance of state-owned enterprises. Lack of resources has broken down the state capital formation system which previously consisted of two elements: centralised investment funds and the investment funds of state-run enterprises. According to the prognosis of the Economic Ministry of Russia, by the end of 1992, as against 1990, capital investment from the first source would fall, in comparative prices, from 53.5 billion rubles to 13.5 billion rubles, and from the second source from 73.8 billion rubles to 36.5 billion rubles (*Ekonomika i zhisn'*, No. 23, June 1992, p. 1). In other words, the prognosis in 1992 predicted a decrease of two and a half times in new investment in fixed capital over two years (in 1990–91 the decrease was about 11 per cent).

Simultaneously, the tight monetary policy of the Russian Federation Central Bank caused a shrinkage in working capital. The accretion of money supply in circulation was kept tens of times below the increase in prices while the access to bank credit was restricted. As a result, the economy was hit by an unprecedented payments crisis as businesses did not have enough working capital to pay for deliveries, to promote sales and repay credit. The debt of state enterprises in the course of mutual settlements increased within the first quarter of 1992 from 32 billion rubles to two trillion rubles (a sum greater than all cash in circulation) (*Isvestia*, May 20, 1992; *Ekonomika i zhisn'*, ibidem.). The crisis pushed to the edge of bankruptcy thousands of enterprises, including the acknowledged leaders of Russian industry such as KAMAZ, the largest and one of the most modern truck plants in Europe.[11] One of the first joint-stock companies in the country, it was often praised as an example of efficient management and production. Ironically, the firm was found to be delaying the repayment of over ten billion rubles of short-term bank credits only a few days after one of the major national newspapers alluded to it in support of the thesis that public enterprises were run incompetently and therefore failed to resist the crisis while private and semi-private firms were more prepared to face it.

Inter-enterprise arrears became a form of unauthorised spontaneous monetary emission. They practically nullified the results of the policy of economic atrocity introduced by the government at the beginning of 1992. This fact was officially recognised in August 1992 as the Russian Central Bank injected into the economy hundreds of billions of roubles of extra credit in order to help enterprises settle their mutual debt. The credit expansion increased the budget deficit dramatically, but this sacrifice in terms of monetary stabilisation did not bring long-term results as it was not followed by any serious change in the reform strategy. A bias on monetary stabilisation combined with a hands-off policy in respect to industrial enterprises proved to be inadequate as a reform strategy. The enterprises had reputedly failed to adjust thereby calling into question the belief that macro stringency alone would be enough to press firms into spontaneous adjustment measures. By the end of 1992 there was again evidence of an enormous accumulation of inter-enterprise debt.

Under these conditions prospects for both the privatisation of the economy and its sectoral and technological restructuring looked bleak. The majority of enterprises to be privatised did not belong to what might be called a competitive, market type. Withdrawn from their habitual environment within protracted productive chains, and deprived of state financial support, they have become a tough and risky investment for domestic investors, but no less so for foreign capital. Against an unfavourable political risk background, the demolition of industry and the suppression of the consumer power of the population represented the two most improbable prerequisites for promoting integral-type foreign direct investments. However, this does not exclude the possibility of some important acquisitions of the Russian industrial property by non-residents as a predictably low juncture in Russian industrial property market is likely to make almost any deal a bargain for foreign currency holders.

5.2.2 Privatisation and Bankruptcies

The performance of state-owned enterprises is central to the formation of the pattern of foreign direct investment in the Russian economy. Indeed, privatised state property will inevitably be the main object for foreign investment until progress in privatisation changes the balance between public and private sectors in favour of the latter. On the other hand, during a certain transition period, the activities of state and municipally-owned enterprises will still determine the business environment for foreign ventures in the country. Hence the conclusion that government policy towards state-run firms has and will have important consequences for the type of inclusion of a foreign-controlled sector in the national economy.

Some Russian reformers seem to share the belief that privatisation, in particular with foreign participation, is able to transfer automatically both enterprises and the economy as a whole to a new higher level of efficiency. In reality the link between the cause and the result proves to be more complicated. A shift to a modern level of efficiency is impossible unless there is a persistent effort to strengthen national competitiveness. Therefore, it would be disastrous for all practical purposes if policy-makers in Russia confused the reorganisation of the public sector with its simple demolition. To do this would cause heavy damage to the national industrial complex and weaken the Russian position in the world economy in the future. On this point, Professor Mario Nuti inferred a significant generalisation from the experience of Central and Eastern Europe:

The state sector, which in the necessary delays of privatisation continues to exist and to provide the bulk of productive capacity, should not be ignored, neglected and penalised [original underlined]. (Nuti, 1992, p. 17)

Many experts in Russia fear that the absence of an efficient industrial policy may lead to yet another economic bloodletting. Yurii Ol'sevich (1992, p. 36) writes: 'to "frighten" producers, make them reduce the output and cut down costs, wages in the first place, seems to be yet another aspect of the "shock therapy" policy. The inevitable curtailment of public production would cause bankruptcies and mass unemployment thus establishing a climate characterised by the underemployment of all the types of resources and high prices which are necessary for domestic and foreign capitalists to unfold private entrepreneurial activity'.

The strength of monopolies in the Russian economy is widely acknowledged. However, it is a mistake to combat these monopolies with market instruments alone. First, the market has yet to be developed. Second, Russian monopolies are not conventional market monopolies which emerge as a response to competition. They have their origins in the technological structure of the economy as left over from central-planning days. At that time the national economy was perceived as a large single household, and economy of scale was considered to be the major means to cut costs. Statistics demonstrate that ex-Soviet industry appears to be particularly subject to monopolies at the level where it really counts: individual and narrowly-defined product groups.[12] In other words, ex-Soviet enterprises are more narrowly specialised than is usual in the West. As a result, there is often just one national producer of a particular product.[13] According to Aleksandr Vladislavlev, Chairman of the presidential Council on Entrepreneurship, the bankruptcy of even a few and, on the face of it, insignificant enterprises is able to put the whole economy in coma.[14]

Creating a monopolies dominated economy was a deliberate choice of Soviet planners concerned with the task of establishing a managerial system especially adapted to administrative supervision. The negative consequences of monopoly in a shortage economy, that is the desire of the producer to increase prices while decreasing the output or diminishing the quality of the product, were neutralised, though not completely of course, by a close state control. As with the beginning of reforms the government abstained from traditional administration of the economy without shifting to any coherent industrial policy, producers responded as effort-minimising monopolists, ending up with higher prices and lower output, overemployment and the accumulation of arrears.

Russian reformers seem to have put all their trust in the privatisation of state owned enterprises as a method to increase the efficiency of the Russian industry. They also promote bankruptcies as a way to speed up privatisation. The strategic importance of privatisation is beyond any doubt. What causes scepticism is that neither policies are likely to bring short-term results. The fate of the Presidential Decree on bankruptcies (August 1992) is a case in point. When introduced this very radical regulation inspired many hopes. However, during the six month period it was effective not a single firm was forced into bankruptcy. Industrial enterprises have a powerful lever against the government: once started, bankruptcies are likely to have a protracted chain effect owing to the structural specifications of the ex-Soviet economy described earlier. This will cause mass layoffs leading to dramatic social and political consequences.

It is not difficult to see that the monopolistic structure typical of the Russian industry is a restraint for foreign investors unless their intention is to detach their acquisitions from their previous environment and include them in a new one. Under these circumstances, the fixed assets of Russian enterprises can be of interest to foreign investors. The claim that the level of production of Russian industry is considerably below world standards is correct as a general description. Many production chains included both modern and outdated enterprises, and the condition of the weakest link often determined the quality and the technological level of the end product as well as the efficacy of the whole chain. Moreover, modern and efficient enterprises were penalised by the centralised system of profit redistribution. Profits above industry-assigned averages were claimed by the state while high-cost producers were compensated. There were no incentives to fully utilise the capacities of new technologies and modern plant or to increase productivity. It was common that many new factories failed to achieve projected output figures for decades.

All or many of these bottlenecks and deficiencies inherent in the administrative-command system cease to be an obstacle for return-generating investment as soon as the object of investment, usually an enterprise with a sufficiently high technological level, is transferred into a new stimulative environment. The experience of Eastern and Central Europe demonstrates that, though transnational corporations seek to invest in the most competitive and modern plants and factories, they none the less usually find it necessary to 'streamline' their new property. This is exactly the process of detaching the competitive core from the ballast, which often includes cutting out the network of traditional suppliers. Hence the threat that the most modern and efficient enterprises, after having become foreign property, will be reoriented in such a way that they can no longer be considered integral-type investments.

This threat tends to increase because of the stresses of landslide privatisation. The government has opted for a give-away scheme of privatisation based on investment vouchers. Voucher-holders will not be the only category of buyers. A certain number of shares may rest with the state or be acquired at an advantageous rate by the workers and employees of privatised enterprises. None the less, the issue of participation certificates will entail a tremendous fragmentation of capital ownership rights. Probably the main problem with this scheme is that it does not provide any visible evidence that the change in ownership will promote profit maximisation and business efficiency. No new capital or expertise will be introduced into troubled companies. Furthermore, the individuals receiving a share in privatised enterprises, if ownership is broadly spread, will not have any influence over the specific competitiveness of the companies they come to own. Since, with so little information available, the acquisition of assets will comprise a considerable chance element, new owners may soon discover their property to be uncompetitive and unprofitable. In other cases enterprises which are competitive in their operations may fall into the hands of entrepreneurially incompetent individuals who could ruin the business. As a result business conditions in the country may become even more chaotic and insecure making the inclusion of foreign owned ventures in the national productive system still more questionable.

5.2.3 How Much Foreign Investment is Enough?

President Bush, following continuous appeals for aid from Russia, once commented: 'I don't know that there's enough money in all the world to solve Russia's economy'. He touched upon a very sensitive point. There is a growing awareness that, quantitatively, foreign capital's involvement in reorganising the Russian economy, either as aid or in the form of private investment, will remain modest in comparison to the scope of the process itself.

The declared needs of separate firms may be helpful in establishing an approximate figure. A giant heavy-machine producer, Uralmash Zavod, alone needs 500 million dollars in investment to pull through the reconstruction stage, according to calculations presented by its management to a group of six American banks.[15] In the rust-belt cities of Russia there are dozens of plants like Uralmash. They all constituted part of the military–industrial complex of the USSR, the conversion of which will need, argue government experts, a further 150 billion dollars in investment.

These demands may appear to be inflated. However, the following brief comparative study demonstrates that the total expenses of market transition can be expected to reach exceptionally high levels. The methodology uses extrapolations for Russia based on the amount of investment considered by foreign experts necessary to integrate the former German Democratic Republic (GDR) into the Federal Republic of Germany. As a minimum they estimated this sum at 2000 billion DM (1120 billion dollars) to be spent within 10 to 30 years. For the purpose of our argument this figure may be taken as the price of transition from the economy of 'really existing socialism' to a highly developed modern industrialised economy.

The Commonwealth of Independent States lagged behind East Germany in almost all relative indicators such as the number of telephones, or cars, or personal computers, etc. per thousand inhabitants. The railroad density in the CIS was 25 times lower, and the automobile road density 15 times lower than in the GDR. To achieve an equal result, per head investment in reconstruction in the CIS has to be higher, but for simplicity let us assume it to be at the same level. By population the CIS was 17.6 times and Russia nine times bigger than the GDR. Hence, the Commonwealth's demand in capital would be 19 700 billion dollars and Russia's 10 200 billion dollars. Russia would need hundreds of years to put this capital into operation.

On the one hand, as the author of these calculations, Professor Kovalevsky (1992) writes:

[it] is possible, of course, to create a market at smaller costs and within shorter time, but then we shall get only a semi-colonial market in the form of a raw-material appendage to developed countries.

On the other hand, it is utopian to imagine that this money will ever come to Russia. Even within the most developed triad of the world – the

United States, the EC and Japan – foreign direct investment stock has never exceeded 4 per cent of the gross domestic product.

The answer to this dilemma is to attempt to bypass some stages on the road to a post-Communist economy. To this end it is necessary to overcome a natural desire to mechanically imitate patterns which were once successful and instead to try to evaluate without prejudice the main trends in the international economy and the country's own heritage. One of the major lessons to be learned from the economic history of the twentieth century is that only a mixed economy has the potential to concentrate resources in priority spheres essential to the implementation of technological renovation and the achievement of an independent policy of development. The policy of relying on a government's skill in mixing market mechanisms and government planning, as the example of Japan and the ASEAN countries has demonstrated, is particularly attractive when the private sector is still in the infant stage (Okita, 1990).

Implementing a monetarist 'model' has deprived the government of any levers of influence on the evolution of economic process. Meanwhile, incomplete system transformation – e.g., undeveloped financial markets, a lack of satisfactory functioning labour markets especially with respect to the determination and the differentiation of salaries, persistent monopolistic markets, state ownership, general impoverishment of the population – implied the persistence of structures and rigidities unsuitable for market signals to emerge or be received and responded to effectively. Indeed, the increase in prices resulted in the cutting down of the output of all manufactured goods instead of stimulating their production as one would expect. Simultaneously, the chaotic curtailment of investment activities gave an impulse to dangerous structural processes the progress of which might undermine Russian industrial competitiveness even further. Price liberalisation contributed to a shift of financial resources to the extracting sector while manufacturing industries, in particular machine-building and chemical production, found themselves decapitalised (a 60 per cent and 66 per cent decline in capital investment respectively). This has only consolidated the most serious defects in the Russian economy: an excessive bias towards a capital- and labour-intensive mining industry and dependence on imported technology.[16]

Price equilibrium and even privatisation, important as they are, are not sufficient to halt recession of production, prevent the erosion of national industry, raise productivity and efficiency and eventually to impede national competitiveness from sliding down into an irrecoverable position. This is the case for industrial policy. The earlier stated reform priorities must be complemented by a commitment to pursue profound structural changes in the economy.

Sometimes it is argued that the open declaration of a move towards a mixed economy as the objective of reforms in Russia would be a concession to the 'old guard', leading eventually to the restoration of an administrative economy. In fact, it is the hasty enforcement of the market that has already brought about the restitution of some of the most rigid forms of administrative interference in the economy.[17] It is fair to point out that recent years have seen a shift of emphasis in Western academic research from market failures to 'regulatory failures' as it was discovered that the cost of public intervention might exceed the benefit. In practical terms, however, this did not prevent industrial regulation from remaining an important part of policy-making in the modern industrial state.

In this context a foreign capital entry management system should be seen as a component of a national industrial policy. A relative (compared to the maxi-demand prognosis outlined above) shortage of foreign investment in Russia, as well as in other CIS countries, can be overcome through channeling the available resources according to preselected objectives. This should be done on the basis of the principles of 'new' market-friendly interventionism that favours policies with the potential of broadening the scope and increasing the effectiveness of markets while recognising that the primary responsibility for industrial development rests with enterprises.

5.3   SELECTING PRIORITIES FOR FOREIGN INVESTMENT

The problems facing Russia's economy are mostly structural in nature. Some of them are products of the administrative–command system and bear the stamp of its main defect – the domination of politics over the economy. These problems will be solved as new forms of property and business relations spread across the country. Others are similar to those that all industrialised countries are forced to deal with, though the peculiarities of Russia's previous development add to them certain country-specific features. The latter range of problems includes, *inter alia*, the shift of capital and labour from old and 'dying' industries (shipbuilding, coal mining, metallurgy, textile industry, etc.) to new booming high-tech industries, and from industrial production to services; the strengthening of society's capacity for sustained technological innovation; the protection and cleaning-up of the environment. Worldwide, governments are engaged in helping national economies to cope with these challenges, whether it be called guidance planning in one country, or the Strategic Defence Initiative in some other.

Taking into account the seriousness of problems of this type in Russia, it would be shortsighted to delay working out relevant structural policies. Following the experience of industrialised countries, structural policies can raise potential output by improving the allocation of resources, by promoting technological change, by improving the quality of the factors of production and by eliminating financial market rigidities and tax distortions. Below I will attempt to identify some of the most immediate structural problems and to analyze the role of foreign capital in dealing with them.

5.3.1 The Industrial 'Overhang'

Russia is over-industrialised, that is it has more industry than a country of its size and its level of development should have. According to Marvin Jackson (1989, p. 12), the percentage of actual to expected normal share.[18] of the labour force in Soviet industry was 145 in 1975 and 154 in 1980. In absolute figures this means that about 16 million workers and employees in excess were employed in industry. Consequently, the share of employment in services was below normal. The Soviet economy did not follow the main trend in labour force and capital allocation of the 1970s and the 1980s towards the redistribution of resources in favour of services and infrastructural branches. This explains quite a sharp variation between the figures for 1975 and 1980: it reflects not only the further expansion of the country's industrial sector but even more so the withdrawal of capital and labour from industry in the rest of the world.

In its turn, Soviet industry itself was suffering serious structural deviations. Capacities were located in the wrong branches and sectors as the economy remained immune to the tremendous international relative price changes that occurred in the world markets in the 1970s and 1980s and led to major structural shifts worldwide.

First, most capacities were developed to produce machines and materials for the purpose of producing other machines and materials rather than to supply products for personal consumption, or for the needs of the social infrastructure, or for exports. According to available calculations, by the end of the 1980s, 80 per cent of industrial production was consumed within industry and only 20 per cent found its way to household consumption (Pervushin, 1991). Correspondingly, over 55 per cent of the aggregate labour pay went to workers who were neither directly nor indirectly (through intersectoral links) associated with production of consumer goods and services (in the United States this proportion was 33 per cent).[19] Counter to the world tendency, the amount of investment destined for the complex of industries providing for the needs of the inhabitants of the country had been decreasing in the total sum of investment up to 1990. Only 6–8 per cent of the country's productive capital stock was engaged in producing consumer goods.

Second, the balance between the capacities allocated for the production of materials and mineral resources and those manufacturing equipment and machinery was also distorted. The output of the primary sector rose to 40 per cent of all industrial production. As a result, in the Soviet Union the share of extracting industries in the gross national product was twice as large as in the developed countries of the West. The hypertrophy of the primary sector was caused not least by the fact that the economy of the country was developing on an unchanging technological base (the coefficient of new plant brought into operation yearly fell from 10.5 per cent in 1970 to 5.9 per cent in 1990). Under these conditions increment in industrial production was achieved by employing a constantly increasing amount of resources, hence the enormous consumption and waste of resources. This could have been avoided if enterprises had been transferred to a new technological platform.

Drastic structural changes can no longer be delayed. What makes this task somewhat delicate, also from the point of view of employing foreign capital, is that it involves two very sensitive strategic areas: the utilisation of the non-reproducible component of national wealth – oil, gas and other mineral resources – and the fate of the military–industrial complex (MIC).

5.3.2   The Development of Natural Resources

The oil and gas industries in Russia have become matters for great concern. While experts point out that known oil reserves, at current extraction rates, will be exhausted in thirteen years, many Russians fear that these resources can be misused and their country might become (or remain) a raw-material appendage to the West. Such a prospect cannot be completely excluded though it has very little, if anything, to do with the issue of whether foreign capital should or should not be allowed to develop the country's natural resources. The crux of the matter lies elsewhere. To be a major exporter of resources does not preclude the possibility of also being a successful and important producer of manufactured goods. If a country has a weak standing in international markets it is not because one of its sectors has a developed export capacity, rather the problem lies with those sectors which do not show such a capacity. Russia's future and the future of its natural resources are linked mostly to improvements in the general efficiency of the national economy: the higher the productivity level, the less is the relative consumption of raw materials. At present, the energy efficiency of the

GDP in Russia is 2.2 times lower than that in the United States and more than three times lower than in former West Germany, Great Britain and South Korea. In fact, on this account Russia was placed 103rd in the world classification compiled by Illarionov.[20] More specifically, the prospects of the oil industry in Russia depend very much on the technological renovation of the industry itself. Russia may well have up to a quarter of the world's undiscovered oil but only a major technological effort can bring it to the surface. Another promising possibility is to recover previously developed oil fields using up-to-date extracting processes.

Taking into account the current economic situation in the country, the maximum possible utilisation of foreign investment for developing national natural resources appears to be indispensable to the successful restructuring of the Russian economy. This will, first, take a great burden off the financial system of the country and, second, prevent pumping over resources from manufacturing to oil extracting and processing with the risk that the former remain undercapitalised. In fact, encouraging the inflow of foreign capital in this sector is probably the only way put an end to the dependence of Russian exports on mineral resources in the long run. For decades the economy of the country was locked in a vicious circle as the costs of oil and gas exportation came to absorb the lion's share of the revenues it brought. In general, the energy complex consumed about 40 per cent of the Union's industrial investment budget, yet coal and especially oil production were falling, gas output growth was slowing and the economy was facing energy shortages. A considerable part of Russia's foreign debt has been accumulated owing to the mass acquisition of tubes and equipment for export pipelines. Now foreign consortia, despite the political and policy risks involved, are willing to provide capital for the exploration and development of Russia's oil fields. This opens a possibility to channel released national funds to the development of those sectors which are important for improving national competitiveness but, at least at the current stage, cannot count on any serious interest on the part of foreign investors. Together with other measures aimed at rationalising energy consumption, energy price correction included, this investment manoeuvre will have very positive structural consequences.

Now, and even more so in the future, foreign participation in the development of Russia's oil and gas might give an example of the type of textbook reciprocity between foreign and home producers that leads to technology spill-over and stimulates a competitive environment. This effect could be brought about by the favourable combination of factors that has formed in the country. The most important of these is the acute interest that foreign investors have been demonstrating in Russian oil and gas exploration. The extraction industry is probably the only area in which Russia as a host-country can benefit from the rivalry of foreign firms. A second factor has to do with the state of the Russian oil industry itself. It would be erroneous to disregard completely the value of the experience it has accumulated. Some of this experience, especially in developing oil under extreme natural conditions, is indeed unique. It may be traded for technology and know-how with those foreign companies which need it to operate in Russia.

On the other hand, it is no less true that on the whole the Russian oil industry lags behind Western firms, which can only hamper the advancement of mutual interest in co-operation. This may be compensated for by state regulation which may become as important a factor of co-operation between Russian and foreign firms as the previous two. Extracting companies in general demonstrate more propensity to co-operate with host-authorities since their investments are more tied and more exposed to political risk than investments in manufacturing. Besides, as a lever on foreign companies, Russia may use its control over the vast network of pipelines in its territory (for example, the average length of a gas-line in the former Soviet Union was 3500 kilometres). Experts agree that access to the existing network is crucial to the profitability of foreign ventures as production tends to move eastward to more remote deposits.[21]

The Russian authorities have been under great pressure to ease the public grip on the oil sector. This pressure has been exerted by such unlikely parties as international agencies, transnational corporations and local interest groups. The first criticised, in the name of price equilibrium, the practice of oil price fixing. The second expressed discontent with chaotic and inconsistent regulations that increased investment risk and impeded any serious long-range planning. The latter sought more control over oil revenues. Much of this criticism is relevant. A substantial increase in the relative prices of energy products is likely to reduce the waste in the short run and encourage supply in the longer run. Coherent foreign investment policy could provide a welcome boost to royalties and other taxes paid by foreign companies engaged in the exploration of energy resources. Finally, the settlement of the ownership rights dispute between different levels of authority is important for the establishment of due legal prerequisites for the development of the industry.

At the same time, any adequate reaction to this criticism should allow for the fact that the exploration of natural resources and the energy sector were and remain among the most regulated areas of economic activity worldwide. Russia, in a sense, is in a situation similar to the one the North Sea countries addressed themselves to twenty years ago. It has to rediscover its natural wealth and to find ways to utilise it in the best way. The necessity for foreign participation is obvious, but it should not be expected to be without conflict. This is not because of government interference *per se*, but simply because national and foreign interests cannot coincide completely. Thus, for reasons of petroleum conservation, the Russian state wants foreign companies to rehabilitate old fields (about 20 000 wells with the capacity of 500 000 barrels a day) or to tackle technically demanding fields. Naturally enough, the companies instead want access to the biggest, cheapest reserves. This example once again demonstrates that capital entry regulations cannot take shape other than under conditions of a serious conflict of interests. The struggle for Russian oil has already begun. Numerous articles in foreign specialised journals, based on interviews with high-ranking employees of oil firms, give the impression that, despite considerable general interest, international oil producers practically exclude the possibility of expanding or starting business in Russia under present conditions. These publications are the background for the claims of some Russian authors for developing the capital entry management system by adding new privileges. However, in reality, according to the information of the Ministry of Fuel and Energy of Russia, in 1992 foreign firms have so far signed over 5000 contracts for the development of Russian oil fields.

Clearly, this does not imply that the investment climate in the oil industry is generally good. Foreign investors undoubtedly have a hard time running their oil ventures in Russia. However, the increasing inflow of capital suggests that some variant of equilibrium between the interests of the investors and the host-country has been established. This is a new situation for Russian regulators which, probably for the first time since the opening of the country to foreign capital in 1987, offers a possibility for viewing the task of developing the CEMS not simply as the perpetual escalation of incentives. Oil policy is of vital importance for Russia and the CIS as a whole. The future of reforms and, in a sense, of democracy in the country depends on the degree to which oil revenues will compensate for the default of other industries and ease the material hardships of the population during the transition period. The state must preserve its role as a guarantor in respect to foreign and domestic oil producers, ensuring that natural resources bring maximum returns to the national economy.

5.3.3   The Conversion of the Military Industry

The conversion of Russia's military–industrial complex (MIC) to civil objectives has been of tremendous importance considering its position in the economy. About 80 per cent of the MIC is concentrated in Russia's territory. The military–industrial complex included 70 per cent of mechanical engineering,

90 per cent of all chemical industry and 75 per cent of the production of combustible and lubrication materials that made it practically synonymous with national industry (Piskunov and Lomakin-Rumjancev, 1992, pp. 67–8). It employed directly 4.4 million persons, compared with 1.5 million employed in the Western European military industry; suppliers included, the number rocketed to 12 million (another estimate is 16.5 million). Military production consumed no less than 40 per cent of electricity and textiles, more than 50 per cent of steel, aluminum, plastics, motor oils, etc.

The conversion of the defence industry is more than just the introduction of changes in one, albeit large, industrial sector. It is an attempt to break away from a militarised economy, which the Soviet economy actually was, and thus to eliminate the fundamental cause of many of its structural deformations. In the militarised economy civil branches cannot compete with privileged military industries. For years the latest equipment and most skilled labour were allocated to military production. Civil industries were forced to compensate for the poor quality of machinery and labour by extra investment in productive capital stock. This did not solve the problem because, for the very same reason, new productive capacities also could not be employed efficiently. Capital injections did not and could not result in any substantial breakthrough in the technical and quality levels of the plant used by civilian industries as the money was to be spent on the maintenance of cumbersome and obsolete stocks of equipment and on increasing the gross volume of output in order to counterbalance the low quality and the short life-span of manufactured products. Hence the wasteful consumption of metal, energy and resources generally, as well as other structural deformations discussed above.

The first State Conversion Programme, endorsed in December 1990, proceeded from the assumption that cuts in the output of weapons and military hardware would immediately free resources for developing civilian production at defence complex enterprises. In reality no actual redundancy of productive capacity followed (Khokhlov and Samsonov, 1992). A partial cut in the volume of military production was not enough to allow the equipment to be re-tooled to manufacture civilian production. Besides, producers experienced a decrease in economy of scale: for example, a planned cut in production of tanks led to the cost of each unit nearly doubling (Ibidem, p. 57).

As in the second half of 1992 the political and economic situation in the country changed dramatically, planned conversion was aborted and the stage of 'wholesale' or 'landslide' conversion began. The military sector found itself completely deprived of any state financial support as military orders shrank abruptly by 70 per cent. Within months the output of weapons and accompanying products was down by a substantial number of percentage points while civilian production, due to the absence of conversion subsidies, remained at best stagnant. Lack of resources emerged as the main obstacle standing in the way of conversion.

Under these conditions a search for funds has become one of the principal tasks facing conversion. It cannot be adequately supported by state financial injections while the consumer market for durable civilian goods and agricultural machinery, produced by converted industrial capacities, has virtually collapsed following the price reform. At the same time, the foreign capital-based privatisation of MIC enterprises raises specific questions. National security aspects apart, the MIC remains a particular object for privatisation as it incorporates the core of the technological and industrial potential of the country. It has a pyramid structure. Resources-producing enterprises constitute the base. Then follow factories supplying intermediate products. The manufacturers of technology-intensive final products are at the top of the pyramid. Analysts point out that the network of MIC firms is especially fragile because it represents a protracted industrial chain with a high degree of specialisation and interdependence. This was one of the main arguments in favour of a very gradual approach towards the reform of military industry. It was often claimed that the closure of the elite enterprises of the upper level would have a multiplying effect owing to the devastating impact on their dependent industries.

In reality, top-level producers appear to be most vulnerable. Suppliers of mineral and other resources could easily find outlets both inside and outside the country. The producers of general-purpose components have a chance to adjust them to civilian needs at relatively little cost. Only final producers are specialised to such an extent that changes in the production profile inevitably entail a dramatic, from 30 to 50 per cent according to some evaluations,[22] fall in productivity. Moreover, because it is known that adjustment under competitive conditions is the more difficult the more sophisticated the product, one may expect that high-tech industries will suffer most from the opening up of the domestic market. Already converting enterprises tend to choose for civilian production articles which are technologically inferior to those they produced for the military.

In addition, in the Soviet Union four fifths of research and development financing was spent on military research.[23] This money was also an important source of support for fundamental research and academic science, as a part of the military R & D budget used to be allocated eventually to civilian research centres. As conversion started, the number of people employed in military R & D decreased by 40 000 in 1990 and by 160 000 in 1991. To appreciate the implication of these figures it is enough to compare them to the number of staff in the Academy of Sciences of the USSR: 60 000 in 1991.

Clearly, it is of paramount importance for the future of Russia to preserve the industrial and technological potential accumulated by the military–industrial complex. It is not entirely clear that this task may be resolved by purely market methods, in particular by the adoption of economic openness. The point is that the military sector had already been formed as an industrial enclave under the central-planning system. It was fenced off not only organisationally but even more by the technological gap which existed between the military and civilian sectors. In the latter the general technological level of enterprises was so low that they were often not capable of finding use for materials, products or technologies offered by military branches.[24] The mutual isolation of the two sectors, the technical incompatibility of many of their products, and the difference in standards and technological levels, all contributed to a difficulty for military industries to supply the internal civilian market (Krutsky and Kochetkov, 1992). At the same time, MIC enterprises, possessing state-of-the-art equipment and qualified workers to run them, can be very good subcontractors capable of manufacturing both mass and unique products for international markets. However, their isolation from external markets is by no means less than from internal markets. In these they have no marketing positions of their own and must win orders starting from scratch.

Optimally, conversion should retain the high quality of MIC manufacturing, eliminate the gap between military and civilian sectors and promote the expansion of national industry into international markets. The way conversion has been developing since the dissolution of the Soviet Union, military enterprises have been forced to pass from the manufacture of products of special technological value to the manufacture of simple consumer articles. The above-mentioned gap has been narrowing following the downgrading of a more advanced sector to the level of a less advanced sector which is distinctly counterproductive. Under these conditions, encouraging foreign assistance appears to be a step in the right direction. After the extraction industry, elite converted enterprises may be estimated as the most attractive object for FDI,[25] in particular as many of them do not need a massive infusion of new capital but rather access to international distribution networks in tandem with the relevant management expertise and marketing skills to disclose their competitive strength.

Predictably, different groups of experts maintain contrasting positions concerning the role of foreign capital in conversion. One group argues that 'creating assembly plants based on enterprises undergoing conversion and belonging to foreign corporations and joint ventures is the most rapid and effective way to integrate our processing industry into the international division of labour' (Khokhlov and Samsonov, 1992, p. 62). The other group demands that 'producers in [high-tech] sectors must at least be put into conditions more favourable than any type of joint venture or foreign companies' and that Russian ex-military enterprises should be equal partners when co-operating with foreign firms (Krutsky and Kochetkov, 1992, p. 89; pp. 91–4). It may be noted that the first proposal does not correspond to the goals of conversion as outlined above. It clearly bears the impress of the change in priorities in public mentality: from progress to survival. The second proposal pushes towards protectionism and has a visible relationship with the 'infant industry' argument so often raised in trade theory discussions.

These two positions mark the range of choices for government policy. The uniqueness of the Russian military industry is in a halfway position in terms of technology and quality between the level of performance of domestic civilian sectors and that of the leaders of the international market. It is one of the greatest assets the country has and the basis for its competitiveness in industrial markets. As regards high-tech enterprises, it seems reasonable to protect them from becoming a bargain for foreign competitors. Financial bottlenecks may be overcome through the injection of portfolio investment. This form of investment is rarely discussed in Russian publications. Indeed, taking into consideration the magnitude of the problems in the ex-Soviet economy, it will not be common for other industries that the foreign investor would easily agree to be a minor shareholder. Especially as this type of investment is in practical terms penalised or at least discriminated against by existing legislation which does not foresee any privileges for firms with foreign participation below 30 per cent. However, MIC enterprises are clearly a case apart as is evident from the persistent interest that foreign companies show in establishing business relations with Russian former and current arms producers. Hence, the government should not delay in introducing initiatives establishing a favourable legislative and organisational framework for these relations. Portfolio investment will permit the preservation of competitive producers under national control. In turn, joint ventures with global companies will provide a bridge to world markets.

Modern competitive producers may not include a majority of defence enterprises. Hence, raising portfolio investment from abroad will not be feasible for all of them. Others should be protected in a different way, and some should not be protected at all. Different approaches have to be applied to different cases. However, the one that should be avoided is 'wholesale' landslide conversion of the type that has been effective recently.

5.3.4   Technological Challenge

The Soviet centrally-planned economic system was infamous for its inability to provide for sustained technological innovation. In the 1970s and especially in the 1980s this defect became the cause of particular concern against the background of two pronounced tendencies. One was presented by the increasing worldwide evidence that innovation capacity had turned into a major strategic strength. The other was a progressive imbalance between the amount of material and financial resources and manpower invested by the Soviet Union in research and development and its inadequate technological performance in comparison with other industrialized countries. In the 1990s, technological innovation in the ex-Soviet economy slowed even further. Financial tension undermined the government's role as a consumer of scientific and technical products. In turn, in industry, there was no incentive to use new and up-to-date technology. As a result, 1991 saw a levelling out of effective demand for R & D products.

The Soviet technological lag can be attributed in part to the existence of the two-tier structure of technology creation, diffusion and adoption. The lion's share of research was carried out for military objectives. Naturally, it was concentrated on basic issues thus requiring a gigantic infrastructure and maximum spending. Civilian R & D instead was insufficient. The two tiers barely overlapped in the same way military innovations barely trickled down to civilian industries. Although military R & D enjoyed privileges unknown to its civilian counterpart, both faced similar problems: high costs, low quality and most of all the very slow pace of the introduction of R & D results into production. As for the latter, the reasons lay outside research institutions. The monopolism of producers and the pertaining scarcity of all types of manufactured items deprived the country's economy of whatever incentive it might have for technological innovation.

This must change if Russia is to have any future in the approaching technological age. The conventional advice is to create as soon as possible a competitive environment and to open the economy. This is by no means inappropriate. However, the following questions should be asked. What will help Russian R & D to survive before competition among producers boosts interest in innovation? Will this interest be strong enough to pay the high price of technological progress? Why is technology policy not alien to countries with developed modern market systems?

The structural problem with Russian science is that it has to become more integrated with industry, and to focus on generating new technologies, on engineering, and on the adaptation of basic research to industrial needs. The accelerating 'brain drain' from Russia indicates a precarious situation in national R & D since state funding has been largely withdrawn. Some state laboratories in the sphere of basic research are going to survive but otherwise research has to pass through privatisation and reorient itself towards commercial sources of finance. Meanwhile, research institutions have come to face higher requirements in terms of quality and efficacy. Applied research has to meet ever more rigorous standards as technology becomes increasingly expensive and the life-cycle of many products shrinks. This signifies that the ability to commercialize technology, to move a product from a concept to market quickly and efficiently is crucial for the prospects of both Russian science and industry.

World leaders in innovation differ from laggards in several respects (Nevens *et al.*, 1990). They get products or processes to markets faster, use new technologies in products across a wider range of markets, introduce more products, and incorporate in them a greater breadth of technologies. Clearly, under present conditions Russian firms cannot follow this pattern. Incorporation of some of research centres into the structures of trans-national companies may reduce tension in the upper-grade sector of the labour market. But, as yet another form of the export of highly-educated labour force and know-how, this settlement cannot solve the problem entirely.

What Russian R & D needs is the inflow of venture capital that would help to transform the accumulated intellectual potential into such ready-for-sale products as licenses, patents, samples of technology-based products and processes. These could be supplied to both domestic and international markets and would contribute to the welfare of the country in a much more positive way than the export of labour. There is no doubt that, at least in the visible future, venture capital as well as expertise in venture business can only come from abroad. Foreign investment for these purposes should be encouraged but traditional incentives may not be enough. Venture projects are known to be particularly dependent on the business environment. If national companies remain slow in responding to innovation no incentives to foreign capital will change the situation.

Hence what is necessary is a technology policy which, while helping to bridge modern research with actual production, would also serve as a component of a capital entry management system. In the United States where R & D, since the Second World War, has also come to depend on basic research for the military, the amount of venture capital has recently risen to 15 billion dollars. Much of this money is busy 'translating' the outcomes of basic research into commercial products. If in the first instance just a fraction of this money was to do the same job in Russia, it would none the less have a very positive structural impact.

Technology policy may concentrate either on the supply side or the demand side, or both. In the first case the government stimulates innovation through state financed science and grants to private research, proceeding from the assumption that industry would eventually benefit from technological spin-off. This 'model' is unlikely to prove instrumental in recruiting foreign venture capital under Russian conditions. First, because of the dramatic budgetary situation which will remain, according to all realistic hypotheses, a major constraint on all forms of government funding for many years to come. This does not suggest that state grants could be substantial enough to become a sufficient incentive for foreign capital. Second, it is quite predictable that government spending will essentially go to defence-related R & D thus restricting the possibility for foreign ventures to benefit from state technology policy. Besides, the unaided diffusion of military technologies is too slow to cause a radical change in national competitiveness.

The foregoing model once again puts trust in basic research as a generator of new products and new industries. It does not differ greatly from the traditional Soviet approach, with the minor variation that it allows for the existence of a non-state sector. Recently, under the influence of Japanese successes, the supply side concept has been increasingly criticized as misplacing the source of competitive strength. Instead, authorities are recommended to stimulate *demand* for innovative ideas. For Russia this type of technology policy promises tangible advantages. It does not require massive budget expenditure or involve the government in the precarious business of picking losers and winners among rival technologies and products. At the same time it contributes to the establishment of such an environment that would help domestic companies to become eager consumers of technology and aggressive innovators. In fact, an increasing domestic market for cut-edge technology is a fundamental prerequisite for the survival of Russian R & D and, eventually, for turning science into a profitable export industry and for attracting foreign money to it.

Unfortunately, no trace of any specific technological policy can be found in the actions of the government. At the same time, one can see statements such as that made by Igor' Nit, the head of a group of experts working for the president of the Russian Federation, maintaining that Russia was not yet ready to accept foreign high-tech investment. Thus he insisted that such investment would not be covered by the guarantees of a state foreign investment insurance fund to be established in the country in the near future (*Izvestia*, May 12, 1992). These are very alarming signs that suggest that innovation policy does not receive the necessary attention from the government.

5.3.5 Averting Environmental Collapse

Many of the industrial and agricultural regions of the former Soviet Union are on the verge of ecological breakdown posing an imminent threat to the health of present and future generations inside and outside the borders of the country. The 1988 official State of the Environment Report identified 290 'ranges of severe ecological conditions'. These ranges cover 3.7 million square kilometres, equivalent to an area ten times larger than unified Germany. Nearly 60 million people live in severely degraded environments. The acuteness of the pollution situation demands that the state should regard it as a major priority that foreign investment contribute to the improvement of environmental conditions.

The greatest effect can be expected to come from the correction of those structural imperfections of the post-Soviet economy discussed earlier. Industrial restructuring, the elimination of 'overindustrialisation', should lead to the closure of inefficient plants, and increase efficacy in the use of inputs per unit of output and spur technological renovation with positive consequences in terms of pollution. However, there remain some specific ecology-related issues requiring the particular involvement of the state.

The first group of issues is linked to the absence or near absence in the country of an industry specialised in the supply of technology necessary to tackle environmental problems. For decades environment protection targets have not been achieved because of failure in the production and supply of pollution control technology and waste-treating technology. This has been one of the most underinvested sectors of national manufacturing. Its budget constituted only a fraction of the costs of environmental damage which has been estimated at some 100 billion rubles per year. This disparity has been translated into the continuous degradation of the quality of life and natural resources. In 1989, life expectancy in the USSR fell below the 1965 level. The gap between the USSR and the OECD countries has increased, leaving Russia out of the top fifty countries with the highest average life-expectancies.

The pollution problem has been underplayed for many years. Russian and foreign experts agree that there are many of its aspects still waiting to be discovered, such as the burden of hazardous waste increasing at the rate of 20 million tons per year. This only stresses that ecology deserves all the attention it claims. It should not be overlooked, however, that the establishment of a new market-oriented system and the privatisation process also appear to be dependent on ecological conditions. Liability for existing environmental damage and the costs of environmental reconstruction interfere in the cost-benefit considerations of potential investors. Besides, the population would estimate the new system, *inter alia*, by the change it brings to the quality of life.

The industry supplying technology, appliances, measuring and screening instruments, and so called 'attachable' equipment (designed to complement existing technologies to clean waste) for environmental protection can become, with some government help, one of the hinges of the structural renovation of Russia's economy. It is technology-intensive, has an expanding and secure market at home and abroad (the market in environmental goods and services comes to 200 billion dollars a year) and, on the whole, provides for higher production efficiency. It is a field with very good prospects, in which Russian basic research and Russian cheap factors of production can merge with foreign capital in a potentially booming industry. Its output, among other things, may help save jobs at polluting factories which would have to be closed if cleaning equipment were not installed. Moreover, private foreign investments in the environment protection industry are likely candidates to obtain support from the governments of capital exporting countries that generally rank environmental protection high and are sensitive to the threats of transfrontier pollution. As a result, investors may receive risk guarantees and other incentives in home-countries as a form of environment-saving aid thus decreasing the cost of capital import for Russia.

The second group of issues reflects on the ecological dangers which may emerge following Russia's opening to foreign capital. The country's environment can fall victim to the consequences of the immigration of dirty industries from the OECD countries. A relocation of pollution intensive activities, in experts' jargon, 'from regions with a low level, or a high use, of assimilative capacity to regions where the assimilative capacity is still largely available'[26] is a pronounced tendency. Though the situation as discussed so far in this research may indicate that it is unlikely that the ex-Soviet Union would enter into the latter category, there are good chances none the less that Russia and the other CIS countries could become recipients of dirty production which other nations are no longer willing to tolerate in their territory. This will happen if the former fall prey to the temptation to trade whatever is left of their clean environment for some extra material wealth. Of course, this would not necessarily take the form of physical transference of polluting enterprises. Taking into account that anti-pollution protection in many Russian enterprises is still inferior to what is considered unacceptable in countries with more environmental awareness, such a transference could somehow be justified if respective domestic productive capacities were closed.[27] What is likely to happen, however, is that foreign firms will shift production from their own 'dirty' factories to even more 'dirty' Russian factories. If this trend is not resisted, Russia will find not only its environment deteriorating but also the objectives of industrial restructuring frustrated because healthy, growing and future-oriented companies are usually able to pay for pollution control out of rising profits rather than avoiding it while firms which are forced to shift their production to cheaper locations with lower ecological costs are likely to be behind in their technological development.

Environmental problems in Russia may be settled only if there is relevant state regulation. That markets by themselves cannot internalise environmental costs has become conventional wisdom almost everywhere in highly developed industrialised countries. Russian neo-liberals have still to learn that. Appropriate environmental laws, institutions and policies are central to environmental awareness and behaviour. Hence, it is crucial how high environmental policy stays on the government agenda. Inflation control, budget equilibrium, rouble convertibility and privatisation seem to have completely absorbed the reform effort of the government. However, it is not acceptable that a passage to capitalism should include the repetition of all the awful environmental mistakes of capitalism to add to the already tragic experience of socialism. Besides, the neglect of ecological issues will eventually put Russia in opposition to other European countries where environmentalism is in the ascendent. The European Community is imposing increasing pressure on trading partners to conform to their environmental standards and is willing to use tariffs and other fiscal instruments to enforce such requirements (Baumgartl and Stadler, 1992). Therefore, environmentalism should already be a part of reform strategy at this point, the capital entry management system included.

Foreign investors, when establishing plants inside Russia, should be called on to meet those environmental standards which will permit Russia to form a unified regime with other European countries. In practice this means that Russian environmental norms must be oriented towards the EC. So far there have been no clearly defined environmental standards. An attempt to create a competitive advantage on the basis of incorrectly defined environmental standards has no prospects because, if environmental problems are allowed to accumulate, they become more expensive to remedy, thus undermining the chance to reinforce competitiveness in the long run.[28] Due attention must be given to the opinion that better environmental conditions would favour future investments. Russia should stick to codes of practice and guidelines, now being elaborated at the international level, that have as their final objective such a global harmonisation of principles concerning environmental protection costs that it shall be ensured that polluters cover the full environmental cost of their activities (the 'Polluter Pays' Principle).

Unfortunately, the practical implementation of measures preventing the CIS from becoming a 'dustbin' for more prosperous countries is hampered by the critical state of the national economy and a pertaining political crisis. In the central-planning days powerful industrial lobbies succeeded in effectively blocking attempts at making nature-protecting legislation more demanding and punitive. Recently, possibilities for working out and in particular for enforcing unified standards and policy in this field have shrunk even further. As has been stated previously, the environment does not seem to be high on the government's economic agenda. However, even if we assume that the government at some point would be recruited from the influential part of the opposition that represents industrial circles in the country, this is still unlikely to introduce many positive changes in environmental policy. The 'captains' of big industry, who would then actually control decision-making, can be expected to be no less inventive in finding excuses to spoil the environment as they were during the Soviet period. One way or another, there is a danger that environmental issues will be pushed to the margins of the reform debate. Hope lies with the growth of public[29] and international pressure for an environmental clean-up, on the political side, and with the growing awareness of the importance of environment stabilisation for national competitiveness and import of capital, on the economic side.

Notes

1.   *Dialogue*, No. 4, 1991, p. 4.
2.   *World Investment Report 1991*, UN, New York, p. 35.
3.   *Izvestia*, June 9, 1992.
4.   *Dialogue*, No. 83–1, 1989, p. 5.
5.   Two indices may help to quantify the difference between enclave and integral foreign industrial investment. One is the index of 'related party' trade, i.e. the share of the trade between a foreign-owned subsidiary and a parent company in the total exports and imports of the host-country. This index is not easy to calculate because of source problems. The other index is similar to the first one though not identical to it. It depicts the share of the affiliates belonging to mother-companies from the same home country in the host-country's bilateral trade with the respective home country. For the countries in which these indices are small there are more reasons to believe that foreign investments are better integrated than in those countries where they are high. In 1989, among the seventeen developing countries in Asia and Latin America belonging to the United States trade and investment cluster, the United States affiliate percentage share of bilateral trade was

below 10 per cent for South Korea, Taiwan, Venezuela and Thailand. It was about thirty per cent and over for Mexico, Brazil, Singapore and Malaysia (*World Investment Report 1991*, United Nations, New York, p. 73).

6. In the frame of the Marshall plan the United States allocated to Western Europe a sum equal to 77 billion dollars at 1992 prices, which made up 14 per cent of the federal budget for 1948. Forty four years later US Congress failed to decide on aid to Russia at the level of 620 million dollars, representing four-tenths of 1 per cent of the current federal budget.

7. See Chapter 6 for further analysis.

8. *World Investment Report 1991*, p. 32.

9. In December 1992, there were about 600 000 officially registered unemployed in Russia. The figure in the main text allows for different forms of hidden unemployment, such as sending on 'vacation' the employees and workers of those enterprises which stopped production due to the shortage of supplies.

10. *Kommersant*, No. 6, 15 February 1993, p. 1, p. 16.

11. The chain reaction of defaults on current payments, in fact, *was* a latent form of mass bankruptcy which did not turn into a storm of formal bankruptcies only because, before the decree of President Yeltsin, there was no legal possibility to proclaim a state-owned business bankrupt.

12. *Vestnik statistiki*, No. 1, 1991, pp. 4–7.

13. The survey of 7664 items produced in five sectors (machine building, metallurgy, chemical and timber, construction and the 'social sphere') revealed that 5884 product lines, or 77 per cent, were supplied by only one producer (*Vestnik statistiki*, ibidem).

14. *Ekonomika i zhizn'*, No. 23, June 1992.

15. *Business Week*, April 20, 1992, p. 18.

16. *Financial & Business News from Moscow* No. 51–2, 1992, pp. 3–4.

17. For example, regional authorities have received from the centre the obligatory privatisation targets which they have to fulfill by the end of 1992. They are the products of generalised statistical calculations and completely ignore the actual state of affairs in different regions of the country. Some historians were quick to draw an analogy between this 'marketisation planning' and the methods of the mass collectivisation of Russian agriculture in the 1930s.

18. 'Normal shares' are calculated from an equation matching the share of industrial labour force to the level of GNP per capita for 35 capitalist countries, using each country's actual GNP per capita.

19. *Communist Economies and Economic Transformation*, Vol. 4, No. 2, 1992, pp. 269–70.

20. *Voprosy ekonomiki*, No. 4–6, 1992, pp. 133–6.

21. *East European Markets*, June 12, 1992, p. 11.

22. *Izvestia*, February 2, 1992.

23. *EKO*, No. 2, 1992, p. 6.

24. Krutsky and Kochetkov (1992) report the following case. A chemical company in the Volga region produced 'kevlar', an extremely resistant material, on the development of which the American company Dupont had spent 700 million dollars in 25 years. Not finding industrial buyers in the internal market, the enterprise started to manufacture artist's brushes with

this material. These were sold in the domestic market at 2.5 roubles. It should be noted that this material cost in the international market (at the 1990 dollar exchange rate) almost one thousand times more than the producer was trying to obtain in the internal market for its 'finished' product.

25.   Academician Yevgeni Velikhov, a noted expert in electronics, was quoted as saying that if the rouble exchange rate had been calculated on the basis of technical equipment and the technological potential of top-level military producers it should have been established at 10–15 US dollars (*Moct-Most*, No. 2, 1992, p. 90).

26.   *1992 – The Environmental Dimension*, Brussels, 1991, cfr.11.2.3.

27.   In 1988, on average Soviet factories and plants were twice as polluting as similar American production facilities (*Planovoe khoziastvo*, No. 4, 1991, p. 99).

28.   Experts generally agree that a one to ten ratio correctly reflects the relationship between what it costs to prevent pollution and what is necessary to eliminate its consequences (*Planovoe khoziastvo*, No. 4, 1991, p. 100).

29.   The 'green' movement in Russia is disjointed and has not yet gained the political weight and mass support that environmentalists enjoy in Western Europe. In part this is due to the secrecy which surrounded environmental issues in general and environmental accidents in particular under the Soviet regime. Only in 1988 and 1989 for the first time were reliable environmental statistics revealed. With the dispersion of the knowledge of real environmental deterioration and the further liberation of political mentality in the country, Russian 'greens' have a good chance of developing into an influential political force.

6 The Political Economy of Free Economic Zones

6.1   THE RISE OF FREE ECONOMIC ZONES IN RUSSIA

6.1.1   Joint Ventures and Free Economic Zones in the USSR and Russia

Joint ventures with foreign firms are historically the first and, at present, the most diffused form of foreign participation in the ex-Soviet economy. In Russia's industry joint ventures play a noticeable role. At the beginning of 1992, they employed 130 thousand persons and had a volume of sales above eleven billion rubles. In some branches their presence was quite substantial: by mid 1991, their share in telephone production was 10 per cent, in computers 7 per cent, in textile equipment 4 per cent and in footwear output over 2 per cent.[1] However, according to widespread opinion, joint ventures have failed as an attempt to induce foreign capital to participate more actively in restructuring and modernising Russia's economic potential. Major firms with solid reputations, modern technology and huge capital, have shown no particular interest in participating in JVs so far. Foreign partners prefer to invest in services rather than in industrial production. With few exceptions they have been keen to extract short-term profit instead of embarking on long-term projects as was initially hoped. Foreign firms have also brought with them a sophisticated technique of disguised transmission of profits abroad. Therefore, shortly after the green light was given in the Soviet Union for the creation of joint ventures with the participation of foreign firms, a search started for additional instruments to precipitate the inflow of production assets from abroad.

In this context special (or free) economic zones were regarded by many Soviet experts as the next major step towards the opening-up of the national economy and the intensification of foreign investment in the country. In recent years this topic has been the focal point of a heated and controversial discussion. Though having contributed a great deal to creating a clearer and more objective picture of the nature of the phenomenon of free economic zones, it has failed, however, to produce a unanimous view on the degree of the applicability of these entities under the particular conditions of the Soviet economy. In the meantime, the authorities have been surprisingly quick to pass decisions legalising free economic zones in the country. First, in the autumn of 1990, the Russian Parliament, following President Yeltsin's initiative, authorised the establishment of 'free enterprise zones' in the territory of the Russian Federation. Several months later, President Gorbachev issued a decree approving the creation of zones throughout the whole Soviet Union. The dissolution of the union state has not weakened interest in developing economic zones. In summer 1992, the Russian President signed an extensive decree on some measures promoting the development of free economic zones. Similar legislation was endorsed in the Ukraine, Belarus and Kazakhstan.

At present, on paper at least, Russia is second probably only to China in the spread of free economic zones. Twelve officially proclaimed zones cover a territory of 1.2 million square kilometres with 18 million inhabitants, making up 12 per cent of the population of Russia. At the same time, the performance of these zones in terms of attracting foreign capital has been negligible. This contradiction deserves attention. Analysis may be expected to reveal some interesting details concerning Russia's investment climate. Besides, the formal inauguration of a number of free economic zones has not dismissed two main questions: (i) if a workable model, both adapted to the demands and conditions of the Russian economy and attractive to foreign investors, has been found, and (ii) if free zones are able to facilitate the transition of the national economy to a market system.

6.1.2   Theoretical Debate and Practical Politics

The early stage of the theoretical debate on free economic zones was characterised by the pronounced divergence, sometimes even the polarity, of opinions on the social and economic nature of these structures. The initial negative reaction on the part of some critics had its roots in a dogmatic Marxist mentality treating the export of capital almost exclusively in terms of exploitation and dependence. This sort of criticism, at least at the level of an academic debate, was soon overcome as the society disposed of many of its prejudices. As for constructive criticism, it was directed mainly against the excessively euphoric evaluations of the contribution of free export zones to the success of newly industrialised countries. It also placed in question the universality of a zone type prevalent in these countries. This latter criticism proved to be very helpful as it drew attention to the necessity of making a distinction between different types of free zones. Initially it was rather common that the desirability of developing free economic zones in the USSR was deduced simply from the fact that they were widespread globally. In the course of discussion it became clear that in reality different countries had different types of zones. In industrialised countries free trade zones, enterprise zones, technological parks and free banking zones usually served as instruments for encouraging selected industries and services as well as a means of regional planning, with no special bias being placed on incentives to foreign capital. In developing countries, however, free economic zones mainly existed as export processing zones specifically designed to attract a massive inflow of foreign capital. As each zone type could be seen as representing a particular combination of interests and contradictions characteristic of relations between involved parties, a clear vision of the specifics of existing zone profiles was essential as a premise for choosing the right prototype for future Soviet zones. Thus, it became obvious that the experience of developing countries appeared to be more relevant to the needs of the Soviet economy as it was also struggling to attract foreign investments.

Amazingly, the discussion did little to address the problem of the political and economic nature of free export zones.[2] The arguments of domestic and foreign advocates for the creation of free economic zones in the Soviet Union proceeded from the assumption that the zones were basically favourable to the host-country's economy by way of definition. In numerous publications the zones were depicted as an efficient instrument for the importation of modern technology and management, and an increase in productivity and, eventually, living standards. Under the pressure of this propaganda the emphasis of the discussion shifted to the debate of technical aspects of zone programmes, first of all the type and scale of incentives and privileges to be granted to foreign investors, including tax reductions and exemptions, the elimination of tariffs and trade barriers, reinforced legal protection of property rights, etc.

6.1.3 Economic Romanticism as a Concept of Survival

Official plans to promote free economic zones (FEZ) in Russia received very favourable response from regions. The prospect of opening up the regional economy within a short period of time and obtaining additional financial resources through capital import proved to be of great appeal to local leadership. The existing procedure of organising a FEZ leaves the right to initiative with the local authorities. In the absence of a state concept of the free economic zone they are encouraged to develop their own projections. What consequences might this spontaneous approach have for the development of the zones themselves and for the interests of regions and the country?

The Polish expert on free economic zones, Professor Jan Monkiewicz (1989, p. 4, p. 13) once pointed out that the regional authorities had a tendency to fall into what he called 'provincial economic thinking'. He held it typical of this to disregard the fact that FEZs potentially carried many threats to the national economic regime such as disintegration, the reallocation of resources at the cost of other regions, and environmental and social problems. He marked 'economic romanticism' as another feature of this type of thinking. It usually reveals itself in simplified ideas of what should be done in order to attract foreign investors and ensure the success of the zone.

These observations came to be very relevant to the situation in Russia, in which local interests appear to dominate the process of zone creation. Meanwhile, it seems to be quite obvious that any zone-related decision, if it is to be constructive, must not ignore certain general considerations following from international practice and national vital concerns.

First, the success of the zone depends on a complex of economic, social and geographical factors effective within the country and abroad. It is important not to overlook the fact that the free economic zone, taken in general, is a mature phenomenon of the international economy. Many different types of zones have evolved: free trade zones, enterprise zones and technological parks, export producing zones and special economic zones, etc. Each type has its own logic of development which cannot be neglected. A clear understanding of the specifics, objectives and the mechanism of the zones and their role in the global economy is essential to the success of every new zone.

Second, a newly organised zone, particularly specialising in manufacturing, immediately enters into competition with hundreds of other zones worldwide. As a result the economy of the zone becomes subject to the direct influence of international market forces. All the main parameters of the zone, including employment, output volume, demand for infrastructural objects, tax revenues and other income, become a function of foreign investment which is, at the moment the zone is created, a quantity both undefined and variable. In turn, the foreign investor enjoys the liberty of choosing among a vast variety of zones. Rivalry between the latter has resulted in the standardisation of conditions in which foreign capital shows readiness to come to a zone. It is impossible to ignore these standards, including a certain package of incentives, especially in view of the extremely high 'footlooseness' of zone firms. At the same time it is important to find for every project a specific 'argument' that would favourably distinguish it from others.

If at this point we turn to free zone development programmes worked out in Russia at a regional level we may see that they reflect distinctly different considerations. Let us take as examples the two largest zones: Altai (262 000 square kilometers) and Chita (432 000 square kilometers).

The document entitled *The Concept of the Altai Zone of Free Entrepreneurship* (1990, p. 3) outlines the following motives for establishing a free zone in the region:

> ... the accumulated enormous lag of the Soviet economy, Altai included, in comparison to international experience, ... the lack of means for the substitution of obsolete equipment, for solving ecological and social problems; extremely limited possibilities to retain means for productive, social and ecological purposes from the income generated in the *krai* [region].

The same motives lie behind the establishment of the Chita zone. Once again in concept documents one reads about the economic degradation of the region, the absence of new centralised investment, the lack of infrastructure and energy supply, poor social conditions, etc.

Are these good reasons for creating a free economic zone? Judging from the above, they certainly are from the point of view of the local authorities. When evaluated from any other position, however, the case leads to many doubts.

First, the aforementioned conditions are not unique properties of the two regions in question. Many other Russian territories have experienced similarly severe consequences of centralised economic administration. Thus, among newly proclaimed FEZ-candidates one finds such privileged and relatively well-off centres as St. Petersburg and the Moscow satellite-city of Zelenograd which also claim that their economy lies in ruins and insist on the urgent injection of funds.[3] If the presence of ailing industry and ravaged infrastructure were taken as a sufficient premise for creating a free economic zone, the country would soon arrive at an absurd situation in which the whole national economy would become a conglomerate of such zones. This plainly contradicts common sense. The excessive proliferation of the FEZs would mean that either they became a formality as, by definition, the FEZ is an exception to a conventional order, or, conversely, there would no longer be a single national economy. Clearly, free economic zones should be created where (i) zone related expenses can be brought down to a minimum and (ii) prerequisites for attracting foreign investment are most solid. But this suggests that the establishment of the free zones should be co-ordinated on a scale wider than strictly regional. Otherwise it will be a problem to provide a balance between costs and returns as territories with similar starting conditions will begin to compete one with another.

Second comes the problem of financing the FEZs. It is well known that their preparation requires billions. According to available information, in South Asian countries a square kilometre of a free zone's territory costs on average 25–40 million dollars in infrastructural investment alone. In China a square kilometre costs 70–80 million dollars.[4] Russian FEZs are not going to be cheap either. However, the draft-budgets of some Russian zones recall Monkiewicz's remark on provincial economic romanticism. The further to the east of Moscow, the more optimistic preliminary budget outlines are. Whereas one of the most developed industrial and cultural centres of the country and a would-be economic zone, the city of St. Petersburg, estimated its requirements (at 1990 prices) at 7.5 billion rubles, and a tiny but prosperous city of Vyborg, situated 70 kilometres to the north-west of St. Petersburg, at 2.0 billion rubles, the enormous and backward Altai region evaluated its needs at only 2 to 2.5 billion rubles.[5] Moreover, the vice-governor of the Chita region maintains:

> ... we don't need the money, we need a mechanism to compensate us for those particularly unfavourable starting conditions we found ourselves under when entering the market. (*Rossiiskaia gazeta*, July 18, 1992)

This is, of course, either an illusion or a play upon words. One way or another, a compensative mechanism will always become a mechanism for the redistribution of funds. Many of the financing blueprints of free economic zones (Chita's included) are based on the idea of 'budget credit'. According to this, regions stop paying taxes to the federal budget for a period of five or ten years, whereafter they start returning the debt accrued by the sum of the interest. It would be naïve to claim that this scheme does not involve a reallocation of resources as the burden of carrying the budget during 'tax holidays' falls on other regions. The same effect will result from any other privilege granted a zone, for example a special tariff regime. At least two basic observations follow from this. First, the decision to organise a zone, even when taken by a territory independently, affects interregional relations. In the initial stage the zone is financed, directly or otherwise, by other regions. In the long run this places extra responsibility and obligations on the zone-creating territory. Second, now that relations between various regions of the country have become so tense and economic and market disintegration is a reality, the financial aspect is more than ever likely to result in still greater antagonism at an interregional level. This highly undesirable effect can be avoided only if there is confidence that established zones are able to bring tangible results on a national scale.

This leads us, *third*, to the question of the return of zone projects. The host-region is likely to gain in any case, although gains might prove to be short-term. At the very least, new infrastructural objects may remain the property of the region irrespective of how successful the project will prove in other respects. For interregional and national economies extra benefits may never be forthcoming taking into account how badly many of the announced zones are prepared and equipped to become instrumental in attracting foreign investment.

As regards Altai and Chita, this is already quite clear from the quotations above. Let us now turn, however, to the locational aspect of these two projects. Changes in production technology and the organisation of production have made it more economical for global companies to locate both intermediate production and final assembly of many goods closer to their final markets. Jan Winiecki (1991, p. 188) cites a recent Austrian research which shows that 40 per cent of world exports is shipped no further than 400 kilometres. As for the two zones in question, each is situated several thousand kilometres away from both the western and eastern borders of the country, and from sea ports. Each has very poor communications with the outer world and seems geographically to be the least appropriate place for an export production platform.

What do the organisers of zones like Chita and Altai then count on? Valentin Fyodorov, the Governor of Sakhalin and a fierce proponent of special economic zones, is explicit on the point:[6]

Sakhalin is ideally suited for the immediate establishment of a Free Economic Zone designed to: 1) Develop our natural resources – oil, gas, forest products, coal and marine life; 2) Market these resources in East Asia, and 3) Put the revenues back into social infrastructure... Oil companies stand to recoup up to $200 billion in the next 20 years on their investment of roughly $20 billion...

Also Chita and Altai, as is clear from documents, rely on their enormous natural resources. In the territory of Chita *oblast'*, for example, there is a unique molybdenum deposit big enough to meet the demand of the global market for years to come. However, this orientation of Russian free zones towards the extraction of raw materials is very debatable, and the *fourth* question mark comes here. Indeed, international practice does not know another example of this kind. Special economic zones are usually organised to precipitate the development of the industrial potential of a country or a region, but so far never to speed up the extraction of products in high demand on international markets such as oil or gas, or some rare metals. On the contrary, the development of raw materials by foreign firms is normally subject to additional taxation. In China, for instance, in which special economic zones play a notable role, joint ventures in mining and extracting industries have no special advantages. Instead they are taxed at a maximum rate (Campbell and Adlington, 1988).

Not all of the twelve Russian FEZs will specialise in raw materials, but the emergence of extraction zones brings about many serious problems. Clearly, they are far from the originally endorsed official concept of the free economic zone as a means to encourage the inflow of foreign capital, modern technology and up-to-date management in order to secure a technological breakthrough in national industry, an increase in the production of high quality goods for domestic and external markets, and the improvement of the position of the country in the frame of the international division of labour (see *The Strategy of Foreign Economic Relations of the USSR*, Moscow, 1988). Instead 'raw materials' zones represent a drastic attempt to survive on a regional level in a situation in which the local authorities have lost faith in government regional policy and seek to solve their problems on the basis of isolationism. This leads to very precarious possible consequences; rapid exhaustion of resources, environmental degradation, and the conservation of a monoculture economic structure are just a few of them. A conflict with central authorities concerning control over natural resources seems very plausible too inasmuch as manipulating hard currency income generated by mineral exports remains the last resort of the government's economic policy.

The situation of free economic zones is in itself a strong argument in favour of implementing a new policy in this sphere. It should be based on the awareness that, though the regime within the FEZ may be the incarnation of liberalism, the idea of the zone emerged from the practice of state economic regulation and worldwide the zones are its instrument. There is a need for a state programme determining unified criteria for zone formation in the territory of the country. This will provide a possibility to execute methodologically coherent expertise in consideration of various proposals and to exclude competition between zones. It is none the less important that a clear and explicit programme will also be helpful in promoting Russian free zones in the international arena. Such a programme would be both evidence of the seriousness of intentions on the side of the host-country and a valuable source of first-hand information for potential investors. This will lead to a climate that both protects national interests and reduces risk – and hence costs – to foreign investors by moving towards some degree of stabilisation of business parameters.

Until recently, slow progress in the development of 'raw resources' zones has suggested that the Federal authorities are still undecided on this issue. On the one hand, the government and the Parliament have issued a sequence of decrees, directives and orders designed to facilitate and precipitate the establishment of free zones. On the other hand, none of them in reality has been implemented. The only privilege that the zones may actually offer the foreign investor is a 50 per cent cut in trade tariffs. This dualism can be attributed, to an extent, to difficult general conditions in the national economy which interfere with many government plans. At the same time this may be taken as an indication that the central power would prefer that the zones were more in line with their initial design, i.e., that they are developed as technology intensive production sites.

6.2 ACHIEVEMENTS AND FAILURES OF FREE EXPORT ZONES

6.2.1 The Mythology of Free Economic Zones

As is clear from the available documents of the Central Planning Committee (Gosplan), the State Commission on Foreign Economic Relations (GVK), the Ministry of Finance and other ministries, prepared in the period from 1985 to 1991, the official Soviet viewpoint on the merits and defects of the free economic zone as an instrument of foreign economic policy was based on the perception that other countries' experience of them was on the whole positive. How well founded was this opinion? Surprisingly, it is not easy to answer this question.

To start with, the evaluation of the performance of free zones is usually based on expert assessments. Quantitative information on zone economies is scarce and erratic, probably because host-countries prefer to treat it as confidential. Statistics are conspicuous by their absence even in the case studies contained in the UN Centre on Transnational Corporations 1990 and 1991 reports on free economic zones. Some data are included in foreign trade gross figures and similar data but typically it is difficult, if not impossible, to extract them from these sources. Therefore, the studies of FEZs must rely on sporadic information gathered by research missions and individual investigators in various zones. This is clearly not sufficient for extensive comparative studies.

On the other hand, it must be admitted that a certain tradition has emerged in the depiction of FEZs generally in positive terms. By nature the FEZs are a type of expensive commercial enterprise and their patrons, governments and local authorities, have a vested interest in ensuring them a good reputation. But there were also other forces with motives for giving good publicity to the zones. This played a decisive role in the fate of free economic zones to the extent that, at a certain point, they became something like the symbol of an export-led economic growth model for developing countries. This happened largely because of the efforts of the UNIDO (United Nations Industrial Development Organisation) which, from the beginning of the 1970s, has been issuing surveys, feasibility studies and promotional literature, and organising workshops on industrial free zones and incentives to promote export-oriented industries. It should also be noted that the 'clients' of free zones, different categories of investors including transnational corporations who, thanks to the zones, obtained additional privileges for their off-shore production, were also inducing 'Third World' countries to experiment in this field.

Finally, it is necessary to note that free economic zones have never been the object of a complex fundamental study. The exhaustive and meticulous bibliography of international investment literature compiled by the UN Centre on Transnational Corporations staff (UN, New York, 1988) contains over 70 titles of books and articles devoted to FEZs. Acquaintance with these and later publications demonstrates that they address themselves mostly to historical topics, to host-country conditions and legislation, or to some particular, often technical, aspects of the functioning of the zones. Publications attempting to contribute to what might be called the political economy of free economic zones in developing countries, especially its international component, are in reality rare.[7] The most comprehensive and ambitious attempt to study the phenomenon of 'zones' in the wider context of the international economic regime was made by Folker Fröbel, Jürgen Heinrichs and Otto Kreye in the monograph *New International Division of Labour* (1980). Probably for the first time, the FEZ was examined as a category of the international political economy (IPE), more precisely, the 'new' IPE, as they included in the analysis not only states but also firms and international organisations. They effected a synthesis of economic, political and social studies offering a unifying concept that allowed connections to be made between the origin of free economic zones and important shifts in the global economy and politics in the 1970s and the 1980s triggered by the evolution of transnational corporations into major agents of bargaining relationships. As a result they reached what appears to be a very harsh conclusion:

The process of the world market oriented industrialisation of the underdeveloped countries as determined by the rationality of the valorisation of capital is found in its ideal-typical form, or to put it more concretely, in its most undisguised and brutal expression, in the free production zones. (Fröbel, Heinrichs and Kreye, p. 292)

Although the book did not pass unnoticed (originally written in German, it was later translated into English), it has had more influence on research on the transference of industry from Western to 'Third World' countries and 'imported' industrialisation than on works on free economic zones. More exactly, the principal criticism of the zones contained in the book did not have a great effect while the criticism of some particular features of the zone economy, for example, the exploitation of female labour, was elaborated further very intensively by other authors.

Taking into consideration that the export-oriented type of zone is likely to become prevalent in Russia and other CIS states, it may be useful to verify once more, based on the evidence of the last ten years, some of the hypotheses which reflect the most widespread assertions concerning the contribution of free economic zones to the economy of the host-country. In the economic literature four possible merits are most often attributed to the FEZs (see, for instance, Maex, 1983; Warr, 1988; Yakovleva, 1989; Crane, 1990): (i) the increase in employment; (ii) the inflow of foreign currency, leading to improvements in the balance-of-payments; (iii) the transfer of modern technology; and finally, (iv) the promotion of national products in international markets.

6.2.2 What is an FEPZ?

At this point some introductory remarks are necessary. The generic term 'free economic zone' describes a phenomenon the origins of which may be traced back to medieval 'city-states' and 'free merchant cities'. As has already been mentioned, nowadays it has a wide but often loose and confusing usage, being applied to economic territories and entities very different in their status and purposes. In a more traditional sense, under the name 'free economic zone', a part of sovereign national territory is designated in which goods of foreign origin can be stored, sold or bought free of usual customs duties, i.e., it is a duty-free market-place or a warehouse which, although situated within national borders, for fiscal reasons is regarded as being outside the frontier. Such zones exist in many countries (not to mention numerous duty-free shops in international airports). Less frequently one may come across the term 'free zones' in the descriptions of special banking and insurance zones, enterprise zones and even technological parks.

In the following section, however, attention will be given primarily to territories designated to serve as the sites for foreign direct investment in industrial production and services. Therefore, in order to avoid ambiguity, the term 'free export promoting zones' (FEPZ) will in preference be used in this chapter. This choice is not accidental. It is a term which most adequately summarises three salient features characteristic of the zones in question. First, that they are designed to serve world markets. Second, that they are exempt from certain regulations in force for the rest of the territory of the host country. And finally, that these zones, although explicitly organised in accordance with the principle of *laissez-faire*, are implicitly an extension of, and thus subject to, the economic policy of the host-country's government.

Formally the name FEPZ should be reserved for the specialised industrial estate located physically and/or administratively outside the customs barrier, oriented to export production. Its facilities serve as a showcase to attract investors and as a convenience for their establishment, and are usually associated with other incentives (Basile and Germidis, 1984, p. 20). However, in general it is justifiable to extend this name also to separate entities enjoying special legislative treatment and designed to function as world market factories, such as 'maquiladoras'[8] in Mexico. In fact the FEPZs themselves are conglomerations of the world market factories; hence the term FEPZ may be used both in the sense of territory and in the sense of status.

6.2.3   Eight Theses on the FEPZ

1. *Free export promoting zones are an attribute of underdeveloped economies.*
Territories designated to serve specifically as sites for foreign direct investment in industrial production and services, and this is precisely what is awaited from free zones in Russia and other Commonwealth member-states, are not spread in industrialised countries at all (maybe with the exception of the Republic of Ireland). Free economic zones did not gain widespread recognition until the mid 1970s, when they became strongly associated with a major change in the orientation of the development strategy of third world countries from import substitution to export promotion. They finally evolved into a symbol of outright success in the 1980s as a number of less developed countries (LDCs) had spurted into the league of newly industrialised countries. Despite many notable failures, the proliferation of the free economic zones in the LDCs during those years was uneven but ever growing, with only two of them in operation in 1966, 79 in 1975 (Fröbel *et al.*, 1980, p. 306) and over 260 by the end of the 1980s.

2. *Free export promoting zones evolved as a product of bargaining between less developed countries and transnational corporations concerning conditions necessary for attracting foreign investment into those countries which initially can propose international investors no other advantages than abundant labour force.*

All FEPZs irrespective of their location are strikingly similar in terms of the commercial and financial incentives and technical equipment they provide to investors. The most important privilege granted to foreign capital there is simply the lack of any restrictions on foreign investment and capital transfer. This is the case even in those countries in which serious restrictions are placed on foreign capital outside the zones. Other common features are numerous incentives for foreign investors including full or partial exemption from duties and taxes, tax holidays, freedom from foreign exchange control as well as the assurance of free repatriation of earned profits, preferential financial facilities, the simplification of red-tape through 'one-stop' administration.

The last but not least important general feature of the FEPZ in a LDC worth mentioning is a special regime which regulates labour relations within the zone. In some countries workers are not allowed to organise trade-unions on zones' territories, in others the zones are exempted from labour legislation, especially those articles which deal with the social rights of employees. This involves the elimination of minimum wage ordinances, exemption from the obligation for firms to pay social security contributions, etc. Even in the People's Republic of China, which according to its Constitution is a state of workers and peasants, enterprises in special economic zones are free to manage their labour in accordance with the priorities of profit optimisation (Sklair, 1991).

The previously outlined similarity of the FEPZs reveals their one very peculiar feature: *unlike other development programmes the installation of a free zone does not presume any particular tailoring of the general design in response to the specific needs of a given country.* This observation deserves special explanation. The above description of the characteristics of the FEPZ in legal, spatial and organisational terms, gives a definite idea that the FEPZ is skillfully designed to meet any possible needs of a foreign investor, while providing no clear answer to the question of why developing countries have found this concept appealing. The apparent explanation is that the host countries are not so much interested in the zones themselves, but create them for the sake of possible positive impact they may have on their development as a whole.

The concept of FEPZs gained popularity with LDCs in the late 1970s and early 1980s as a result of a growing disappointment in the import substitution policy. In this situation the introduction of FEPZs seemed to many to be an excellent intermediary step facilitating transition towards export oriented growth, providing good possibilities for attracting foreign capital, technology, know-how and management expertise, and creating new working places, while at the same time producing no menace of exposing obsolete national industries to direct competition with foreign producers as the total output of an FEPZ was destined for export.

However important for the development of an LDC such objectives may be, they usually find no direct reflection in the organisational principles forming the legal and financial framework for an FEPZ. This inconsistency indicates, in my opinion, a serious intrinsic contradiction characteristic of the free export promotion zone as an element of international economic relations.

This contradiction is related to the fact that an FEPZ may emerge only as a result of the combination of the interests of the government of a host country on the one hand, and multinationals as the main investors of capital around the world, on the other. It is apparent that initial considerations underlying their decision to co-operate within the framework of the FEPZ cannot entirely coincide. The solution to this conflict of interests is inevitably predetermined by the inequality in economic potential of the parties involved: in negotiating the conditions of participation in an FEPZ the multinational corporations are better placed insofar as, for one thing, they possess at least three of the assets most desired by the LDCs: investment capital, modern skill and technology, an established position in the world markets; for another, they are relatively free to choose countries and regions in which to make direct investments, while the developing countries are forced to compete with each other on the grounds of abundant and easily accessible resources (an unskilled labour force most importantly) and under limitations imposed by the geography and geology of their national territory. This means that to be successful an FEPZ should first of all correspond to certain demands of the multinational corporations, which raises the question long under discussion in academic circles, namely, what makes a firm operate abroad? A number of hypotheses explaining this phenomenon with varying degrees of sophistication have been introduced in recent years, the most notable among them briefly discussed in Chapter 2. However, the success of FEPZs in developing countries suggests that FEPZs' experience may be very useful in identifying possible answers to this question.

Modern theory suggests that a multinational will invest in the following cases. First, when organising industrial production in a foreign country promises to be more profitable than simply using it as another export market. Second, when foreign investment provides real or potential advantages over competitors (local firms as well as other multinational companies). Among possible examples the most important may be considered to be those which reflect the TNCs' global approach to market strategy and profit optimisation. Third, when by doing so the multinational seeks to protect its interests when other less costly methods (licensing, for example) fail to give results or do not seem to be reliable.

In this context a free export promoting zone in a developing country may become a success if it provides foreign investors with at least one of the following advantages: cheap factors of production; a proximity to main markets and/or sources of supply; a special financial and regulatory 'climate' to allow TNCs to capitalise on their 'transnationality'. The LDCs which are not generously endowed with natural resources and do not occupy the strategic geographical position in the region have to compensate for this, if they want to compete for foreign investments, by selling what they possess in abundance not only cheaply but also in a very attractive package. This is what FEPZs in general are meant for: *to export labour, some raw materials and few locally made components which would hardly attract any attention of the multinationals were they not supplied under very favourable conditions at the expense of a host country.*

An FEPZ ceases to be an integral part of the national economy of the host country and extends the sphere of 'supranational' business activities of transnational corporations. In this connection FEPZs appear to be something more complex than solely the outcome of bilateral relations between TNCs and LDCs. The involvement of the third party – the regulatory authorities of industrialised countries – impose further constraints on the ability of a host country to influence the development of FEPZs on its territory.

3. *FEPZs are insufficient to establish long term relationships with foreign firms as the 'footlooseness' of foreign capital is characterisitc of these zones.*

The problem of the 'footlooseness' of TNCs is one of those very often addressed in the literature on FEPZs. This issue is far from being purely of academic interest. For host-countries the readiness of the TNCs to leave entails additional strains and costs: if it happened the host country would lose not only a source of hard currency receipts, working places and a hope for technological progress, but would be forced to write off a considerable amount of spending on infrastructure and would never recuperate other expenditures on organising a zone.

Statistics which can be helpful in testing the hypothesis of the 'footlooseness' of TNCs are rather scarce. In Warr's *Export Processing Zones* one may find an analysis of aggregate economic performance of Bataan FEPZ (Philippines) (Warr, 1988, p. 11). The total number of firms occupying the zone at the beginning of the years 1979 to 1982 remained almost constant, increasing from 51 to 52 firms during 1980. But during 1979, four firms entered the zone and four others left. In 1980, five entered and four left. During 1981, three entered and three left and during 1982 two entered and four left. All in all this signifies that in the duration of only four years, the composition of the zone had changed by an impressive 56 per cent.

Even in the absence of comprehensive statistics it looks possible through deduction to arrive at the conclusion that firms in FEPZs are especially mobile since the zones are in fact purposely designed to be in conformity with what may be called the 'easy come – easy go' principle. Other things being equal, a foreign investor would be fastened more firmly to those outlets which propose some special advantages either not easily available or too resource-consuming to be developed elsewhere. In contrast to this the FEPZs are all cut from the same model and provide a standardised package of incentives, thus being intentionally deprived of national features. As such they embody the previously immaterial category of an extra-territorial (in economic terms) world production (more precisely, assembly) centre.

When a foreign firm comes to an FEPZ it finds factory buildings which it can lease on advantageous terms, workers ready to work overtime and under other discriminative conditions, local administration eager to provide maximum hospitality (which does not mean, of course, that foreign firms do not encounter bureaucratic obstacles). These favourable conditions might have provoked the investor into a long term deal were they not also available in at least 29 other countries. This factor reverses the situation. The 'footlooseness' of TNCs in free export zones can also be attributed to the fact that TNCs' interests in the zones concentrate mainly around a cheap labour force. This attraction is very unstable by nature, as comparative labour advantages may change very rapidly under the influence of a variety of social and economic factors. A general tendency towards diminution of the competitive importance of unit-labour cost[9] increases the vulnerability of the FEPZs by making foreign investors even more sensitive to the slightest changes in labour conditions there. It is quite comprehensible that for companies with highly labour-intensive technologies the relationship between investment and social stability tends to be stronger than for companies in industries which are not labour intensive.[10] as the former are more dependent on the state of social environment.

Is there a possibility for an LDC to find an 'antidote' against TNCs' 'footlooseness'? As will be shown in this chapter elsewhere, the pure escalation of financial privileges does not help much. A lot depends on TNCs' attitude towards a particular zone. If the TNC regards it simply as another suitable site for one of its world factories, the 'footloose' approach will be an integral part of its strategy. On the contrary, the TNC will demonstrate more loyalty and tolerance if it regards a zone's activities to be a stage in opening up the internal market of the host country as is the case in China and India in which enormous but undeveloped markets are gravitation centres for foreign companies.

4. *In establishing an FEPZ the balance of costs and gains is especially precarious.*
The cost of a zone is crucial for any host-country. The costs of establishing and running an FEPZ can be considered in two categories. The first may be called direct capital costs and cover all money spent on supplying the zone with an infrastructure, factory buildings and other necessary facilities plus an international advertising campaign, the training of officials, etc. These are actual costs as opposed to what may be called missed gains which constitute the second category and comprise the revenues which the state could have received if firms in the zones had no financial and tariff privileges.

Direct costs may achieve very substantial amounts. The case study of FEPZs in 26 countries undertaken by the experts of the Institute for Oriental Studies of the Academy of Sciences of Russia has shown that host countries spent at least four dollars in investments in infrastructure and other zone facilities in exchange for every single dollar of foreign direct investment. In China, for example, initial zone investments have totalled 22 billion dollars with the result of only four billion dollars of foreign direct investment attracted to four special economic zones of the country by 1989.[11] From the economic point of view such expenses may be justified only if these special economic zones function for a very long period of time with a very high rate of efficiency. This means that host countries become in a sense the hostages of their own FEPZs: after all the gigantic investments made they cannot risk losing foreign investors. As any large investment project, an FEPZ, once launched, tends to gain its own momentum threatening to escape the control of its initiators. More arbitrary are the evaluations of the necessary scope and type of financial assistance to be rendered by the host country government to firms active in the zone. From the very beginning such assistance (interest subsidies, state guarantees, tax advantages, interest advances, etc.) was envisaged as one of the main attractions of an FEPZ. After a lapse of time two facts have become evident. The first and most obvious is that incentives in the form of direct money transfer or subsidies (like the interest rate subsidy) have proved to be more effective than non-fund using incentives (like accelerated depreciation). The second is more striking. Numerous examinations and interviews have shown that foreign investors are not inclined to place too much importance on these types of incentives at all, considering other factors as more decisive. Oman in his notable *New Forms of International Investment in Developing Countries* (1984, p. 73) comes to the conclusion that:

> the overall state of the host economy and the world-wide business cycle are more important than the regulatory or incentive-oriented nature of host-government investment policies per se.

According to Basile (1989, p. 4), an OECD expert on export processing zones, potential investors give considerations in the first place to political stability in the recipient country, to the attitude of the government and the population as a whole to private investments, to the tradition of respecting international agreements existing in the country. Some zones (in India, for instance), which are generally acknowledged to be successful, offer very limited tax advantages to the investors.

It would be wrong, however, to deduce that multinationals are completely indifferent to financial conditions prevailing in an FEPZ. Yet, apparently, there are circumstances making them less receptive to such incentives, which means that those LDCs especially generous in providing them have in fact been running unnecessary costs.

More important is the assumption which one quite often comes across in books on multinational corporations that the latter have developed an efficient system for the intrafirm redistribution of financial resources free from public control and monitoring. For obvious reasons exact figures are not available, but considering the data which can be judged to reflect the respective activities indirectly, it may be safely maintained that LDCs face a very serious challenge which, in the case of developing an export promoting zone, may cause a considerable income drain for the state.

5. The potential of FEPZs to trickle-down modern technology and know-how to the mainland industries of host-countries is greatly limited.
Access to modern technology remains one of the highest priorities of developing countries. It is not by chance, therefore, that FEPZ projects inspired high expectations of help to bridge the technological gap between the LDCs and industrialised countries. But it did not take long to realise that the simple fact of functioning of a number of individual foreign-owned high-tech enterprises does not entail any improvement in the technological level of an economy as a whole. Under these conditions the disappointing remarks concerning the role of foreign direct investments in the technology

distribution process in the LDCs, which may be found in the UN Centre on TNC report *Transnational Corporations and Technology Transfer* (1987, pp. 33, 35 and the following), are not unexpected. Also a number of special studies on export promoting zones and joint ventures in the LDCs have given the same results (see, for instance, Campbell and Adlington, 1988; Warr, 1988; Dörrenbächer, 1991).

It is not difficult to deduce what makes TNCs so reluctant to share modern technology. Patents, know-how, trade marks and management skills are commonly evaluated by corporations as their most important 'intangible' assets. Technology, especially that which originates in-house, appears to be the major source of competitive advantage for multinationals, maintains one of the studies (Bertin and Wyatt, 1988, p. 23). Managers in TNC headquarters are well aware, though, that under certain circumstances this advantage tends to be very fragile as worldwide the army of imitators is ready to exploit ideas that do not belong to them and that cost them nothing to develop. For this reason, and also because the resources demanded for protecting technological rights abroad are enormous in terms of organisational and financial outlay, the transnational corporations show an obvious propensity for transferring R & D results 'internally', i.e. through the net of controlled companies. This implies that *foreign affiliates are not established in the FEPZ to serve as technological 'supermarkets' but, on the contrary, to provide the TNCs' R & D with the highest rate of protection.* The transfer of imported technology into other firms in the same and/ or closely related industries is highly restricted by foreign partners through special clauses or through daily business practice.

In the economic literature two possible ways in which foreign companies may contribute to the technological development of a host country are mentioned most often: (i) through training of national workers, engineers and management and (ii) through so-called 'backward linkages'. But it is not difficult to discover that both variants are deeply inconsistent with the nature of the FEPZ as a phenomenon and that the lack of serious progress in the field is not in the least incidental.

One of the main characteristics and attractions of the FEPZ is the easy availability of a cheap but disciplined and hard-working labour force. It is cheap because it is poorly educated and has no previous experience in professionalised work although the literacy rate can be relatively high. These qualities match the demand of many industries, ranging from textiles to semiconductors, which still rely upon labour dependent technologies. The zones provide them with an extremely advantageous opportunity for locating primitive assembly production. That this is really the case is supported by the fact that in the 1970s the annual amount of foreign direct investments per working place was less than 2000 dollars.[12] However, as it is rightly stressed by the authors of *The New International Division of Labour* (p. 328), this does not imply, as it is often claimed, that FEPZs are destined only for labour-intensive production. Modern capital-intensive production, due to the separation of operations, is equally as open to operation by unskilled and semiskilled workers.

The bulk of the FEPZs' workers are thus engaged in simple routine operations which they can normally learn in a few weeks or even days. Hence, foreign companies investing in the FEPZs face no need to improve the quality of the labour force. On the contrary, when the cost of labour rises, they tend to move away to other countries as the example of South Korea, Singapore and Hong-Kong has proved.

There is substantial evidence to confirm the above assertion.[13] Companies in the zones do not seek to consolidate their staff as is usually the case with highly-skilled professionals. The bulk of employees is hired on the basis of monthly or even daily contracts. It is not surprising that the author of a study on the technological effects of foreign direct investments in South Korea (Doo-Soon Ahn, 1983, p. 213) has arrived at the conclusion that:

> there is no evidence for diffusion effects of technology through mobility of workers and technological personnel between FDI-firms and other firms.

The concept of 'backward linkages' assumes that by placing orders with local businessmen, and demanding high quality and reliable supplies, TNCs force local producers to modernise and improve their operations. However, once again evidence contradicts such optimistic assumptions. From the survey of 33 enterprises in the free economic zones of the Philippines and Malaysia it was discovered that almost 70 per cent of the zones' enterprises bought less than 1/10 of raw materials, components and parts on the domestic markets (Maex, 1983, p. 39). In 1978 in the FEPZ of Penang (Malaysia) zone enterprises imported 87 per cent of raw materials from abroad, 9.6 per cent from firms within the FEPZs and only 3.2 per cent was supplied by the domestic economy. In electronics in particular the share of domestic supplies was negligible. In Sri Lanka local supplies for FEPZs' garment manufacturers were also very marginal and mostly confined to services and packing material. The case of Masan zone in the Republic of Korea in which local contents component runs at about 44 per cent in 1991 is rather an exception.

TNCs in free export promoting zones in LDCs prefer to rely on their international partners as suppliers and do not invest in local producers as the TNCs find it expensive to raise the quality of their products to acceptable levels. Reluctance to rely upon local raw materials also derives from the global strategies of the corporations involved. Parent firms wish to preserve a high level of international mobility for their processing operations and developing long-term commercial relationships with local suppliers in the host countries does not serve this goal. If the corporation wishes to retain the capacity to relocate its processing activities internationally at short notice it is more expedient to purchase these inputs from the cheapest reliable international source. They are also not inclined to sell technology through patents for the reasons discussed earlier.

6. *FEPZs help increasing employment in host-countries, though their role in improving the quality of labour is limited.*
One of the main reasons for the enthusiasm of host countries about FEPZs was the assumption that they could assist in solving the two-digit rate of unemployment problem typical of a great many developing countries by serving as export outlets for an excess of labour. As such they have quite a good record, having absorbed as many as 1.5 million workers by the end of 1980s (UNCTC, 1990, p. 1). The rate of job creation in the zones was usually higher than in mainland economies. In Jamaica, for example, in 1981–84 employment rose by only 2.4 per cent as compared with 1100 per cent in export promoting zones. These impressive figures, however, should not conceal the fact that the FEPZs still account for a less than moderate share in the host countries' total employment (from 15 per cent in Malaysia to below 1 per cent in Jamaica).[14] Employment effects of FEPZs may be seriously diminished by the following: (i) the demand for workers in the FEPZ is a function of foreign capital and as such is unpredictable and unstable; (ii) owing to restricted horizontal integration of zone enterprises with mainland enterprises the augmentation of employment in the former has only an insignificant multiplier effect for the host economy as a whole.

One remarkable fact deserves special attention. In comparing the characteristics of the typical worker employed in FEPZs nowadays and twenty years ago no tangible changes can be discovered. Thus, recent articles on Chinese zones demonstrate that there is no considerable difference in the structure of the labour force of a zone irrespective of how long the zone has been in operation. Such stability suggests that years and novelties in technology have not affected the orientation of TNCs' investments towards the cheapest and less protected sector of the reserve labour army of the LDCs.

Some authors claim that the discussion on working conditions in FEPZs has often not reflected familiarity with the employment conditions and wages existing outside the FEPZs in the developing countries concerned and has ignored the obvious fact that unless workers were better off being employed in an FEPZ than otherwise, FEPZ firms would find it impossible to hire. References are often made to investigations which have revealed that a zone worker's income in national currency was as a rule equal to or higher than that of a worker employed at a firm outside the zone either because of appropriately higher salaries or favourable foreign currency/ national currency exchange rate (if zone workers were paid in hard currency).

But the question is not whether zone workers' salaries are above or below the average rate for a host country but whether they cover the costs of the reproduction of the labour force. Being employed by a zone firm local workers get involved in technological processes which might have no analogies in the traditional industries prevalent outside the zones, in terms of the intensity of labour first of all. A historical parallel suggests itself at this point. After implementing conveyor methods of production Henry Ford was forced after a while, for the first time in American history, to introduce a guaranteed minimum salary rate at $5 a day to compensate for the drastic discrepancy in labour intensity at his plant and in the rest of the automotive industry. The intensity gap between zone and non-zone enterprises could hardly be less profound, which implies that any direct comparison of average FEPZ earnings with average mainland earnings can be only deceptive if it does not refer to comparative working conditions.

7. *Increase in zone exports does not imply the strengthening of a host-country's national competitiveness in world markets.*
FEPZs have made a certain contribution to the growth of industrial exports from host countries. Thus, in the Republic of Korea, FEPZs exports accounted, in 1986, for around 4 per cent of the total exports of manufactures. In the Philippines and Sri Lanka in 1980, FEPZs accounted for 12.3 per cent and 25.8 per cent of the total exports of manufactures. Labour-intensive off-shore production by TNCs accounted for roughly 10 per cent of the manufactured exports in Hong Kong and for 40 per cent in Singapore (Maex, 1983, p. 18).

Especially impressive are the figures of electronics industry export from Malaysia, in which about 90 per cent of the production are concentrated in FEPZs. In the 1970s the electronics industry grew at an average annual rate of 13.3 per cent, and Malaysia became the world's largest exporter of semiconductors, overtaking Singapore. Export earnings from the industry increased from M$ 15.7 million or 1.8 per cent of total export earnings of the manufacturing sector in 1970 to M$ 2.7 billion or 37.5 per cent of total manufactured exports in 1980, and M$ 7.0 billion or 53.3 per cent of total manufactured exports in 1986. In 1987, exports reached M\$ 16.7 billion. Employment had increased from less than 600 in 1970 to 85 000 in 1985 (Lee and Fong, 1988, p. 25).

Exports statistics, however, can be misleading if they are to be taken as an indicator of free export zones being a source of gain for national economies. Because of the negligible domestic component of FEPZs' products, exports is almost balanced with imports, resulting in low net foreign exchange earnings. These earnings are even further diminished as a result of the repatriation of profits and capital by TNCs. Actually, profits and interest payments may account for substantial portions of the value added by FEPZ firms owing to privileges granted to them. In general, according to UN statistics, the share in value added by FEPZ enterprises does not exceed 25 per cent of the total value of goods produced or assembled there.[15] An Asian Regional Team for Employment Promotion (ARTEP, Bangkok) report showed that, in 1981, 51 per cent of total value added (net production value) was accounted for by capital service (interest) and profits. The importance of potential resource flow from the host country is demonstrated in the case of Sri Lanka for garments, which had a value added ratio of only 0.28 and a foreign component in equity and loans of about 68 per cent. Furthermore, in Malaysia, in a case study of two typical FEPZ firms in electronics and garments, profit rates on investment capital seemed very high in comparison to benefits accruing to the government and to workers (Maex, 1983, p. 38). It is also characteristic of FEPZ enterprises that they prefer not to reinvest the income in the zones and tend to repatriate even amortisation accumulations.

Taxes raised from FEPZ firms, for the reasons discussed earlier, are generally small. Tariffs for the utilisation of the infrastructural facilities also cannot yield a lot with subsidies being one of the incentives for investment. The major source of gain for host countries are foreign exchange earnings of those employed in the zones. In South Korea, Malaysia and the Philippines they account for one half of the total amount, which only confirms that for the host countries the FEPZs represent a form of indirect labour export (UNCTC, 1991, p. 331 and further). But this source is confined at its origins by low-wage policy inalienable any FEPZ.

8. *FEPZs can have contradictory effects on the regional economic structure of the host-country.*

One of the qualities often attributed to FEPZs is that they may serve as a vehicle for strengthening the regional structure of a host country acting as an industrial pole for depressed or underdeveloped areas. Their alleged contribution to regional development may be suggested as threefold:

through the accelerated development of infrastructure; through the creation of new working places at zone enterprises; and through the general revival of the regional economy and the labour situation because of the zone stimulated demand for services and to co-operative ties between local and zone firms. This explains why local authorities usually actively support the plans for the implementation of FEPZs. The example of Shenzhen in China, which has developed within only ten years from a provincial town of seven thousand inhabitants to a modern industrial city with a population of one million spread on the territory thirty times the size it originally was, shows very clearly the possibilities a special economic zone may open up for the region.

On a national scale the efficiency of FEPZs' contribution to regional development seems less indisputable. In fact, almost every regional development programme ever conceived or implemented has been a ready victim for criticism as excessively capital-consuming and too unreliable in respect of results. These reproaches may well be addressed to FEPZ projects, even more so in that they are meant to attract foreign capital in the first place thus multiplying the cost and uncertainties of regional planning.

The fact that FEPZ construction programmes are extremely expensive have been mentioned earlier in this chapter. However, there are reasons to think that the degree of the utilisation of infrastructure in FEPZs in general fails to reach its optimum parameters because of the special incentive regime effective there (*China's Special Economic Zones*, 1986, p. 62). This inefficiency may be short term: as more and more firms enter a zone the usage of social overhead capital should increase. Another thing is that zone authorities, in anticipating future unpredictable developments, have to assume maximum demand and therefore over-provide, thus constantly running up extra costs.

Studies on regional planning have revealed a strong inverse correlation between variables such as profitability, productivity and demand and the propensity of a particular firm to invest in depressed areas. Conversely, those firms of a given industry that tend to select locations in the depressed areas are more labour intensive than those that invest in 'normal' areas.

Zone implications for the development of regional industrial potential are also debatable. There are few doubts that the presence of an FEPZ promotes the raising of consumer demand for services and dwelling on the part of the zone firms' employees arriving from other parts of the country. At the same time, consequent upon the lack of backward linkages between zone and local industries, the expansion of local production does not take the shape of a breakthrough in quality and technology but is effectuated on the basis of previously assimilated technologies, which in the case of developing countries tend to be obsolete. The multiplier effect of the zone is also diminished as a result of special consumption patterns of zone employees who have high propensity to accumulation (young female workers, for instance, go to free zones with the intention to make savings for their future matrimonial life).

In some cases FEPZs may cause adverse social consequences especially where local currencies are nonconvertible and the market of goods and foodstuffs payable in these currencies is scarce, as is actually true of many developing countries. Under these conditions the possession of a hard currency is a serious advantage in terms of well-being, dividing people into two categories: those who through their free currency assets have access to better quality goods, foodstuffs and services and those who have not. This situation may cause even more profound social strains in countries with a long term egalitarian tradition. Another undesirable consequence is the inevitable development of a black market in foreign exchange, goods and foodstuffs, as well as of smuggling. Host-countries take different measures in order to prevent this development or diminish its scale, including the construction of internal borders as the Chinese did by encircling Shenzhen with another 'Great Wall' – this time made of 80 kilometres of barbed wire. This measure and the like are hardly able to change radically the social climate around the zones as long as economic preconditions for tension and criminality are preserved.

6.3 SOME PROBLEMS OF ESTABLISHING FREE ECONOMIC ZONES IN RUSSIA

The above discussion provides grounds for maintaining that the phenomenon of the free export promoting zone has taken its present shape as a result of the interplay of three major factors. One was the aspiration of the governments of developing countries to open new outlets for excess labour. On the other hand, new technological developments opened up the possibility of breaking down the manufacturing process first into labour-intensive and capital-intensive phases, and then splitting the former into its most basic parts to enable the utilisation of the unskilled labour force. Finally, the progress in transportation and communication systems allowed the reduction of transportation and management costs to a minimum, making a worldwide production scheme profitable.

The gains of the host-country are predominantly indirect. In fact, it is possible to maintain with a considerable degree of certainty only that *FEPZs provide labour opportunities for a specific category of workers as described above while other tested consequences such as the dispersion of technology and know-how, the revitalisation of national industry through the backward linkages of zone firms, contribution to regional programmes, and the improvement of the balance-of-payments of the host-country are either untraceable or play a substantially less important role than that often attributed to them.* This can be explained by the enclave nature of the FEPZs and their outward rather than inward orientation. In a sense, the export promoting zone is a well equipped selling point for the labour force more than anything else.

The enclave character of FEPZs also suggests that it is wrong to expect that participation in the world market through the zones will help the host-country to find a more appropriate niche there or to identify itself in the international division of labour. The specialisation of a zone, being defined by the investment decisions of TNCs which reflect their own global profit optimisation strategy, does not usually reflect any specific quality of the host-country's national economy. While the FEPZs fail to integrate the mainland economy of host-countries into the world market they exert considerable pressure on their finances and are likely to provoke an increase in their external debt.

One of the most frequently stated purposes of establishing the free export promoting zone is to learn the newest methods of capitalist management and to adopt the latest developments of modern capitalism. However, zone capitalism bears only a slight resemblance to the western pattern with features such as the social state, sophisticated labour legislation, etc. The zones look more like the preserves of 'old time capitalism', providing foreign capital with the complete freedom to exploit local labour coupled with the exemption from state monitoring and control.

FEPZs cannot be regarded as a solid basis for the development of the national economy also because they tend to be quite unstable in terms of economic performance. The latter depends, to a great extent, on factors which are out of the control of the host-countries. For instance, much of a zone's success depends on the comparative development of wages in competing countries, on changes in technology, on trends in tariff and tax regulations in industrialised countries, etc. Generally, transnational corporations come to the free zone in search of quick profit. The zones are unable to tie up foreign capital insofar as the supply of cheap labour in developing countries exceeds the demand.

As it is not the absolute low price of labour that attracts foreign investors to FEPZs but a relative wage rate with respect to productivity of labour, such zones may exist even in countries with a comparatively more expensive labour force. The phenomenon of the FEPZ has been evolving, demonstrating its potential for further development. More simple industries move over to new free zones leaving older ones clear for more sophisticated production. This does not necessarily have beneficial consequences for host-countries: the more sophisticated the production in the zone, the bigger the gap between the mainland and zone economies, and the fewer 'backward linkages' such production induces.

The exhaustion of the reserves of cheap labour does not threaten the future of FEPZs as long as *comparatively* cheap labour is always available. Nevertheless, with a cheap labour force being the main justification for their existence, there are strong reasons for considering the FEPZs a temporary phenomenon. Indeed (i) changes in production technology and the organisation of production have made labour costs less important in many industries as wage costs have already fallen to a very limited weight in total production costs; (ii) foreign firms are tempted to choose highly automated methods of production in an attempt to minimise other costs associated with an abundant labour force (such as the risk of more frequent labour conflicts) (UN Document E/C.10/1991/7). Under these conditions the desire to preserve the attractiveness of the FEPZs in the eyes of foreign investors tends to result in even greater pressure on zone employees.

The conclusions above inspire serious doubts as to the expediency of the large-scale implementation of free export processing zones in Russia. China is the only example of a large country which is progressively enlarging its 'special' economic sector. Much of the success of Chinese coastal provinces in terms of attracting foreign capital must be attributed to a unique factor, namely, to the role played by Hong Kong capital and entrepreneurs, and the capital of the Chinese diaspora outside China.[16] Russia is in no position to enjoy the same advantage. As for problems generated by zone development, the Chinese experience appears to be more universal. One of these problems is the threat of political and social disintegration within the country which many in China take very seriously.[17]

This does not mean, of course, that the idea of creating specialised zones is not valid at all under Russian conditions. Rather it requires further elaboration based on expertise, skill and imagination. As long as the conceptual framework of free economic zones in Russia remains as ambiguous as it has been of late, any serious expressions of interest on the part of foreign investors are unlikely. While it is beyond the scope of this analysis to attempt a comprehensive projection of such a concept, it seems to be appropriate to put forward some considerations.

First of all, it is crucial to decide on the purpose of free zones in Russia. Leaving aside those groups for which the turmoil around the free zones is just a convenient ground for achieving certain political ends, there are people who believe the FEPZ to be a tool for the profound social and economic reorganisation of the society on the basis of market relations, the nuclei of a new efficient and modern economy. These expectations by far extend the true, rather limited, opportunities opened by the zones. If the FEDPZs can help to establish a new way of life in Russia it is only following their contribution to the solution of some particular economic problems. The most fruitful and practical approach would be to treat them for what they are, i.e., as specific instruments of foreign investment and trade regulation, and an element of regional policy. Seen thus, the zones lose much of their mystery and become manageable at a conceptual level. The practical outcome of this approach is that the efficiency of a zone would depend ultimately on two factors: (i) how well the concrete objective, justifying the establishment of the zone, is defined and (ii) how well the characteristics of the zone conform to the specifics of this objective.

In other words, it is necessary to move away from the creation of free economic zones *in general*, especially founded on a territorial principle, and begin establishing clearly specialised tailor-made zones: customs zones and free-trade zones in place of transportation junctions; export-processing zones in industrial centres situated close to foreign borders or on international trade routes; technological parks in the vicinity of university centres, etc. The clarity of criteria would be a sort of guarantee that returns cover costs, and it would also allow the correction and improvement of the mechanism of the zone economy so that it better suits the interests of the host-country. The interests of investors would also be better served. Distinct specialisation would allow the introduction of laws and incentives, distinguishing the FEZ opportunity from direct investment opportunities elsewhere in the host-country. Besides, such an approach would eliminate a situation in which the burden of identifying and pursuing investment projects is largely shifted to the party least equipped to do the job, namely, the prospective foreign investor. Last but not least, foreign investors are known to have more confidence in a zone if they feel that the development of their particular industry was a predominant consideration for the establishment of the zone. As a survey of 180 transnational corporations has shown (*CTC Reporter, No. 28, Autumn 1989), the respondents strongly preferred 'single-purpose' to 'multi-purpose' FEPZs. 'No zone can be all things to all investors', conclude the authors of the survey (p. 32).*

Free export promoting zones have the right to exist on equal terms with other zone types. There are no reasons to discriminate against them. On the other hand, it must be clear that there are no logical grounds either for expectations that the export of labour can help improve the national competitive position whereas the export of crude oil and timber – in the past, the two basics of Soviet foreign trade – have failed to do so. Organising export production for transnational corporations may be a good solution for some military enterprises undergoing conversion. They may be given a special status to function as world market factories, such as 'maquiladoras' in Mexico. The creation of special 'import' processing zones, however, appears to be potentially even more promising. This type of special zone was never seriously investigated in the Russian economic literature. They can be helpful in diminishing the burden of import generated money transfers on the balance of payments, but not only that. The production of the 'import' zones may be expected to be sold more cheaply and be more adaptable to local market conditions than purely import products. Finally, 'import' zones are certain to be more integrated into the national economy. Hence, they are more instrumental in contributing to the breaking down of monopolistic structures in the Russian market.

Lastly it is necessary to underline that, under the present unstable conditions in the Russian economy, free economic zones demand the special attention of authorities as they can easily become centres of activities in contradiction to the national economic interests of Russia. There is no doubt that not only foreign producers will be eager to utilise the advantages resulting from the relevant extraterritoriality of the zones. Consequently, the zones may facilitate the flight of capital from the country (already the illegal assets of Russian firms and residents abroad are estimated at 20 billion dollars) and play the role of transit points for wholesale black market trade. The current confusion about the status of the zones, loose and unclear regulations, and the emergence of 'accidental' zones in territories unfit for this purpose have meant that potential threats have become a reality. A quite obvious but necessary conclusion follows from the above observations: the government should not 'toy' with the Free Economic Zones; if they are not treated skillfully they will bring more losses than gains.

Notes

1. *Ekonomika i zhizn'*, No. 5, 1992, p. 13.
2. For details see O. Bogomolov, 'Apertures to the business world', *Sovetskie profsouzy*, No. 15, 1989; I. Ivanov, 'Free Economic Zones in the USSR', *EKO*, No. 2, 1990; A. Kuznetsov, 'Some particularities of Free Economic Zones in the USSR', *Voprosy ekonomiki*, No. 10, 1991; S. Lavrov, S. Prichod'ko, 'Some problems of establishing Free Enterprise Zones', *Voprosy ekonomiki*, No. 6, 1990. For foreign representation of the debate see H. Dörrenbächer, 'Sonderwirtschaftzonen – Ein Beitrag zur wirtschaftlichen Entwiklung der UdSSR?' *Osteuropa Wirtschaft*, Juni 1991, pp. 81–105.

3. *Voprosy ekonomiki*, No. 10, 1992, pp. 80–6.
4. *Variants of Conceptions*, International Association for the Development of Free Economic Zones, Moscow, 1991, p. 5.
5. *Ekonomika i Zhizn'*, No. 2, January 1990, p. 10.
6. The International Economy, March/April 1992, p. 40.
7. A recent monograph on the zones is entitled *The Political Economy of China's Special Economic Zones*. It is written by George T. Crane. The book is largely concerned with the intricacies of policy and the personal and inter-departmental rivalry around the special economic zones within Chinese bureaucratic structures. There is practically nothing in the book on management, labour, foreign-invested factories, the distribution of benefits between the host-country and TNCs, subcontracting operations, etc. As a result of his research Crane reaches the conclusion that while the SEZs may not have entirely succeeded in accounting terms, 'SEZs have fostered a sense of economic vitality that has helped energize the country as a whole'(p. 165).
8. 'Maquiladoras', or border plants, emerged in Mexico in the course of the initiation of Mexico's Border Industrialization Program launched in 1965. They were mainly US assembly plants placed along the US border, producing electric and electronic products, textiles, foodstuffs, sports equipment and toys, as well as a variety of other goods.
9. In Detroit, of the total direct cost of assembling a car, labour's portion is now a mere 10 per cent to 15 per cent, down about 20 per cent since the early 1980s. 'We have seen a recognition that unit-labour costs by and large are not the big problem', says an automotive analyst in his interview to *Business Week*. 'If it's not the problem for the industrial nations, it's not the advantage for the developing nations' (*Business Week*, January 16, 1989, p. 19).
10. Lars H. Thunell failed to find empirical support to this hypothesis in the case of a number of Latin American countries (see L. Thunell, 1977, pp. 77–9), which does not, however, refute it in general because of the weaknesses of his methodology: a) he examined only three countries; b) he considered only major political changes such as the replacement of ruling parties, neglecting less evident events which none the less could be very decisive for the social climate as a whole.
11. *Socialisticheskaya industriia*, November 30 1989, p. 3.
12. Document UNCTAD TD/B/C.2/211/Rev.1, p. 22.
13. See, for example, R.Mallic *To Serve Them All My Days? Multinationals as 'Tutors in Technology' in Indonesia*, University of Tasmania Economic Discussion Paper 85–5 (Hobart: University of Tasmania).
14. *Employment Effects of Multinational Enterprises in Export Processing Zones in the Caribbean*, 1986, p. 53.
15. *CTC Reporter*, 1986, No. 21, p. 55.
16. *The Economist*, Survey 'Asia's Emerging Economies', November 16 1991.
17. See *Far Eastern Economic Review*, April 5, 1991, pp. 21–9.

Bibliography*

ALWORTH, J. S. (1988) *The Finance, Investment and Taxation Decisions of Multinationals* (New York: Basil Blackwell).

AMANN, R. (1986) *Technical Progress and Soviet Economic Development* (Oxford: Blackwell).

ÅSLUND, A. (1991) *Gorbachev's Struggle for Economic Reform* (London: Pinter Publishers).

BAIROCH, P. (1976) *Commerce extérior et developpement economique de l'Europe au XIXe siécle* (Paris: Mouton).

BASILE, A. (1989) *Financial Policy, Economic Regime and Regulative Structure in Free Economic Zones* (in Russian). A paper presented at the international seminar on Joint Business Zones in Countries with Centrally Planned Economies, Moscow (mimeo).

BASILE, A. and D. GERMIDIS (1984) *Investing in Free Export Processing Zones* (Paris: OECD Development Centre Studies).

BAUMGARTL, B. and A. STADLER (1992) *East–West Relations in Change.* Seminar Paper in International Political Economy, EUI, Florence, May 1992 (mimeo).

BAYKOV, A. (1950) *The Development of the Soviet Economic System: An Essay on the Experience of Planning in the USSR* (Cambridge: Cambridge University Press).

BERGSON, A. (1989) *Planning and Performance in Socialist Economies: the USSR and Eastern Europe* (Boston: Unwin Hyman).

BERLINER, J. (1988) *Soviet Industry: From Stalin to Gorbachev* (Aldershot: Edward Elgar).

BERTIN, G. V. and WYATT, S. (1988) *Multinationals Industrial Property: The Control of the World's Technology* (Worcester: Billing and Sons).

BEYME VON, K. (1991) 'Social and economic conditions for ethnic strife in the Soviet Union', in A. McAuley (ed.), *Soviet Federalism: Nationalism and Economic Decentralization* (Leicester and London: Leicester University Press).

CABLE, V. and J. PERSAND (eds) (1987) *Developing with Foreign Investment* (New York: Routledge).

CAMERON, R. (1975) *France and the Economic Development of Europe 1800–1914* (New York: Octagon Books).

CAMPBELL, N. and P. ADLINGTON (1988) *China Business Strategies: A Survey of Foreign Business Activity in the PRC* (Oxford: Pergamon Press).

CARR, C. (1990) *British Competitiveness: The Management of the Vehicle Component Industry* (London: Routledge).

CARR, E. H. (1978) *Socialism in One Country, 1924–1926* (London: Macmillan).

CARSON, G. (1959) 'The State and Economic Growth: Russia', in Aitken H. (ed.), *The State and Economic Growth* (New York: Social Science Research Council).

*Where the work is in Russian, the translations are my own (unless otherwise stated).

CAVES, R. E. (1982) *Multinational Enterprises and Economic Analysis* (Cambridge: Cambridge University Press).

CEC (1991) *1992 – The Environmental Dimension* Task Force Report on the Environment and the Internal Market (Brussels: CEC).

CHUDSON, W. A. (1981) 'Intra-Firm Trade and Transfer Pricing', in R. Murray (ed.), *Multinationals Beyond the Market: Intra-Firm Trade and the Control of Transfer Pricing* (Sussex: The Harvester Press).

COLDOUGH, C. and J. MANOR (eds) (1992) *States and Markets: Neo-Liberalism and the Development Policy Debate* (Oxford: Oxford University Press).

COOPER, R. (1968) *The Economics of Interdependence* (London: McGraw-Hill).

CORDEN, W. (1979[1971]) *The Theory of Protection* (Oxford: Oxford University Press).

COX, R. (1987) *Production, Power and World Order: Social Forces in the Making of History* (New York: Columbia University Press).

COX, R. (1991) 'The Global Political Economy and Social Choice', in Drache D. and M. Gertler (eds), *The New Era of Global Competition* (Montreal: McGill-Queen's University Press).

CRANE, G. (1990) *The Political Economy of China's Special Economic Zones* (New York: Armonk).

CRISP, O. (1976) *Studies in Russian Economic History before 1914* (London: Macmillan).

D'ANDREA TYSON, L. (1991) 'Foreign Investment and National Politics', *Dialogue*, 4/91, pp. 2–6.

DAVIS, R. (1990) 'From Tsarism to NEP', in R. Davis (ed.), *From Tsarism to the New Economic Policy: Continuity and Change in the Economy of the USSR* (London: Macmillan).

DE WOOT, P. (ed.) (1990) *High Technology Europe: Strategic Issues for Global Competitveness* (Oxford: Blackwell).

DEVOS, T. (1989) *Multinational Corporations in Democratic Host Countries: US Multinationals and the Vredling Proposals* (Aldershot: Dartmouth).

DOHAN, M. (1990) 'Foreign Trade', in Davis R. (ed.), *From Tsarism to the New Economic Policy. Continuity and Change in the Economy of the USSR* (London: Macmillan).

DONGAROV, A. G. (1990) *Foreign Capital in Russia and the USSR* [in Russian] (Moscow: Mezshdunarodnye otnosheniia).

DOO-SOON, A. (1983) 'Foreign Direct Investment in Korea and its Economic Effects', in Hottes K. and C. Uhlig (eds), *Joint Ventures in Asien: Eine Form internationaler Productionskooperation* – München.

DÖRRENBÄCHER, H. (1991) 'Sonderwirtschaftzonen – Ein Beitrag zur wirtschaftlichen Entwiklung der UdSSR?', *Osteuropa Wirtschaft*, Heft 2, Juni 1991, pp. 81–105.

DRUCKER, P. (1986) 'The Changed World Economy', *Foreign Affairs*, Vol. 64, No. 4, pp. 768–91.

DUNNING, J. (1979) 'Explaining Changing Patterns of International Production: In The Defence of the Eclectic Theory' *Oxford Bulletin of Economics and Statistics*, Vol. 41, No. 4, pp. 269–95

DUNNING, J. (ed.) (1985) *Multinational Enterprises, Economic Structure and International Competitiveness* (Chichester: John Wiley & Sons).

ELSTER, J. (ed.) (1986) *Rational Choice* (Oxford: Basil Blackwell).

EVSTZATOU S., KOZLOV N. and KUZNETSOU A. (1991) *Foreign Investment in the USSR: The Problems of Financial Regulation* [in Russian] (Moscow; Finansy i statistika).

FALKUS, M. (1972) *The Industrialization of Russia 1700–1914* (London: Macmillan).

FLINK, F. (1988) *The Automobile Age* (Cambridge, Mass.: MIT Press).

FREY, B. (1984) *International Political Economics* (Oxford: Basil Blackwell).

FRÖBEL, F., J. HEINRICHS and O. KREYE (1980) *New International Division of Labour: Structural Unemployment in Industrialized Countries and Industrialization in Developing Countries* (Cambridge: Maison des Sciences de l'Homme and Cambridge University Press).

GATRELL, P. (1986) *The Tsarist Economy 1850–1917* (London: B. T. Batsford Ltd).

GATRELL, P. and R. DAVIS (1990) 'The Industrial Economy', in R. Davis (ed.), *From Tsarism to the New Economic Policy: Continuity and Change in the Economy of the USSR* (London: Macmillan).

GRANT, W. (1982) *The Political Economy of Industrial Policy* (Cambridge: Butterworths).

GREGORY, P. (1980) *Comparative Economic Systems* (Boston: Houghton Mifflin).

GREGORY, P. (1982) *Russian National Income, 1895–1913* (Cambridge: Cambridge University Press).

GRUBEL, H. (1982) 'International Capital Movements', in J. Black and J. Dunning (eds), *The Theory of International Capital Movement* (London: Macmillan).

HANSON, F. (1981) *Trade and Technology in Soviet–Western Relations* (London and Basingstoke: Macmillan).

HARSANYI, J. (1977) *Rational Behaviour and Bargaining Equilibrium in Games and Social Situations* (Cambridge: Cambridge University Press).

HAUMANN, H. (1980) *Kapitalismus im zaristischen Staat 1906–1917. Organisationformen, Machtverhältnisse und Leistungsbilanz im Industrialisirungsprozess* (Königstein/Ts.: Hain).

HELLEINER, G. K. (1981) 'Intra-Firm Trade and the Developing Countries: an Assessment of the Data', in R. Murray (ed.), *Multinationals Beyond the Market. Intra-Firm Trade and the Control of Transfer Pricing* (Sussex: The Harvester Press).

HEWETT, E. (1983) 'Foreign Economic Relations', in A. Bergson and H. Levinne (eds), *The Soviet Economy: Toward the Year 2000* (London: Allen & Unwin).

HEWETT, E. (1988) *Reforming the Soviet Economy: Equality Versus Efficiency* (Washington: The Brookings Institution).

HOLLAND, S. (1987) *The Global Economy: From Meso to Macroeconomics* (London: George Weidenfeld and Nicolson).

HOLSTI, K. (1991) *Peace and War: Armed Conflicts and International Order 1648–1989* (Cambridge: Cambridge University Press).

HONG, W. (1987) *Export-Oriented Growth of Korea: A Possible Path to Advanced Economy* (Stockholm: University of Stockholm, Institute for International Economic Studies).

HOOD, N. and J.-E. VAHLNE (1989) *Strategies in Global Competition* (London: Routledge).

HOTTES, K. and C. UHLIG (eds) (1983) *Joint Ventures in Asien. Eine Form internationaler Productionskooperation* (München: Thienemanns).

HUTCHINGS, R. (1982) *Soviet Economic Development*. Second Edition. (Oxford: Basil Blackwell).

HYMER, S. (1976[1960]) *The International Operations of National Firms: A Study of Direct Foreign Investment* (Cambridge, Mass.: MIT Press).

HYMER, S. (1979) *The Multinational Corporation: A Radical Approach* (Cambridge: Cambridge University Press).

ILLARIONOV, A. (1992) 'Former Soviet republics in the world system of economic coordinates' [in Russian], *Voprosy ekonomiki*, No. 4–6, 1992, pp. 122–43.

ILO/UN (1986) *Employment Effects of Multinational Enterprises in Export Processing Zones in the Caribbean*. A Joint ILO/UNCTC Research project. Working Paper No. 42 – Geneva.

IMF, World Bank, OECD, EBRD (1990) *The Economy of the USSR* (Paris: OECD).

IMF, World Bank, OECD, EBRD (1991) *A Study of the Soviet Economy* (Paris: OECD).

JACKSON, M. (1989) 'Opening the Soviet Economy: Structural Deviations, Systemic Reforms in Foreign Trade, and Western Trade Barriers', *Berichte des Bundesinstituts für ostwissenschaftliche und internationale Studien*, No. 74.

JAO, Y. C. and C. K. LEUNG (eds) (1986) *China's Special Economic Zones: Policies, Problems and Prospects* (Oxford: Oxford University Press).

JONES, G. and G. GERENSTAIN (1983) 'Introduction' to P.V.Ol' *Foreign Capital in Russia* (New York: Garland Publishing).

KAGARLITSKY, B. (1990) *Farewell Perestroika* (London: Verso).

KAHAN, A. (1989) *Russian Economic History: The Nineteenth Century* (Chicago: The University of Chicago Press).

KENNEDY, P. (1988) *The Rise and Fall of the Great Powers: Economic Changes and Military Conflict from 1500 to 2000* (London: Unwin Hyman).

KENWOOD, A. and A. LOUGHEED (1977) *The Growth of the International Economy, 1820–1960* (London: Allen & Unwin).

KENWOOD, A. and A. LOUGHEED (1982) *Technological Diffusion and Industrialization before 1914* (London: Croom Helm).

KEOHANE, R. and J. NYE (1977) *Power and Interdependence: World Politics in Transition* (Boston: Little, Brown and Co.).

KEOHANE, R. and J. NYE (1987) 'Power and Interdependence Revisited', *International Organization*, Vol. 41, pp. 725–53.

KHOKHLOV, O. and K. SAMSONOV (1992) 'Conversion of Russia's Defence Industry', *Most-Moct*, No. 2, 1992, pp. 55–65.

KNUDSEN, H. (1974) 'Explaining the National Propensity to Expropriate: an Ecological Approach', *Journal of International Business Studies*, Spring 1974, pp. 51–71.

KOBRIN, S. (1978) 'When Does Political Instability Result in Increased Investment Risk?', *The Columbia Journal of World Business*, Fall 1978, pp. 113–22.

KOVALEVSKY, A. (1992) 'The formation of the market'[in Russian], *Ekonomika i zhizn'*, No. 20, May 1992.

KOZLOV, N. and A. KUZNETSOV (1989) 'Joint Ventures: Problems and How to Solve Them' [in Russian]. *Finansy SSSR*, No. 6, 1989.

KRUGMAN P. (1990) *The Age of Diminished Expectations: US Economic Policy in the 1990s* (Cambridge: MIT Press).

KRUTSKY, V. and G. KOCHETKOV (1992) 'The Conversion Experience of Military Enterprises in Russia', *Moct-Most*, No. 2, 1992, pp. 81–94.

LAUX-MEISELBACH W. (1989) 'A Note on Import Substitution versus Export Promotion as Strategies for Development', *Kyklos*, Vol. 42, pp. 219–29.

LENIN, V. I. (1923) 'On Cooperation' in *Collected Works*, 1973 (London: Lawrence & Wishart).

LIASCHENKO, P. I. (1948) *The History of Russian Economy* Vol. II [in Russian] (Moscow: OGIZ).

LIM and FONG (1988) *Foreign Direct Investment and Industrial Restructuring in Newly-Industrializing Asia*. An unpublished paper for the OECD, Paris (Mimeo).

LIPSEY, R. and I. KRAVIS (1987) *Is the US a spendthrift nation?* (Cambridge: National Bureau of Economic Research).

LIST, F. (1977) *The National System Of Political Economy* (London: Kelley Fairfield).

MAEX, R. (1983) *Employment and Multinationals in Asian Export Processing Zones*, International Labour Office Working Paper No. 26 (Geneva: International Labour Office).

MALLIC, R. (1985) *To Serve Them All My Days? Multinationals as 'Tutors in Technology' in Indonesia*, University of Tasmania Economic Discussion Paper 85-5 (Hobart: University of Tasmania).

MAYALL, J. (1990) *Nationalism and International Society* (Cambridge: Cambridge University Press).

MARNIE, S. (1992) *The Soviet Labour Market in Transition* (Florence: European University Institute).

MCKAY, J. (1970) *Pioneers for Profit. Foreign Entrepreneurship and Russian Industrialization 1885–1913* (Chicago: University of Chicago Press).

MURRELL, P. (1990) *The Nature of Socialist Economies: Lessons from Eastern European Foreign Trade* (Princeton: Princeton University Press).

MONKIEWICZ, J. (1989) *Free Economic Zones in Poland* [in Russian], paper presented at the International Seminar 'Joint Enterprise Zones in Countries with Centrally Planned Economics', Moscow.

NEUBERGER, E. and L. Tyson (eds) (1980) *The Impact of International Economic Disturbances on the Soviet Union and Eastern Europe: Transmission and Response* (New York: Pergamon Press).

NEVENS, T. M., G. SUMME and B. UTTAL (1990) 'Commercializing Technology: What the Best Companies Do', *Harvard Business Review*, May–June 1990, pp. 150–63.

NAGELS, J. (1993) *La teirs-mondisation de l'ex-URSS?* (Brussels: Editions de l'Université de Bruxelles).

NOVE, A. (1989) *An Economic History of the USSR* (London: Penguin Books).

NOVE, A. (1991) *The Economics of Feasible Socialism Revisited* (London: Harper-Collins Academic).

NUTI, M. (1992) 'Economic Inertia in the Transitional Economies of Eastern Europe', the paper presented at the conference 'Impediments to the transition: The East European countries and the policies of the European Community', European University Institute, January 24–5, 1992 (Mimeo).

NYE, J. (1990) *The Changing Nature of American Power* (New York: Basic Books).

OHMAE, K. (1985) *Triad Power: The Coming Shape of Global Competition* (New York: The Free Press).

OKITA, S. (1990) 'The Dazzle of the Asian Economies', *The International Economy*, August/September 1991, pp. 65–70.

OL'SEVICH, Y. (1991) 'Recommendations of an outsider' [in Russian], *Voprosy ekonomiki*, No. 8, pp. 19–27.

OL'SEVICH, Y. (1992) 'Economic Crises: the Cause or the Consequence of "Perestroika"?', *Voprosy ekonomiki*, No. 4–6, pp. 26–37.

OMAN, C. (1984) *New Forms of International Investment in Developing Countries* (Paris: OECD Development Centre Studies).

OS'MOVA, M. and O. STULOV (1990) 'Foreign capital in our country: something new or well forgotten old' [in Russian], *Kommunist*, No. 18, pp. 51–8.

PENROSE, E. (1959) *The Theory of the Growth of the Firm* (Oxford: Blackwell).

PERVUSHIN, S. (1991) 'One of the fundamental causes of the crisis of Soviet economy' [in Russian], *Voprosy ekonomiki*, No. 5 1991, pp. 3–10.

PISKUNOV, D. and I. LOMAKIN-RUMJANCEV (1992) 'Economic Reform and Scientific Research', *Moct-Most*, No. 2, 1992, pp. 67–79.

PORTER, M. (1990) *The Competitive Advantages of Nations* (London: Macmillan).

PREBISCH, R. (1950) *The Economic Survey of Latin America, 1949* (New York: United Nations).

PREBISCH, R. (1978) *The New International Economic Order and Cultural Values* (Madrid: Instituto de Cooperacion Intercontinental).

REICH, R. (1989) 'Corporation and Nation', *Dialogue*, 1/89, No. 83, pp. 2–6.

REICH, R. (1990a) 'Who Is Us?' *Harvard Business Review*, January–February, pp. 53–64.

REICH, R. (1990b) 'Beyond Economic Nationalism', *Dialogue*, 4/90, No. 90, pp. 30–5.

REICH, R. (1991) *The Work of Nations: Preparing Ourselves for 21st Century Capitalism* (New York: Alfred A. Knopf).

ROBINSON, R. (1976) *National Control of Foreign Business Entry: A Survey of Fifteen Countries* (New York: Praeger).

ROBINSON, R. (1988) *The International Transfer of Technology: Theory, Issues and Practice* (Cambridge: Ballinger).

RUGMAN, A. (1987) 'Strategies for National Competitiveness', *Long Range Planning*, 20, No. 3, pp. 92–7.

SCHWARTZ, H. (1951) *Russia's Soviet Economy* (London: Jonathan Cape).

SERVAN-SCHREIBER, J.-J. (1967) *Le défi américain* (Paris: Denoël).

SHITOV, V. (1989) 'Free Export Promoting Zones' [in Russian], *MEMO*, No. 7.

SKLAIR, L. (1991) 'Problems of Socialist Development: the Significance of Shenzhen Special Economic Zone for China's Open Door Development Strategy', *International Journal of Urban and Regional Studies*, Vol. 15, No. 2, 1991, pp. 197–213.

SMITH, S. (1991) *Industrial Policy in Developing Countries. Reconsidering the Real Sources of Export-Led Growth* (Washington: Economic Policy Institute).

SOKOLOV, V. and SCHISCHKOV Y. (1990) 'How to Measure the Openness of a National Economy' [in Russian], *MEMO*, No. 12, pp. 79–88.

STRANGE, S. (1988a) *States and Markets* (London: Printer Publishers).

STRANGE, S. (1988b) 'The Future of the American Empire', *Journal of International Affairs*, Vol. 43, pp. 5–10.

SUTELA, P. (1990) 'Opening up the Soviet Economy', in V. Harle and J. Iivonen (eds), *Gorbachev and Europe* (London: Printer Publishers).

THUNELL, L. H. (1977) *Political Risks in International Business: Investment Behavior of Multinational Corporations* (New York: Praeger).

TIMMERMANN, H. (1990) 'The Soviet Union and Western Europe: Conceptual Change and Political Reorientation', in V. Harle and J. Iivonen (eds), *Gorbachev and Europe* (London: Pinter Publishers).

TING, W. (1988) *Multinational Risk Assessment and Management* (New York: Quorum Books).

UNCTC (1987) *Transnational Corporations and Technology Transfer: Effects and Policy Issues* (New-York: UN Centre on Transnational Corporations).

UNCTC (1988) *Transnational Corporations in World Development. Trends and Prospects* (New York: UN Center on Transnational Corporations).

UNCTC (1990) *The Role of Free Economic Zones in the USSR and in Eastern Europe* (New York: UN Center on Transnational Corporations).

VAITSOS, C. V. (1974) *Intercountry Income Distribution and Transnational Enterprises* (Oxford: Clarendon Press).

VAN LAUE, T. (1974) *Sergei Witte and the Industrialization of Russia* (New York: Athenium).

VERNON, R. (1966) 'International Investment and International Trade in the Product Cycle', *Quarterly Journal Of Economics*, Vol. 80, pp. 190–207.

VERNON, R. (1971) *Sovereignty at Bay. The Multinational Spread of US Enterprises* (London: Longman).

VERNON, R. (1985) *Exploring the Global Economy: Emerging Issues in Trade and Development* (Harvard: Harvard University Press).

VITTAL, N. (ed.) (1977) *Export Processing Zones in Asia. Some Dimensions* (Tokyo: Asian Productivity Organization).

WADE, R. (1990) *Governing the Market. Economic Theory and the Role of Government in East Asian Industrialization* (Princeton: Princeton University Press).

WALTZ, K. (1979) *Theory of International Politics* (Reading: Addison-Wesley)

WARR, P. G. (1988) *Export Processing Zones: The Economics of Enclave Manufacturing* Working Papers on Trade and Development. (Canberra: Australian National University).

WARR, P. (1989) 'Export Processing Zones: the Economics of Enclave Manufacturing', *World Bank Research Observer*, No. 4, pp. 65–88.

WATT, H. D. (1982) 'The Inter-Regional Distribution of West German Multinationals in the U.K.', in M. Taylor and N. Thrif (eds), *The Geography of Multinationals: Studies in the Spatial Development and Economic Consequence of Multinational Corporations* (London: Croom Helm).

WINIECKI, J. (1991) 'Competitive Prospects in Eastern Europe', *Intereconomics*, July–August 1991, pp. 187–91.

WOOD, A. (1984) *Europe, 1815–1960* (London: Longman).

WU QI (1988) *South Korea and Taiwan: A Comparative Analysis of Economic Development* (Brighton: Institute of Development Studies, University of Sussex).

YAKOVLEV, A. (1991) 'Monopolies in the Economy of the USSR' [in Russian], *Vestnik statistiki*, No. 1, 1991, pp. 4–7.

YAKOVLEVA, H. L. (1989) *Joint Ventures in the Practice of Socialist Countries* [in Russian] (Moscow: International Relations Publishing House).

YAREMENKO, J and V. RASSADIN (1992) 'Conversion and the Economic Structure', *Most*, No. 2, 1992, pp. 39–53.

ZALESKI, E. and H. WIENERT (1980) *Technology Transfer Between East and West* (Paris: OECD).

ZORSKA, A. (1987) 'State Policy Measures for Stimulating Manufactured Exports from the Developing Countries', *Studies on the Developing Countries*, No. 3, pp. 55–75.

Index

Index